"Everything always seems to taste better cooked in a farmhouse kitchen. With this delightful new book, Brian Noyes celebrates our region's culinary riches and captures the true spirit of Southern hospitality. Every well-honed recipe is a gem and Brian's passion for baking is contagious, giving you the feeling that you're receiving a treasured gift from a friend. As you cook your way through these pages, the intoxicating aromas wafting from your kitchen will transport you to the country farmhouse of your dreams. It's reassuring to discover that with food this comfortable, you *can* go home again."

— **PATRICK O'CONNELL,** chef proprietor, The Inn at Little Washington

"Brian makes the food I crave, from Sunday breakfast to Sunday supper, and everything in between. His recipes make you want to cozy up in a big chair and enjoy every sweet and savory bite. Small-town charm with big flavor, *The Red Truck Bakery Farmhouse Cookbook* will have you reaching for your mixing bowl to whip up something delicious. I'm off to pop some Farmhouse Muffins into the oven!"

— **CHERYL DAY,** author of *Cheryl Day's Treasury of Southern Baking*

"It is the Red Truck Bakery that comes to mind when I ponder the perfect bakery: honest, simple, delicious food, sprinkled with love and kindness. I have spent many a night dreaming about their legendary Lexington Bourbon Cake. Now you have that recipe in your hands, along with all the other comforting dishes that will transport your kitchen into the bakery of your dreams."

— **EDWARD LEE,** chef and author of *Buttermilk Graffiti*

"If a cookbook could be a page-turner, this is the one! Brian not only knows how to create comfort in spades, but he writes both the sweet and savory recipes in such a way that you feel like you're part of those five generations who inspired these vittles. I don't know where I'm going to start."

— **CARLA HALL,** chef and author

"A story of rural renaissance and a document of creative life in a country farmhouse, this is also a really great cookbook, with a recipe for a bourbon-and-crystallized-ginger cake so good that you will lie and tell everyone Great Aunt So-and-So handed it down to you."

— **JOHN T. EDGE,** author of *The Potlikker Papers* and host of *True South*

"When I think of Brian Noyes, I think of a fun, warm friend who is always telling great stories and whipping up good food. And lucky for us, *The Red Truck Bakery Farmhouse Cookbook* wraps all of these attributes into one beautiful package. Come for the recipes—Mid-July Tomato Pie, anyone?—and stay for the writing and luscious photography. The only thing better would be to answer a knock on the front door and see Brian standing there with an armful of goodies."

— **DAVID DIBENEDETTO,** editor in chief, *Garden & Gun*

"When you can outbake my great grandmother JoJo, you've reached major hero status. In our collaboration, Brian surpassed my fond memories of her delicious creations."

— **BILLY REID,** fashion designer

THE
RED TRUCK
BAKERY
FARMHOUSE
COOKBOOK

THE RED TRUCK BAKERY
FARMHOUSE
COOKBOOK

*Sweet and Savory Comfort Food from
America's Favorite Rural Bakery*

BRIAN NOYES

PHOTOGRAPHS BY ANGIE MOSIER
FOREWORD BY RONNI LUNDY

Clarkson Potter/Publishers
New York

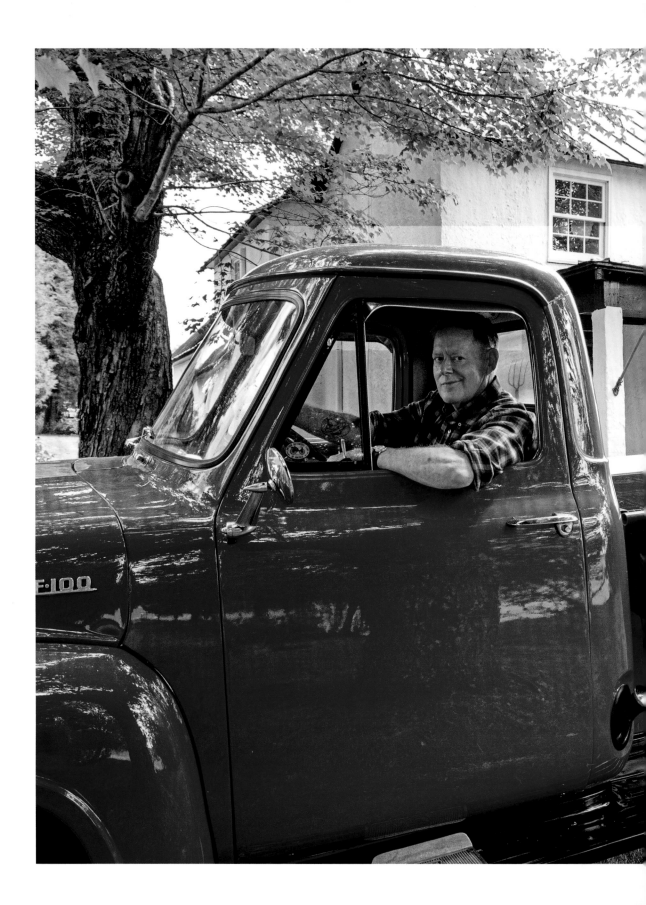

For Willmana Noyes, my grandmother. Originally an Iowa farm girl, she introduced this California boy to North Carolina, taught me to cook Southern (and to not fear okra), and showed me that preparing food is really about creating comfort. I miss her every day.

CONTENTS

9
FOREWORD BY
RONNI LUNDY

15
INTRODUCTION:
THE COMFORT
WE CREATE

26
BEFORE YOU COOK
The Pantry **26**
The Tool Shed **27**
Some Quick Kitchen Advice **28**

31
BREAKFAST

53
BREADS

73
LUNCH

91
SOUPS & STEWS

107
COOKIES & BARS

125
DINNER

147
SIDES

161
DESSERTS

201
CONDIMENTS

212
OUR COMMUNITY
OF ARTISANS

215
ACKNOWLEDGMENTS

220
INDEX

MY HOMEPLACE

Country comfort's in a truck that's going home.

—Elton John and Bernie Taupin

I CAN'T REMEMBER WHERE IT WAS THAT I FIRST MET BRIAN NOYES, OWNER OF RED TRUCK BAKERY, AND his partner, Dwight McNeill. I can see their sweet grinning faces in front of me, in a kind of golden glow from sunlight, but whether that sun was shining on Oxford, Mississippi, or Lexington, Kentucky, or Asheville, North Carolina, I can't say. I met them in the midst of a two-year odyssey as I crisscrossed the South, and a few points north, feasting and speaking at food events, persuading folks to buy my then just-released cookbook *Victuals: An Appalachian Journey with Recipes*. Mine were overwhelmingly joyful journeys, blessed with connections to old friends and new, but reader, I will not lie: two years on the road can be mighty disorienting.

I would straggle home to my apartment in the Blue Ridge Mountains of North Carolina, dump the contents of my suitcase in front of the washing machine, crawl into my likely-as-not still-unmade bed, and sleep the sleep of the dead for a day (or four). And then I'd get up, repack, and hit the road once more. What I most frequently did not do during these quick pit stops at my apartment was feel as if I were really, truly home.

It was on my return from a particularly grueling journey that I climbed the stairs to find a cheery red truck outside my door. Okay. Not an actual truck. They don't even make an ATV that could have taken those stairs. But it was a heavy cardboard shipping box with a decal sticker in the corner that I would soon come to adore. Up against that happy sky-blue background, on a field of pasture grass, sat a bright crimson pickup truck and the words *Red Truck Rural Bakery*, shipped from Brian himself.

I scooched the box across the floor into my apartment, emptied my suitcase, found my box cutter, and pulled up the flaps into a world of joy. There was an old-fashioned cake tin, two bags of chunky granola, a cellophane wrapper with iced sugar cookies inside, and one generous bag I tore open on the spot because, Lord knows, I do love a cheese straw. So much so that I plopped right down on my mound of waiting laundry, put that bite of spicy goodness in my mouth, and proceeded to happy cry.

Look, I'm not trying to sell you salvation in a cheese straw, but here's the truth: Red Truck food doesn't just taste divine, it makes you feel cozy. After I'd had a pot of tea and a few more of those straws, then a bite of granola, then discovered a Triple-Chocolate Cake in that tin, I realized that this time around I felt as if I had actually come home. The kind of home where somebody loves you and made you something really special to eat.

It's not really surprising that Brian knows how to make this mountain girl feel like she's come home. As we continued to run into one another at food events around the country and keep up a lively correspondence, I learned that this fifth-generation California boy nevertheless had a powerful connection to the Appalachian region where I was born. Just like me, Brian spent his summers in the southeastern hills and hollers with his paternal grandmother, Willmana Noyes. From her, he learned to love glistening cornbread, slow-braised green beans, still-warm-from-the-garden heirloom tomatoes, and even okra at the table they shared in Hendersonville, North Carolina. It's obvious from one bite of Red Truck food that the Appalachian foods and flavors that Brian's grandmother introduced him to became an integral part of his cooking repertoire, and that's part of what spoke to both my heart and belly.

Red Truck's food became my new talisman of homecoming. I sent Brian a thank-you email and immediately ordered the Almond Cake for my gluten-intolerant daughter's birthday. Brian added a bag of granola because I'd told him Red Truck's was better than my previously beloved hippie homemade version. We kept writing and I kept ordering: first, the Guinness Stout and Irish Chocolate Cake with Baileys Irish Cream frosting to share with my Hibernian homies for St. Paddy's Day, and then the Old World Stollen for Christmas.

When another friend sent me Red Truck's Applejack Butter Pecan Bundt Cake, I cried again as its caramel butteriness offset with Appalachian apple brandy seemed to combine in one mouthful everything I love about my homeplace.

Brian and I soon discovered that food wasn't our only connection, as we share a passion for much of the same music—Hazel Dickens, the Seldom Scene, anyone who played the Birchmere bluegrass club in the 1970s and '80s—so it's appropriate that it was a New Grass Revival instrumental that finally brought me to the Warrenton, Virginia, doors of Red Truck Rural Bakery. The song is "Lee Highway Blues," which Sam Bush plays with a rippling, soaring, diesel-powered fiddle riff that perfectly matches the curves and swoops of the road it's named after. (That's right, because I love that song, I'd discovered there is an actual Lee Highway, also known as Route 11, that parallels a good stretch of I-81 from the western edge of Virginia east. And whenever I have the time, I try to travel a swatch of it instead of the big-wheel interstate.)

On this occasion in the summer of 2018, I was not on the road for work but headed to a long-weekend party at the Massachusetts home of my friend and agent, Lisa Ekus. Her daughter Sally would be there, along with my food writing buddies Sandra Gutierrez and Virginia Willis. I was going to stop in Baltimore for the night and in the morning pick up one of my best pals in mischief, Toni Tipton-Martin, author of *The Jemima Code* and *Jubilee*, to make the second part of the drive with me. To say that food was on my mind, headed into this auspicious company, is an understatement of spectacular degree. Consulting my trusty road atlas, I realized if I just kept on heading across the Lee Highway, I'd soon be in Warrenton, Red Truck nirvana.

The Warrenton site is a sparkling, spiffy refurbished gas station that looks exactly like a recurring dream I have of opening a sweet community café someday and living happily ever after. The very first thing I did when I walked in was scan the rack of cakes and pies to find just the right treat for sharing with my pals. That's when I discovered something I'd not heard of before: Lexington Bourbon Cake with ginger. Now, I was born in Corbin, Kentucky, a town you may have heard of because a Hoosier huckster set up shop in a motel there and started peddling an herbed and spiced, pressure-cooked travesty he claimed was Kentucky's fried chicken. Therefore I am a little touchy when the Bluegrass State gets invoked. I hesitated to commit to a full cake without tasting it first. But when I walked over to ponder the menu behind the counter, there was one precious (but generous) slice of the bourbon cake still available in the dessert display case. So I ordered it. And a sandwich with Chunky Meatloaf. And Chicken Salad on Harvest Wheat Bread. And, okay, some granola and maybe some Apricot Scones with Cranberries and White Chocolate, and Orange Pecan Rolls.

And I sat down with one of the best cups of coffee I've ever had on the road, ate half a meatloaf sandwich that made me miss my mama (the other half and the chicken salad I was saving for supper in my hotel room), and then broke a corner off that Lexington cake, put it in my mouth, and would have hollered, "Wowser!" had my mouth not been crammed full with sheer delight. That cake is everything: butter-rich and bourbon-heady, sweet but not too sweet, with a sudden sneak-up-and-thrill-you candied ginger bite. I wanted to burst out on the sidewalk and start grabbing strangers and demanding, "Hey, you've gotta taste this."

. . .

LUCKILY, I DIDN'T HAVE TO, as a couple of grandparent types had just walked in and begun a conversation about what pie or cake they should order for a family weekend they were hosting. I tried to pretend I wasn't eavesdropping, but when the grandmother wondered out loud just what the bourbon ginger cake might taste like, I couldn't help myself.

"Here," I said. "You have to try it. Grab yourselves a couple of forks. I only broke off a little piece from this corner . . ." and after only a second of hesitation, that is what they did. And lo, they were immediately converted. They bought the cake, and Red

Truck Brownies and iced cookies for the little ones, and waved goodbye as they carried their bags and cake box out the door. I felt pretty great until I told the clerk I'd take a Lexington Bourbon Cake as well, and she told me that had been the very last one!

Well.

I took another cake instead. Caramel with Pecans? Rum Cake? Orange Cake? I'm not sure, as by now I've had and love them all. But that just-missed bourbon bliss was still on my mind almost a year later when I was in the vicinity again, and this time I went to the Marshall location. A woman on a mission, I went straight to the bakery rack and grabbed my prize before I even ordered brunch, and once I was seated at the long, gleaming community table, I tucked my cake box under my chair, where I could reach down every couple of minutes to pat it, reassuring myself that it was still there.

And this time, when some genial folks sat down across from me and we all started chatting, I didn't offer anyone a spoonful of my Butternut Squash Soup with Apples, Pears & Pecan Butter, even though it was heavenly. Pretty soon the folks and I were chatting like cousins at a reunion, and before you know it, I'd convinced them to buy copies of the *Red Truck Bakery Cookbook*, hot off the presses and stacked on the cookbooks-for-sale table in the next room.

I know that book well, having not only baked from it myself but heard its praises sung by countless friends and colleagues. But it had a funny effect on me. While it satisfied my hunger pangs perfectly, reading it often made me long to head back up the Lee Highway and over to Brian and Dwight's kitchen in their sweet 1850s farmhouse. I dreamed of opening the oven to get a savory, earthy whiff of the Carrot, Parsnip & Leek Potpie that Brian had mentioned he was perfecting. Or to dip my spoon into the pot of sweetly spicy mole sauce while he told me stories of the time he learned to make it in Oaxaca.

Like many travel plans, mine became a dream deferred in the face of the pandemic, but my year-plus at home also brought unexpected pleasure. Brian's recipes for this book, his paean of love to that farmhouse kitchen, began to show up in my mailbox. I discovered that the secret to his root vegetable pie was the creamy sauce that wrapped everything together in a velvety blanket of herbs and spice. And I realized that his thoughtful instructions ("Let the filling cool completely, or you'll melt the dough when you assemble the potpies") were the sort that make you feel as if he were standing at your shoulder, as his grandmother may have once done, making sure you got it right.

And speaking of those old-school kitchens, I whooped with delight when my mail brought what I'd thought was the forever-lost recipe for the Icebox Fruitcake my aunts and mother used to make for childhood holidays.

I fell in love with how Brian spins new twists on classics, not for trendy bragging rights but to make them genuinely better. The Virginia Peanut Pie, dating back to colonial times, is the Commonwealth's pride but admittedly likely to make your tongue cleave to the roof of your mouth with its cloying texture. Brian adds chocolate cake crumbs and coconut to upgrade both the flavor and texture and then—oh, be still, my mountain heart—throws in a dollop of the region's sharp, arboreal shagbark hickory syrup to give the sweetness-perfect counterpoint.

The Red Truck Bakery Farmhouse Cookbook has not only filled my kitchen with warmth and appetizing fragrances but also brought me warming thoughts of some dear and beloved friends. Appalachian orchardist Diane Flynt's bubbly apple butter not only evoked a crisp, tangy Blue Ridge autumn, it made me grin as I remembered her beloved maxim "Eat Ugly Apples." And that kiss of J.Q. Dickinson salt in the Salted Caramel Apple Pie? It took me back to lovely conversations with owner Nancy Payne Bruns at the Malden, West Virginia, saltworks.

The first time that West Virginia–reared, Asheville, North Carolina–based chef and forager William Dissen showed up at my door, he was carrying a mason jar full of his personally picked and pickled ramps. Finding Will's recipe for Wild Mushroom Tartines with Black Pepper Ricotta with those same ramps in Brian's book was almost like having Will at my table again. As for the delicate delight of chef Ian Boden's Corn Ice Cream, kissed with a little sorghum syrup, I savor it with the promise that soon I'll sit down to visit with Ian and his wife, Leslie, in Staunton, Virginia, again.

Well, I could burble on forever—about that fabulous Kentucky-worthy bourbon ginger cake pictured opposite, or the meatless but meaty Beetloaf Sandwiches, or Brian's Aunt Darla's Green Pea Salad—a pure celebration of spring—or savory hand pies. And did I mention Brian's hushpuppies?

But, dear reader, it is now the middle of July and I must stop writing and get myself to the local farm stand for some heirloom tomatoes, like German Pinks, maybe a Mortgage Lifter, and a gorgeous Mr. Stripey, so tonight I can feast on this fella Brian's Mid-July Tomato Pie. And you need to stop reading my raves and discover for yourself the down-home beauty and brilliance of *The Red Truck Bakery Farmhouse Cookbook*, a manual to tell you exactly how to fill your tummy while restoring your soul.

'Cause country comfort's in a Red Truck that tastes like home.

—*Ronni Lundy*

THE COMFORT
WE CREATE

A BEAT-UP OVEN WITH NO EXHAUST FAN AND A WELL THAT PUMPED WATER the color of red clay unwittingly launched the Red Truck Bakery in our circa 1850 farmhouse near Orlean, Virginia. On Friday afternoons I'd leave my job in the nation's capital as the art director of *The Washington Post* to bake all night at our weekend retreat fifty miles west. Even before the roosters raised a ruckus on Saturday mornings, the old red truck I bought from designer Tommy Hilfiger was piled high with warm pies, cakes, and breads. I drove the load to The Village Green, a country store "just over yonder," as a neighbor once directed, where customers were waiting for me in the parking lot long before the store lights were cut on. Food writer Marian Burros happened upon my baked goods at a Rappahannock County picnic and wrote about them on the front page of *The New York Times* Food section in December 2008. Thanks to her, hits on my shipping website went from two dozen to 57,000 in one day, and the mailman scratched his head when he saw my porch piled with a hundred boxes awaiting pickup. I left publishing and eventually opened up two bustling rural bakery locations with four dozen employees, and we now ship thousands of items throughout the United States each year from our little farm town on the edge of the Shenandoah Valley. I first told my story in the *Red Truck Bakery Cookbook*, published by Clarkson Potter in 2018. Barack Obama wrote the back-cover blurb: "I like pie. That's not a state secret, and I can confirm that the Red Truck Bakery makes some darn good pie."

. . .

MY FAMILY GOES BACK five generations in our hometown of Pacific Grove, California. Nestled between Monterey and Carmel on the Monterey Peninsula, it was settled in the 1870s as a Methodist Chautauqua camp. A little ditty from my mom's childhood nails it: "Carmel by the Sea, Monterey by the smell, Pacific Grove by God." Growing up in California really did mean grabbing Meyer lemons, juicy oranges, and black walnuts right off the trees. We looked forward to local artichokes, avocados, and fresh greens from the nearby Salinas Valley, the salad bowl of the nation. Mom's Aunt Helen put up crabapple jelly and apricot jam, made from fruit picked in her yard and sealed back in the day with a pool of paraffin wax (which fascinated me as a youngster). We enjoyed traditional Mexican dishes made by families who settled there even before we did, and we joined surfers drinking fruit smoothies at rustic juice shacks along the coast. I thought everyone ate like this. On Fisherman's Wharf, as pelicans and gulls closed in, we wolfed down abalone sandwiches and chowder until the wharf got too touristy and abalone got too popular, and the delicacy disappeared from menus due to government protection. Cannery Row, made famous by author (and Pacific Grove resident) John Steinbeck, was still around—barely—occupied by the last of the dozens of sardine packing companies. The hulking structures were framed in wood and covered with tin, by then dented with age and streaked with rust, as rickety elevated walkways linked buildings on either side of the street. My older family members recalled the occasional boiler explosions that rocked the area, sending sardine cans flying for blocks and turning the historic wooden structures into smoldering pyres. Our family walks through Cannery Row continued back around Pacific Grove, and mom pointed out the woods near Carmel where she picked huckleberries with her mother.

Flying across the country to my paternal grandmother's house, in the western North Carolina mountain town of Hendersonville, taught me that not everyone ate like we did. Get me talking about my grandmother and I speak of her foreign cooking, heirloom Southern staples unknown to this California kid. I ate what I was served, but Willmana Seeley Noyes, a former teacher in a one-room schoolhouse, knew she had a challenge ahead. During one summer's visit, she met me at the Asheville airport in her black Cadillac and headed directly to a meat-and-three diner aside the French Broad River. We scooched into a booth with a sticky plastic tablecloth. I didn't know what to make of the menu, so she ordered for me, and soon a waitress delivered a heaping tray that sent new smells swirling past my nose. Our tall red plastic tumblers of sweet tea were moved aside to make room for collard greens with country ham, grits, and stuffed pork chops. Fried okra rolled into the stewed tomatoes. My grandmother nudged my elbow off the table as a skillet of silver-dollar cornbread took its place. I ate everything in front of me, although the okra got pushed around a bit. The table was cleared and two slices of buttermilk chess pie arrived. I was surprised that the whole meal was under ten bucks, and I told my grandmother how good I thought it was. She beamed.

I loved her. Her letters arrived weekly, crafted in her beautiful florid handwriting, always mentioning the weather, the birds outside her window, and what she was making for supper. In addition to fueling my appetite for Southern food, she inspired my appreciation of family history. She was a member of the Daughters of the American Revolution, tracing our family tree through two Revolutionary soldiers to ancestors landing in Massachusetts in 1635, and all the way back to my twelfth great-grandfather Robert Noyes (also my dad's name), born in Kimpton, England, in 1465. She typed up the genealogy of her side of the family and that of my grandfather Hiland Batcheller Noyes. She added notes about family highlights and hijinks and mailed it to me while I was in my teens. It took me many years to pick it up and appreciate it. It hurts me to admit that I never thanked her for her hard work.

I always looked for the cardinals in the hedges when she swung the big Caddy into her driveway, and my first chore was refilling her bird feeder with black oil sunflower seeds. Those bright red birds, unfamiliar to me in California, still remind me of my grandmother. After settling into the house, I plopped on her sofa to thumb through issues of *Southern Living*, a new magazine we didn't see on the West Coast that covered regional cooking, architecture, and shopping (those issues inspired me; fifty years later, that magazine would include my bakery in their story "The South's Best Bakeries"). My grandmother's Southern cuisine appreciation project continued in her kitchen the next afternoon. She reminded me that cooking was about creating comfort, not just feeding people. "Grab that bowl and let's make some biscuits," she'd say, as she reached for the White Lily flour and a quart of buttermilk that had showed up on her doorstep that morning.

She taught me that the softer the touch, the lighter the biscuits—and her layering of the dough created pockets of butter that sent those flaky rolls soaring. With my hands floured, I kneaded the ingredients in her white-and-green mixing bowl, its porcelain enamel chipped and dented with scrapes and worn metal spots. "Keep folding the dough until it's as soft as a baby's behind," she advised. That mixing bowl was used for nearly every dish we made: I whisked eggs in it for a breakfast pie, beat a cornbread batter just until the lumps vanished, and sliced veggies as we prepped my grandmother's summer squash casserole, long prized at church potlucks. When that casserole was pulled from the oven, hot and bubbling, she would reach above the stove for her homemade dinner bell. It had a wooden ball for a head and a face drawn in ink and was dressed in a yellowed apron with the name "Isabell" written in my grandmother's printing. "Wash your hands," she said as she rang the bell. "We're fixin' to eat."

• • •

IT WAS DURING THOSE VISITS that I grew to love the South: its tobacco barns, the bottle trees, pottery shacks and kilns in the woods, primitive country stores at rural crossroads, and rows of unfurling collards tumbling down from old farmhouses. Warm, cheery greetings ("Hey, y'all!") welcomed us at storefronts surrounding the courthouse square. In 1984, the South beckoned and I moved to Washington, D.C., and later just across the Potomac to Arlington, Virginia. For twenty-five years I was the art director of, and an occasional writer for, *The Washington Post*, as well as *Smithsonian*, *Preservation*, and *Architecture* magazines. I joined my partner (and now spouse) Dwight McNeill, a residential architect, on weekend explorations of historic homes and tourist sites. Shoved in the glove compartment was a dog-eared copy of Jane and Michael Stern's *Roadfood*. That book fueled my fantasies of owning a rural food business one day.

When Dwight and I flew back to Monterey, California, for a vacation in 2002, we were armed with a list of the sites we wanted to tour and the *Roadfood*-recommended mom-and-pop cafés that were nearby. In a Napa Valley bookstore, I was puzzled by a yellow-and-white-checkered copy of *The Jimtown Store Cookbook: Recipes from Sonoma*

County's Favorite Country Market. I hadn't heard of the place and was intrigued enough to get back in the car to search for it. Out in the boonies of the Alexander Valley, hugging two-lane Highway 128, we found the Jimtown Store, a faded-yellow grocery landmark since 1895, now with a new owner and attitude. A red arrow emblazoned with the words *Good Food* hovered above a vintage fire truck parked out front. Inside was Carrie Brown's ambitious and bustling café, serving breakfast and lunch, with jars of homemade olive tapenade stacked on a rickety farm table. I ordered an egg salad sandwich while Dwight chose ham, fig, and Brie on a baguette. The screen door slammed every few minutes as regulars settled in for lunch. Kids tussled over toys nestled among homemade cookies and pies. I looked at Dwight and thumped the table with my fist. "Man, this is the kind of place *I* want."

. . .

AFTER MY GRANDMOTHER DIED in 1991, I kept for myself the three items that meant the most to me: her mixing bowl, a box of recipes, and Isabell, the homemade dinner bell. She instilled in me a love of cooking—especially Southern food—and that sparked a midlife reckoning of my publishing career in favor of starting a food joint. I trained at the Culinary Institute of America in Hyde Park, New York; at L'Academie de Cuisine outside Washington, D.C.; at King Arthur Baking Company in Norwich, Vermont; with chef Rick Bayless in a former convent in Oaxaca, Mexico; and during early-morning shifts after I talked my way into a three a.m. internship at Connie's Bakery on Cape Cod during my vacation. It all led to launching a rural bakery in a renovated 1921 Esso filling station next to the county courthouse. Five years later our friend and neighbor, actor Robert Duvall, cut the ribbon on my second location twenty minutes north, a 1922 former pharmacy and Masonic lodge on a sleepy Main Street just itchin' for a beloved little bakery to spark a renaissance. That it did.

. . .

THIS BOOK STARTED WITH a busted shoulder and a pandemic. I was on extended medical leave at our Arlington, Virginia, home after a full shoulder replacement and, just three months later, a knee replacement. When our governor issued a home lockdown order during the Covid-19 pandemic, Dwight and I decided to get out of the big city and recuperate at our small farmhouse in the middle of the Virginia Piedmont hunt country. Sheltered under a canopy of 100-year-old red maples and filled with our Southern folk art and North Carolina pottery, the white stuccoed farmhouse is comfy but rustic. With wide-open land and a sparse population, it offered a safe, quiet haven just twenty minutes from each bakery location.

Our farmhouse sits on several acres in the former village of Conde, three miles northeast of Orlean. A large wooden schoolhouse ruin loomed across the road. Originally we had purchased only that property, with our eyes on the seven acres behind the old schoolhouse that offered a future homesite with a view. We drove out from Arlington every few weeks to walk the land and explore the nearby woods. Obscured in an overgrown thicket next door was an abandoned structure that housed, all at once, a corner store and filling station, the owner's residence, and the old Conde post office. The post office had been closed by the US Postal Service in 1955 when

they moved services elsewhere, prompting the demise of Gilbert and Rose Ashby's store and, eventually, the hamlet itself. Dwight and I hacked our way through the bramble surrounding the building and, through broken windows, saw time standing still: after being unoccupied for fifty years, the Ashbys' bed was still made. Dresses hung neatly in the closet. In the next room, evidently the old market, we saw canned goods in neat rows with labels displayed outward. We backed away, just a tad spooked. Returning to our schoolhouse property next door, we could see someone fixing up the vacant little white farmhouse across Conde Road. We wandered over for a chat and tour and ended up shaking hands on an agreement to buy that place; we would have to sell our property to do so. For six weeks we owned two-thirds of what remained of Conde. Dwight named me the mayor.

We purchased the farmhouse in 2005 from the nephew handling the estate of John Butler Ashby and his wife, Mary Lee Weadon Ashby. John Butler was born in the house in 1909 and died there ninety-four years later; their daughter Phronsie died in 2000 and Mary Lee in 2004. The Ashbys hadn't named their farm, as is the custom in the area these days, so we christened it "Cedar Grove" for the towering windbreak of trees that lined our grassy driveway. The house rises on a promontory overlooking rolling fields and a pond that we created after the guy bush hogging our property kept getting stuck in the muck of a swale. I eyed a level site for a decent vegetable garden just behind the house. We've since planted a few legacy trees near there: a sycamore seeding from a tree installed at Graceland during Elvis's day and a chestnut oak and a redbud grown by my friend and former *Washington Post* publisher Don Graham. Adjacent is an existing hedge of ancient blueberry bushes and a grove of peach, persimmon, apricot, and cherry trees. Early revelations: Hungry groundhogs climb fruit trees, and deer eat everything. Two wooden outbuildings are nearby. One of them, a chicken coop (now our garden shed), sits beyond a bed of old-timey yellow irises, and down the steps through overgrown forsythia, home to a flittering family of cardinals, is a curious shed with a swayback roof. I quickly hung a bird feeder there and filled it with black oil sunflower seeds to keep the cardinals happy.

The family cemetery on a knoll overlooking our house dates back to the late 1700s. I walked among the headstones and introduced myself, hoping to make peace with the departed residents and their kin by telling them that we would take care of their former home. During our first few years as owners, small caravans of curious Ashby relatives coasted down our driveway unannounced, wondering what we might have planned there. We gave impromptu tours of the house. Relatives of the old owners told us that Mary Lee Ashby had used our swayback shed as a meat house, partly for making her own sack sausage. Hooks and ropes used to be in the rafters next to wooden peach buckets, and rows of empty canning jars on rickety shelves stretched from front to back. We were sent photos of Mary Lee's crafty scarecrows dressed in wild costumes, created as much for the amusement of passersby as for the protection of her crops. Remnants of the scarecrows were discovered when we poked around a collapsed log shed at the edge of our property.

ON THE FIRST SATURDAY of our state-ordered quarantine, after Dwight and I unpacked both vehicles for a long stay at the farm, we settled into Adirondack chairs at dusk with bourbon in hand. Movement at the edge of the meadow out back caught my eye. Slowly emerging from the woods on the left was a row of fourteen wild turkeys, spread out side by side, making their way in formation across the field as they fed on seeds and insects. We watched them work their way to the tree line on the right, turn around, and head back across the field. Now twenty yards closer to us, they appeared much like a line of police cadets scouting for evidence after a crime.

The solitude at the farm is comforting, although it was interrupted early Sunday morning by the honking of Canada geese circling low over the house and skidding across our pond. An early riser anyway, I got up, cranked over my cherry-red truck (a 1954 Ford F-100), and headed to the Orlean Market to pick up a copy of *The Washington Post*. The peaceful dawn was pierced by the howling of dozens of foxhounds at the Old Dominion Hounds kennels down Leeds Manor Road; it must have been breakfast time for them, too. Our volunteer fire hall next door would normally be bustling with a monthly pancake breakfast, but it was quiet during the lockdown. Mary and Bobby Tarr waved as I drove past (everyone waves when I drive that truck). Before heading home, I ventured a bit east to see how progress was going on the restoration of the old Waterloo Bridge, a one-lane span over the Rappahannock River (pictured on page 124). Our county supervisors had worked with the Virginia Department of Transportation to save the steel-and-iron bridge built in 1878, which replaced an earlier bridge destroyed during the Civil War.

Driving back up John Barton Payne Road, I watched early golden light pan across the hilltop Orlean Cemetery, the site of our town's annual three-congregation Easter sunrise service. One highlight for me on that holiday each year was watching a woman play a large pump organ loaded into the bed of a pickup truck while her husband dozed behind the wheel, and I wondered if that would be happening this Easter. At a farm farther up the road, I stopped to buy a dozen fresh eggs (the rich yolks are the color of marigolds), dropping four bucks into the honor box. Football coach and former Washington player

Andy Heck's farmland near the end of Conde Road was starting to green up; huge round hay bales would soon be strewn across his land, one of my favorite sights out here. Heading back down my driveway I spotted our neighbors' horses rolling around in the pasture. On their backs, their legs swung in the air as they scratched and snorted in pleasure. It felt like spring, a time of renewal and anticipation, yet we were being forced to retreat inside our homes and away from friends and family. Stuck in the house, I started playing with food.

Cooking projects that I had put off for years were now on the front burner. I had a list of the new cakes, summer pies, berry cobblers, and other baked goods I wanted to add to my bakery's lineup. Dwight's mom, Dot, had given me her quirky peach cobbler recipe years before and I was gung ho to finally make it. I yearned to revisit a favorite gazpacho recipe that I first found decades ago. I remembered a summer day Dwight and I had spent in Berkeley, California, in the 1980s, when we ate a clever sandwich of grilled chicken wrapped in pancetta with a garlic aioli and watercress on focaccia at Alice Waters's Café Fanny. I had Alice's recipe and was eager to create a version of it for our bakery customers. At the same time, I dug through my grandmother's pile of recipes searching for forgotten classics that she and I had mastered together.

As I gathered my old recipes and brainstormed about cooking new dishes, a bit of serendipity brought a new project magically into focus. The owner of a home design store near Seattle carrying my *Red Truck Bakery Cookbook* tagged me in an Instagram video. Juleen Pudists had interviewed a customer and daughter who were well on their way to baking every recipe in my cookbook. Corinna Harn, a district court judge in King County, Washington, later emailed me about it. "While at home for several months, my daughter Chelsy and I baked our way through your *Red Truck Bakery Cookbook*. She had been away for many years until the pandemic brought her home for a while, and baking with her has really bonded us. I often shared the results with friends who were working crazy long hours during the pandemic. It made their lives a bit better to find something yummy and comforting at their doorstep or in their refrigerator when they came home late at night and could enjoy their first real meal of the day."

Comforting. I was elated to hear that and thanked her by sending our new Lexington Bourbon Cake with fresh ginger, which I had conjured up too late for publication in the

first cookbook. "Can we have the recipe for *that*?" she laughed. (Before you flip anxiously to the Desserts chapter, don't worry—I have included the recipe on page 183). It quickly became evident that families stuck at home *were* growing closer over my cookbook. Postings of photos on the Red Truck Bakery's Facebook and Instagram pages showed moms and dads and kids together baking our chicken potpies, Meyer lemon cakes, buttermilk chocolate chewies, cranberry muffins, and our Rise & Shine Biscuits (featured, again, this time with ham on page 55). But I got the hint through emails and Instagram comments that they were hungry for more, just as I was yearning to create additional savory and dinner-worthy dishes. With a lot of time on my hands, a second cookbook soon was brewing.

I had been keeping a list of the bakery favorites my customers were disappointed to find left out of the first cookbook, such as our savory Farmhouse Muffins (page 46) and vegetarian Beetloaf Sandwiches (page 79). I had included eighty-five recipes but knew I couldn't please everyone. "I bought your cookbook just for the coffee cake recipe, and it wasn't in there!" grumbled one discouraged cook (cheer up, because it, too, is in this book—see page 40). Others wanted more soups and savory main dishes. I worked on a Bundt-cake version of the caramel-pecan layer cake (page 191) that I wrote about for *Garden & Gun*. Then I added whiskey to it for a Maker's Mark collaboration and later local apple brandy to it for a *New York Times* article about the resurgence of applejack, which included a recipe for our new cake. Since Day One of the bakery, we had been having fun with booze cakes that used rum and local moonshine, and later on bourbon and amaretto. This apple brandy cake cemented our reputation as "the bakery with a drinking problem," although we think we're a bakery that likes to party.

The Red Truck Bakery Farmhouse Cookbook was inspired by my projects at the farm during that time: comforting recipes for family and friends in the style we all want to be cooking, especially these days (and, truthfully, for all time). Some of the dishes are gems shared by friends and relatives, and a few favorite recipes were cajoled from pals in the business. These are classic and, hopefully, familiar dishes that can be shared with family or just enjoyed by yourself, made with simple local ingredients that taste like home, wherever that might be. Most are quick and easy to follow, like Orange Poppy Seed Cookies (page 116), Squash Casserole with Corn & Crunchy Bread Crumbs (page 158), Virginia Peanut Pie (page 170), Gussied-Up Hushpuppies with Country Ham & Pepper Jelly (page 68), and a retro Icebox Fruitcake (page 123) that requires no cooking but, instead, a sense of humor (and it's truly good). I've also included a couple of more-labor-intensive dishes that rank highest among my personal favorites and are cherished at the bakery: a Mushroom-Ricotta Lasagne with Port Sauce (page 140) from Greens restaurant in San Francisco, where my interest in creative cooking was launched forty years ago, and an incredible Oaxacan Mole Sauce (page 137), which is useful in many dishes. These two are projects for the whole family to help with over a couple of days, if you and your kitchen can put up with that. Regardless of the amount of time involved, the recipes in this book will bring folks closer together and encourage slowing down and savoring each meal. Many recipes will introduce kids and kitchen novices to cooking and baking, and offer a chance to bond in the kitchen. These are dishes of cheer, no matter the season—whether it's in the middle of July or with a snowstorm blowing at your door—that will inspire you to wander through your farmers' market or local grocery and fill a basket. Create comfort at home with our tomato sandwiches, a summery gazpacho, and a warm blueberry pie with corn ice cream, and slow down with us.

The
PANTRY

There are ingredients you will see in this cookbook over and over again. Some of them are basics of baking, while others are specialty items that are called for only on occasion. It's worth tracking them down; it makes a difference in the recipe's taste.

WHITE LILY & KING ARTHUR FLOURS

For 130 years, White Lily all-purpose flour, made from soft winter wheat, has been the gold standard for Southern biscuits. If you can't find it in your local grocery store, it's readily available online. If you choose to use self-rising flour for our biscuits, you should eliminate the baking soda and baking powder from the recipes and add an extra 2 tablespoons self-rising flour to the given flour measurement. Otherwise, we use King Arthur Flours for everything else.

BUTTER

We always use unsalted butter; it tastes cleaner and lets us control the amount of salt in a recipe. At home I use a good American unsalted butter, such as Land O'Lakes or Breakstone. And there's nothing better than Kerrygold on Irish soda bread.

BUTTERMILK

Full-fat buttermilk works best in baking; it gives better texture and taste than the nonfat or low-fat version. It's especially vital to use full-fat buttermilk in biscuits and chess pies.

EGGS

Always use large, preferably local and organic, definitely cage-free.

SALT

Readily available, kosher salt is a foundational ingredient for any baker worth his or her . . . well, you know. If a recipe calls for sea salt as a finishing touch, I'm a big fan of J.Q. Dickinson's salt from our friends in West Virginia (see page 213).

BAKING SODA & BAKING POWDER

You should have both on hand, stored in airtight containers. Make sure to replace them one year after opening or after the use-by date to ensure they are at peak strength. Your muffins, coffee cakes, and other baked goods will suffer otherwise.

ACTIVE DRY YEAST

There are several styles of yeast available, but our recipes are designed to work with active dry yeast. Store it in an airtight container in your freezer, where it will stay fresh for a year.

PURE VANILLA EXTRACT

Please avoid using imitation vanilla extract, as it will impart a chemical flavor and create an inferior product; it's not worth the savings. At home and at the bakery, I use Nielsen-Massey Madagascar Bourbon Pure Vanilla Extract.

DARK BROWN SUGAR

Occasionally a recipe will call for light brown sugar; otherwise, use dark. Always pack brown sugar when measuring it. Store-brand brown sugar and granulated sugar are what we use.

DRIED SPICES

Though you may be opening a spice bottle or tin and leaving it on the rack until it's depleted, I urge you to replace your spices after six months: the fresher the spices, the more intense their flavors. Keep the following spices on hand: ground cinnamon, ground allspice, ground ginger, ground or whole nutmeg (a nutmeg grinder makes a big difference), ground cloves, smoked paprika, crushed red pepper flakes, and dried sage. Please use only fresh rosemary, not the dried version.

MEYER LEMONS

There's an intensity and complexity to Meyer lemons that is superior to regular lemons, with a perfumed orange-like zest that's unlike anything else in the citrus world. Meyer lemons are available from November through May in grocery stores, or online at WhiteFlowerFarm.com and other sources. Regular lemons can be substituted, but you'll miss the nuances of Meyer lemons.

SORGHUM SYRUP

A fair number of our recipes are sweetened with this Southern syrup, which is made from juices pressed from the stalks of tall green sorghum plants (not from corn, as many people think). Lighter and less intense than molasses and smoother and more buttery than maple syrup, sorghum has a unique golden flavor. If you don't live where most gourmet stores carry it, you can purchase sorghum syrup online (we carry sorghum on our retail shelves). If you must substitute, use honey, pure maple syrup, or molasses (or, even equal parts of both).

The
TOOL SHED

The majority of the recipes in this cookbook can easily be made using equipment available in most kitchens. However, there are times when specialty tools will make a big difference. Unless indicated otherwise, you can find these items at most kitchen stores or online; we use Williams-Sonoma.com and Webstaurant.com.

STAND MIXER

This will be your workhorse, helping you quickly prep cookies, cakes, and breads and whip eggs and frostings faster and fluffier than if you did it by hand. Make sure you have paddle, whisk, and dough hook attachments to handle a variety of tasks.

HANDHELD ELECTRIC MIXER & IMMERSION HAND MIXER

Though not a necessity, handheld mixers can be helpful in cutting down the prep time and saving your arms a workout. A hand mixer is usable as a substitute for a stand mixer in most cases, but you'll need a more powerful and stable stand mixer when beating or kneading heavier doughs. Immersion hand mixers are useful for puréeing soups.

FOOD PROCESSOR

This is invaluable when you need to finely chop ingredients or blend multiple ingredients together. I like the ones with larger capacity, ranging from 11 to 16 cups, but the recipes in this book will work with a standard 8-cup model. I still prefer chopping herbs, scallions, and bell peppers with a chef's knife and a cutting board.

PASTRY BLENDER OR PASTRY CUTTER

When you're cutting chilled butter into a flour mixture, this handheld tool with narrow metal strips allows you to break it down into pea-size pieces quickly and efficiently.

BISCUIT CUTTER

A circular 3-inch cookie cutter is the perfect size for most biscuits. Make sure the edge is sharp enough to cleanly cut through the dough, and please don't twist the cutter when cutting out your biscuits—you won't get the desired rise.

OFFSET SPATULAS & ROTATING CAKE STANDS

When it comes time to frost cakes, an offset spatula is an invaluable tool for smoothing sides, leveling tops, and ensuring they look as gorgeous as they taste. Rotating cake stands will make frosting those cakes much easier, and they're a great way to show off your creation on your kitchen counter or at the center of the table.

WIRE WHISK

A medium-size whisk works best; too big is unwieldy.

SERRATED KNIFE

Get one with a 10-inch blade to cut breads. I use mine for nearly everything.

RIMMED BAKING SHEETS

A couple of 18 × 13-inch baking sheets, along with raised wire racks that fit into them, are invaluable for a variety of tasks.

BUNDT PAN

When a recipe calls for one, go with a 10-inch, 12-cup fluted Bundt pan. Straightforward, simple designs are fine, but more ornate molds add a little flair to special occasions.

WIRE-MESH STRAINERS

We keep several sizes on hand with various types of mesh. I suggest using these for sifting your flour and confectioners' sugar before each use. I think medium-mesh strainers work best—you don't need to purchase a flour sifter.

CANNING POT WITH JAR RACK

You only need these items if you plan on water processing any of the jams, jellies, or pickles in this cookbook. Find them in the canning section of your local hardware store, the canning aisle of some grocery stores, or online.

SOME QUICK KITCHEN ADVICE

Please first read through these tips and tricks and you'll benefit from my years of trial and error. They will save you time and help ensure your baked goods turn out great. And if you follow the first bit of advice about substitutions, we'll all be happy.

NO SUBSTITUTIONS (AT LEAST THE FIRST TIME)

I put a lot of time, thought, experimentation, and testing into developing this cookbook. All I ask is that the first time you make a recipe, please follow it as I've written. Later you can make all the substitutions you'd like, if that's your thing. I posted a photo of my grandmother's luscious Persimmon Cookies from the *Red Truck Bakery Cookbook*, and someone who made that recipe mentioned in the comments that she substituted chocolate chips for the raisins. That sounded horrific to me and wouldn't have pleased my grandmother— those plump raisins married perfectly with the persimmon and are what makes that cookie so good and succulent. It might be why the commenter thought something was amiss when she tasted them. Thanks for listening.

MISE EN PLACE

The first thing I learned at the Culinary Institute of America was the practice of mise en place (French for "put in place"). It's the routine of having every ingredient measured out, sliced, peeled, and/or grated before you start your baking or cooking. There's a reason instructors and professional chefs start with this and why I insist that my staff do this—having everything ready before you begin eliminates any head-scratching later as you wonder if you've already added baking powder, or you discover that you don't have any fresh thyme or buttermilk on hand. Read through a recipe first, prep each ingredient, and grab all the pans, bowls, and tools you'll need. It really helps.

DON'T CRACK EGGS INTO YOUR BATTER

We like to use farm-fresh local eggs whenever possible. Always crack your eggs into a small vessel or measuring cup first, and you'll be able to pick out any shell fragments—or worse—before ruining your bowlful of ingredients. We learned our lesson once and will never again crack eggs directly into a big mixing bowl of batter: an egg that smelled like it sat for a year in a chicken coop made its way into our supply of eggs and then directly into our batter, which was immediately discarded.

DON'T WASTE ANYTHING

The first baker I hired watched me and observed, "You must come from a rich family!" I was stumped until he pointed out the ingredients—and therefore, the money—that I was wasting as the last bit of the muffin batter was being scraped into the sink. "That cranberry gave up its life for you," he said. Don't waste anything: add that little bit of batter or dough back into what you're baking.

MEASURING STICKY INGREDIENTS

If you're working with sorghum syrup, honey, molasses, maple syrup, or anything else that tends to cause a sticky mess, simply coat your utensils with nonstick cooking spray first. You'll be surprised how easily these syrups slide out of measuring cups, spoons, and bowls.

CITRUS ZEST & SUGAR

You'll notice that if a recipe calls for sugar mixed with grated lemon zest, orange zest, or fresh ginger, I mention it early for a good reason. After you mix the citrus zest into the sugar, a few minutes of sitting allows the sugar to become highly infused with the flavor. It also prevents the pores of the peel from closing up so the zest continues to add flavor and fragrance, giving you more bang for your buck.

ADDING FLOUR TO A BATTER

In our cake recipes, we add flour a third at a time when blending the batter, alternating with a liquid and blending again. It prevents the heavier ingredients from weighing down any light fluffing you've already done and keeps everything mixed evenly. Typically you'll start with the flour and other dry ingredients (except for sugar): add one-third of the total amount of flour needed, mix, then add half the total amount of milk or other liquid and mix again. Repeat with half the remaining flour, mix, add the remaining milk, mix, then add the remaining flour and give it all a final mix.

SPRITZING THE OVEN

This trick only works on quick breads and muffins (don't try it when baking cakes or yeast doughs). Immediately after you

Pies: Poke vent holes in a top piecrust and don't pull it out of the oven until it's bubbling furiously from the very center. It's not fully baked until that happens, and pulling it out too soon will give you a watery pie.

Caramel: When making caramel, cook it until it's a deep brown or it won't be thick enough to use (but watch it closely before it burns).

Baked goods: If breads and cakes don't cook long enough, even if they look done, the center will be gooey since the moisture deep inside hasn't baked off. Don't rush it.

RESPECT YOUR TOOLS

Even as a big-shot bakery owner, I need to be reminded of this practice sometimes. While making wheat bread during a visit to my parents' house, I had just stuck my hands into a running mixer's bowl to feel the dough when my mom walked into the kitchen. My fingers got wrapped up in the moving beaters and were nearly torn off. She rushed to unplug the machine, and I had to grease up my hands to untangle them. Then came her wry observation: "Well, *I've* never done that!" Avoid such embarrassing (and potentially dangerous) moments by working slowly and carefully. Other rules: Don't walk around with a knife pointed out—after too many near stabbings, I have to explain that every time I hire someone; keep knives at your side. Move handles of pots and pans inward—someone walking by will inevitably catch the handle, and that bubbling pot won't remain on the stovetop or counter. And please clean up as you go along (at the bakery, there's always someone waiting to use the area or a mixer).

place your pans in the oven, give a quick spritz to the bottom of the oven with a water-filled sprayer, or splash in a quarter cup of water. Then quickly shut the oven door. The steam created will prevent a skin from forming on your muffins, and they'll continue to rise higher. And our easy way for you to enjoy a muffin quickly: We spray the muffin pans with vegetable oil spray, insert the muffin paper liners, and then spray them also. Catch and release.

WORKING THE DOUGH

When bread doughs require kneading to develop gluten, kneading by hand can provide an immense amount of satisfaction. You can really feel the dough— the texture, the softness, and the elasticity. Conversely, biscuit doughs and piecrusts require a light touch so they don't become tough—handle those doughs as little as possible. When making biscuits, using cold butter keeps it from mashing into the flour too much; the cold bits of butter add rise and texture.

BREAKFAST

32
ORANGE PECAN ROLLS

35
APRICOT SCONES
with Cranberries & White Chocolate

37
HEAVENLY WAFFLES

39
FARMERS' MARKET GALETTE

40
MOM'S SOUR CREAM COFFEE CAKE

41
SUNDAY MORNING PEACH MUFFINS
with Candied Pecans

42
QUICHE LORRAINE
with Bacon & Basil

45
STRAWBERRY BUCKLE

46
FARMHOUSE MUFFINS
with Sausage & Jalapeño

49
PEACH HAND PIES

50
FLOVA'S COFFEE CAKE
(Vegan & Gluten-Free)

ORANGE PECAN ROLLS

These will get the family out of bed in the morning. We bake our orange-cinnamon rolls in trays of a half dozen each weekend at the bakery, and they're the first thing we run out of on a Saturday morning. I've rejiggered the recipe so that you have the option of prepping them the night before, and then all you have to do the next morning is pop them in the oven. These rolls are extraordinary even without nuts, but the combination of orange and pecans is a natural partnership, and I have been known to roll these up with pecan pieces before letting them rise (and the addition is up to you). The double hit of orange in the icing—zest and juice—will brighten up everyone's morning. Let the kids spread on that final touch.

MAKES 12 LARGE ROLLS

FOR THE FILLING:

Freshly grated **zest of 1 orange**

1 cup **granulated sugar**

1½ teaspoons **ground cinnamon**

8 tablespoons (1 stick) **unsalted butter**, at room temperature

1 cup chopped **pecans**

FOR THE DOUGH:

8 tablespoons (1 stick) **unsalted butter**, at room temperature

1½ cups **whole milk**, warmed

1 tablespoon **fresh orange juice**

1 (0.25-ounce) packet (2¼ teaspoons) **active dry yeast**

2 tablespoons **granulated sugar**

1 teaspoon **kosher salt**

4½ cups **unbleached all-purpose flour**, sifted, plus more as needed

FOR THE ICING:

1½ cups **confectioners' sugar**, sifted, plus more as needed

Freshly grated **zest and juice of 1 orange** (2 to 3 teaspoons zest and 2 to 3 tablespoons juice)

1. **Make the filling:** In a medium bowl, use a fork to stir the orange zest into the granulated sugar; let sit for a few minutes to infuse. With a spoon, stir in the cinnamon, then add the butter until well blended.

2. **Make the dough:** In the bowl of a stand mixer fitted with the paddle attachment, beat the butter on medium-low speed for a few minutes until smooth. Scrape down the sides of the bowl with a flexible spatula. Add the warm milk, orange juice, yeast, granulated sugar, salt, and flour. Beat on medium-low speed until a dough forms. If it is sticky, add a little more flour a tablespoon at a time; the sides of the bowl should be mostly clean.

3. Replace the paddle attachment with the dough hook (or use your hands and a floured work surface) and knead the dough on medium speed for 8 minutes. (Don't walk away from the working mixer, as it may travel on the counter.) The dough should be smooth. Cover the bowl with a damp dish towel and let the dough rise in a warm, draft-free spot for 1 hour, or until doubled in size.

4. **Form the rolls (see process photos on page 34):** Dust a rolling pin and your work surface with flour. ① Transfer the dough to the dusted surface and roll it out into a 16 × 10-inch rectangle. Spread the filling evenly over the dough, leaving a ½-inch margin on just one of the long sides. ② Scatter the pecans evenly over the filling. ③ Starting at the long side of the dough with no margin, roll it into a tight cylinder. Pinch the edges of the dough margin against the cylinder to seal.

5. Grease a 13 × 9-inch baking dish or a large cast-iron skillet with vegetable oil spray. ④ Cut the log crosswise into 12 equal-size rolls and lay each one cut-side up in the baking dish so that they are touching one another. Cover the rolls again with a dish towel and let rise in a warm, draft-free spot for 30 minutes. (Alternatively, to bake the rolls the next morning, cover the baking dish with plastic wrap and refrigerate. In the morning, let the rolls rest at room temperature for 1 hour before baking, preheating the oven to 400°F during the last 30 minutes.)

recipe continues

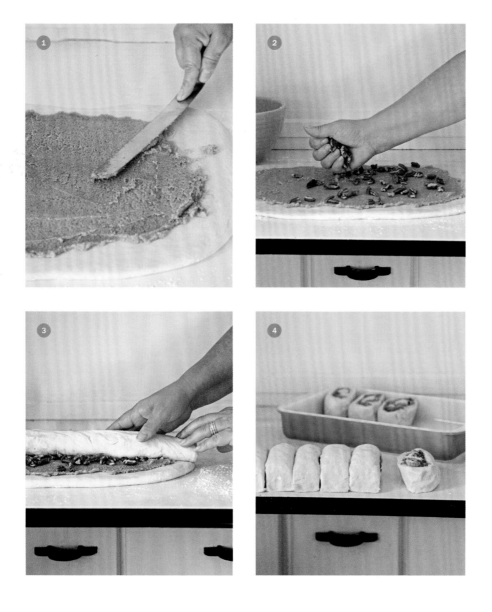

6. While the rolls are rising, preheat the oven to 400°F.

7. Bake the risen rolls 20 to 30 minutes, rotating the baking dish from front to back halfway through, until the tops are golden brown. Let cool in the baking dish for 5 to 10 minutes.

8. **Meanwhile, make the icing:** In a medium bowl, use a fork to combine the confectioners' sugar, orange zest, and orange juice, whisking until smooth, opaque, and barely pourable. If it's too thin and runny, add a bit more of the confectioners' sugar as needed.

9. Whisk the icing once more and use an offset spatula or a large spoon to spread it across the top of the warm rolls. Let the icing set for about 5 minutes before serving.

APRICOT SCONES
with Cranberries & White Chocolate

My friend Ouita Michel is the maestro of Kentucky restaurants. With eight food businesses circling Lexington, she's figured out how to run each efficiently and brought all of her bakers together in one location to bake for all of her properties. Housed in a former high school cafeteria, her Midway Bakery produces, among other delicious items, a sweet scone with dried apricots, which Ouita named the "Betty Ann" after a beloved customer and one-person Welcome Wagon. I bought several of those scones at Ouita's Wallace Station, and more at her Windy Corner, and they were gone before I reached my hotel. I didn't hound her for the recipe but, with her blessing, came up with this version. Now I can enjoy these at home. So can you. **MAKES 12 LARGE SCONES**

---

3 cups **unbleached all-purpose flour**, sifted, plus more for dusting

¾ teaspoon **kosher salt**

½ cup **granulated sugar**

1 tablespoon **baking powder**

8 tablespoons (1 stick) **cold unsalted butter**, cubed

1½ cups (about 10 ounces) **dried apricots**, coarsely chopped

½ cup **dried cranberries**

½ cup **white chocolate chips**

3 large **eggs**

1 cup **heavy cream**

Turbinado sugar, for sprinkling

1. Preheat the oven to 425°F. Line a baking sheet with parchment paper or a silicone liner.

2. In a large bowl, whisk together the flour, salt, granulated sugar, and baking powder. Using your fingers, two knives, or a pastry blender (but not an electric mixer), cut the chilled cubed butter into the flour mixture until it's broken down into pea-size pieces. Stir in the chopped apricots, cranberries, and white chocolate. Using a wooden spoon or your hands, mix in 2 of the eggs and the cream until just combined. The dough should hold together and not flake.

3. Turn out the dough onto a lightly floured surface. Using your hands, gather it up into a pile and mix with your fingers. With the palms of your hands (or a rolling pin), flatten the dough into a roughly 11 × 8-inch rectangle about 1 inch tall.

4. Dip a sharp knife in flour and cut the large rectangle into 6 rectangles of equal size. Cut each rectangle in half diagonally to make 12 scones.

5. Place the 12 scones on the prepared baking sheet about 1 inch apart. Whisk the remaining egg with 1 tablespoon water. Brush the tops of the scones with the egg wash and sprinkle with the turbinado sugar. Bake for 18 to 25 minutes, rotating the pan from front to back halfway through, until the tops are golden brown. Transfer to a wire rack to cool completely. The scones will keep in a tightly sealed container at room temperature for up to a day and in the freezer for up to 6 months.

HEAVENLY WAFFLES

I made these waffles for my mom and my sister-in-law Pam when they were visiting me for the first time after my move to Washington, D.C. Mom hoped that I would be making my lighter-than-air "angel biscuits" (made with yeast for an extra rise) for breakfast, but she was a waffle lover from way back, and I knew she'd enjoy these. So did Pam, who remembered the hint of orange zest even thirty-five years later when I texted her about that visit and this recipe. Mom deemed these "heavenly waffles" because they were just as airy as the biscuits. It's both the yeast and the use of a Belgian-type waffle maker that give them the lift (although a standard waffle iron works well, too). Now they're a staple for Sunday breakfast at the farmhouse, served with Allan Benton's bacon, and we've made a version of these for a horse steeplechase brunch at Great Meadow near the bakery, served with fresh strawberries and a bourbon whipped cream. Make the batter the night before and let it sit in the fridge to develop the yeast. Adding the baking powder just before cooking gives the waffles added height and a crispy exterior.

MAKES 12 TO 16 INDIVIDUAL WAFFLES

1. In a small bowl, combine the yeast and warm water and stir in the sugar until well mixed. Let sit for 10 minutes to allow the mixture to foam and bubble. (If it doesn't, start over with new yeast.)

2. In a large bowl, whisk together the buttermilk, whole milk, melted butter, salt, nutmeg, orange zest, flour, and eggs. Add the yeast mixture and whisk until blended; the batter will be slightly lumpy. Cover loosely with plastic wrap and refrigerate overnight to let the batter rise.

3. The next morning, preheat the waffle iron after applying a light coat of vegetable oil spray to the grid; preheat the oven to 200°F and line a baking sheet with parchment. Whisk the batter again (the mixture will deflate, and that's okay). Whisk in the baking powder and scrape the sides of the bowl with a flexible spatula. Ladle each portion of the batter (amount depends on the type and size of your iron) onto the hot waffle iron grid, close the lid, and cook according to the manufacturer's instructions. Transfer the cooked waffle to the prepared baking sheet and keep warm in the oven while you finish making the remaining waffles.

4. If desired, thinly slice the remaining orange peel, twist each piece, and place on top of each waffle. Serve with softened butter and maple syrup.

TIP: I like to place the waffle iron atop a section of newspaper for easy cleanup.

1 (0.25-ounce) packet (2¼ teaspoons) **active dry yeast**

½ cup **warm (not hot) water**

1 teaspoon **sugar**

1 cup **full-fat buttermilk**

1 cup **whole milk**

8 tablespoons (1 stick) **unsalted butter**, melted and cooled

1 teaspoon **kosher salt**

¼ teaspoon **freshly grated or ground nutmeg**

½ teaspoon **freshly grated orange zest** (save the remaining peel to cut into strips for garnish, if desired)

2 cups **unbleached all-purpose flour**, sifted

2 large **eggs**

2 teaspoons **baking powder**

Softened **unsalted butter**, for serving

Warmed maple syrup, for serving

FARMERS' MARKET GALETTE

A galette is simply a rustic tart with a free-form dough wrapped up and around fresh fruit, and this preparation is especially family friendly, low hassle, and highly rewarding. Your first step: Go to the farmers' market and be inspired by what is in season and ripe. You'll need 6 cups of fruit, so buy what excites you: any combination of berries, apples, peaches, plums, and cherries (I like peaches and blueberries, or just a straight sour cherry tart). This is a relatively quick choice for breakfast, brunch, or dessert, especially if you have some piecrust dough in the freezer, and it can be served straight from the oven. The open-faced recipe calls for a single piecrust; our pie dough recipe makes two, so make the full amount and freeze half, well wrapped, for another use.

MAKES ONE 10-INCH GALETTE

Unbleached all-purpose flour, for dusting

½ recipe (1 disk) **Classic Piecrust** (page 169), or 1 store-bought crust

½ cup **granulated sugar**

2 tablespoons **cornstarch**

Pinch of **freshly grated or ground nutmeg**

Pinch of **kosher salt**

6 cups **fresh fruit** (blueberries, blackberries, pitted cherries, sliced peaches, sliced plums, sliced apples, or any combination)

2 tablespoons **cold unsalted butter**, cubed

1 large **egg**

Turbinado sugar, for sprinkling

1. Dust a work surface with flour and roll out the piecrust dough into a 13-inch round. Slide the dough onto a piece of parchment paper and refrigerate for 30 minutes.

2. Meanwhile, in a large mixing bowl, whisk together the granulated sugar, cornstarch, nutmeg, and salt.

3. Add the fruit to the sugar mixture, lightly stirring until blended.

4. Preheat the oven to 450°F. Line a baking sheet with parchment paper or a silicone liner (or grease a large pie pan).

5. Remove the chilled dough from the refrigerator and let it sit at room temperature for a couple of minutes. Carefully transfer the dough with the parchment to the baking sheet. Spoon the fruit mixture in the center of the dough, leaving a 2-inch margin at the edges. Scatter the cubed butter evenly across the filling.

6. Fold the edges of the dough up and partially over the fruit filling, creating a rustic look all the way around, leaving the center uncovered, and pinching together any adjoining crust folds.

7. In a small bowl, use a fork to whisk together the egg and 1 tablespoon water, then lightly brush the egg wash all around the edges of the dough. Sprinkle the dough and the filling with the turbinado sugar.

8. Bake for 40 to 50 minutes, rotating the baking sheet from front to back halfway through, until the crust is golden and the fruit is bubbling. Serve warm.

MOM'S SOUR CREAM COFFEE CAKE

With five kids under the age of six (including two sets of twins born on the exact same day three years apart), my parents had their hands full. Mom stayed home and did the big work—keeping us fed and out of trouble. I still make her coffee cake, a family favorite, which has been a staple at the bakery since we opened. (If you need a gluten-free and/or vegan version, see page 50.) The recipe appears here thanks, indirectly, to a woman who sent me a terse email saying that she bought my first cookbook "for the one recipe it does *not* contain—the sour cream coffee cake. Wish I had known that before spending $25. Please advise." My advice is to make this coffee cake, and your kids will love you forever. And check the Contents page before buying a book.

MAKES ONE 13 × 9-INCH CAKE

FOR THE STREUSEL:

1 tablespoon **ground cinnamon**

1½ cups (packed) **light brown sugar**

½ teaspoon **kosher salt**

¾ cup **unbleached all-purpose flour**

12 tablespoons (1½ sticks) chilled **unsalted butter**, cut into large chunks

FOR THE CAKE:

½ teaspoon **freshly grated orange zest**

½ teaspoon **freshly grated lemon zest**

1¾ cups **granulated sugar**

4 cups **unbleached all-purpose flour**

1 teaspoon **kosher salt**

2½ teaspoons **baking powder**

12 tablespoons (1½ sticks) **unsalted butter**, at room temperature

3 large **eggs**

2 teaspoons **pure vanilla extract**

1 cup **sour cream**

1¼ cups **whole milk**

1. **Make the streusel:** In the bowl of a stand mixer fitted with the paddle attachment, beat the cinnamon, brown sugar, and salt on low speed just to combine. Add the flour and mix until well combined. Continuing on low speed, add the butter and beat just until the butter breaks up into pea-size pieces; otherwise the streusel will turn to sludge. Transfer the streusel to a separate bowl and wipe out the mixer bowl.

2. **Make the cake:** Preheat the oven to 350°F. Lightly grease a 13 × 9-inch baking pan or dish with vegetable oil spray.

3. In a small bowl, use a fork to stir the citrus zests into the granulated sugar until evenly distributed. Let the mixture sit for a few minutes to infuse.

4. In a large bowl or onto a sheet of parchment paper, sift together the flour, salt, and baking powder.

5. Return the clean mixer bowl to the stand mixer. Using the paddle attachment, cream together the butter and the sugar-citrus mixture on medium-low speed until smooth, about 2 minutes. Add the eggs one at a time, incorporating well after each addition. Add the vanilla and mix until combined, stopping to scrape down the sides of the bowl with a flexible spatula as needed.

6. In a large liquid measuring cup, use a fork to stir together the sour cream and milk.

7. Add a third of the flour mixture to the butter mixture, beating on low speed just until blended. Add half of the milk mixture and blend well. Add half of the remaining flour mixture, beating at low speed just until blended. Add the remaining milk mixture, then the remaining flour mixture, beating for a few minutes after each addition.

8. Pour half of the batter into the prepared pan, smoothing it evenly to the edges. Sprinkle with half of the streusel, covering the batter evenly. Pour the remaining batter over the streusel, again spreading it to the edges, then scatter the remaining streusel evenly over the top.

9. Bake for 55 to 65 minutes, rotating the pan from front to back halfway through, or until the topping is evenly browned and a toothpick inserted all the way to the bottom of the cake comes out clean. The cake's surface should spring back when gently pressed. Let cool for at least 20 minutes.

SUNDAY MORNING PEACH MUFFINS

with Candied Pecans

I usually pair peaches with crystallized ginger in our bakery's recipes—it's a great partnership and the ginger boosts the peach flavor. These simple muffins are loaded with fresh peaches and topped with homemade candied pecans, making these extra special for a Sunday morning. The pecans can be made well in advance, and you should try it this way at least once, but afterward feel free to instead sprinkle the muffins with turbinado sugar just before baking. And if you want to add a tablespoon of finely chopped crystallized ginger to the batter, please do. The muffins at the bakery are jumbo size, but we've adjusted the recipe here to accommodate standard muffin pans. If you want to make the larger version, use a jumbo or Texas-size muffin pan and increase the baking time to 20 to 25 minutes.

MAKES 12 TO 15 REGULAR MUFFINS, OR 6 TO 8 JUMBO MUFFINS

FOR THE CANDIED PECANS:

⅓ cup **granulated sugar**

⅓ cup (packed) **dark brown sugar**

1 teaspoon **kosher salt**

2 teaspoons **ground cinnamon**, or to taste

½ teaspoon **ground ginger**

1 large **egg white**

½ teaspoon **pure vanilla extract**

1½ cups **pecan halves** (about 6 ounces)

FOR THE MUFFINS:

¾ cup **granulated sugar**

3 cups **unbleached all-purpose flour**, sifted

1 tablespoon **baking powder**

¾ teaspoon **kosher salt**

4 tablespoons (½ stick) **unsalted butter**, melted and cooled

¼ cup **vegetable oil**

3 large **eggs**

1½ cups **whole milk**

1 teaspoon **pure vanilla extract**

2¼ cups coarsely chopped, skin-on pitted **peaches** (about 3 large peaches)

1. **Make the candied pecans:** Preheat the oven to 300°F. Line a baking sheet with parchment paper or a silicone liner.

2. In a medium bowl, whisk together the granulated sugar, brown sugar, salt, cinnamon, and ginger. In a separate bowl, with a fork whisk together the egg white, vanilla, and 1 teaspoon water until frothy. Add the pecans and toss to coat evenly. Add the sugar mixture and toss again until the pecans are completely coated.

3. Spread the pecans on the prepared baking sheet in a single layer and bake for 45 minutes, stirring every 15 minutes, until the coating hardens and becomes deep brown. Let the pecans cool on the baking sheet for a few minutes before transferring them to a cutting board and coarsely chopping them. The candied pecans can be kept in an airtight container at room temperature for up to 2 weeks and frozen for up to a year.

4. **Make the muffins:** Raise the oven temperature to 400°F. Grease the wells of a standard muffin pan (or two) with vegetable oil spray, line with paper liners, and spray the inside of the liners.

5. In a medium bowl, whisk together the granulated sugar, flour, baking powder, and salt.

6. In a large bowl, whisk together the melted butter, oil, eggs, milk, and vanilla. Mix until well blended.

7. Add the chopped peaches to the flour mixture, blending gently. Add the flour-peach mixture to the milk mixture and gently fold it in with a spatula. You're simply combining; overmixing will result in a tough crumb. The batter will be lumpy.

8. Scoop the batter evenly into the prepared muffin pan(s), filling each liner nearly to the top. Generously sprinkle the chopped candied pecans over each muffin. Bake for 15 to 20 minutes, rotating the muffin pan(s) from front to back halfway through, until light golden brown and a toothpick inserted in the center of a muffin comes out clean. Let cool slightly in the pan, then transfer the muffins to a wire rack to cool completely.

QUICHE LORRAINE
with Bacon & Basil

I learned to make quiche at L'Academie de Cuisine, outside of Washington, D.C., in a cooking school co-founded by White House pastry chef Roland Mesnier. My instructor, chef Mark Ramsdell (also of the White House's pastry team), taught me to brush the dough with Dijon mustard, which offers a tart little bite and keeps the crust from turning soggy. I was so fixated on creating elevated versions of quiche with ramps, morels, and butternut squash that I never thought to introduce the classic quiche lorraine at the bakery. Customers requested it, but I steered them to our country ham version. Recently I fell in love with it all over again, and added fresh basil to complement the smoky bacon. This recipe calls for a single piecrust; our Savory Pie & Quiche Crust recipe makes two, so freeze half the dough, well wrapped, for another use.

MAKES ONE 9-INCH QUICHE

Unbleached All-purpose flour, for rolling

½ recipe (1 disk) **Savory Pie & Quiche Crust** (page 128), or 1 store-bought crust

1 tablespoon **Dijon mustard**

9 slices **smoky bacon**

1 large **yellow onion**, cut into ½-inch dice

Kosher salt and **freshly ground black pepper**

1 cup **half-and-half**

6 large **eggs**

6 ounces **Gruyère cheese**, grated (about 1½ cups)

¼ cup (packed) **fresh basil leaves** stacked, rolled, and cut into thin ribbons

1. On a lightly floured surface, roll out the dough into a circle 11 inches in diameter. Gently pick up the round (without stretching it) and transfer it to a 9-inch fluted metal or ceramic quiche pan, letting the sides of the round droop over the pan edges while tucking the dough with your fingers against the bottom of the pan. Fold the overhang back over the edge toward the inside of the pan, squeezing it together with the dough in the pan as you turn the pan to give the top edge a bit more thickness. If you're using a fluted metal pan, run your rolling pin over the pan, pressing to trim the dough against the top edge of the pan, and remove the excess dough.

2. Brush the floor of the quiche shell with the mustard. Refrigerate for 1 hour.

3. Meanwhile, in a large skillet over medium heat, cook the bacon until browned but not too crisp, about 5 minutes total. Using a slotted spoon, transfer to paper towels to drain, leaving the rendered bacon fat in the pan. (Alternatively, wrap the bacon in paper towels, put it on a dinner plate, and microwave until the bacon is crispy, 3 to 5 minutes. Let cool slightly and then pat the bacon with fresh paper towels to soak up any excess grease.) Stir the chopped onion into the remaining bacon fat and season with salt and pepper. Reduce the heat to medium-low and cook until the onion is translucent, 8 to 10 minutes. Let cool. Chop the cooled bacon into 1-inch pieces.

4. Preheat the oven to 375°F. Place a wire rack inside a rimmed baking sheet and set the chilled quiche shell (in its pan) on the rack.

5. In a medium bowl, whisk together the half-and-half, eggs, ½ teaspoon salt, and ½ teaspoon pepper.

6. Use the slotted spoon to transfer the cooled onion to the quiche shell, spreading it evenly over the mustard (discard the grease in the pan or reserve it for another use). Scatter the chopped bacon over the onion. Sprinkle evenly with the Gruyère and the basil, then carefully pour in the egg mixture. (Do not fill all the way; the custard will puff up in the oven.) Pour gradually and don't splash any egg mixture over the dough edges, or they will brown too much as the quiche bakes.

7. Bake for 45 to 60 minutes, carefully rotating the baking sheet from front to back after 30 minutes, until the filling is just set and the crust is a deep brown. Let cool before slicing and serving.

STRAWBERRY BUCKLE

An old-timey buckle delivers the most bang for the least amount of work, and it's one of my favorite breakfast treats. The classic buckle is a cross between a light coffee cake and a cobbler, with fresh fruit gently pressed into a quickly made batter. A hefty scattering of turbinado sugar across the top adds a solid crunch, while it also protects the fruit from scorching. Enjoy it throughout the year with other fresh fruit, such as peaches or blackberries (or a combination of the two). When using strawberries or peaches, a pour of heavy cream on top of each serving wouldn't hurt anything—but that's still pretty much true no matter what fruit you choose.

MAKES ONE 9-INCH BUCKLE

---

1 tablespoon **freshly grated lemon zest** (from 2 lemons)

1 cup **granulated sugar**

8 tablespoons (1 stick) **unsalted butter**, at room temperature

1 large **egg**, at room temperature

2 cups **unbleached all-purpose flour**

2 teaspoons **baking powder**

¾ teaspoon **kosher salt**

¼ cup **full-fat buttermilk**

½ cup **heavy cream**, plus more (optional) for serving

1½ teaspoons **pure vanilla extract**

1 pint (about 12 ounces) **strawberries**, hulled and rinsed (if large, cut into halves)

Turbinado sugar, for sprinkling

1. Preheat the oven to 350°F. Grease a 9-inch round cake pan, pie pan, or cast-iron skillet with vegetable oil spray.

2. In the bowl of a stand mixer, use a fork to stir the lemon zest into the granulated sugar until well mixed. Let the mixture sit for a few minutes to infuse. Add the butter to the sugar mixture in the bowl. Using the paddle attachment, beat on medium speed until well combined and pale yellow, about 3 minutes. Add the egg and beat until just combined. Scrape down the sides of the bowl and the paddle (where the zest may collect).

3. Sift the flour, baking powder, and salt onto a sheet of parchment paper.

4. In a large liquid measuring cup, combine the buttermilk, heavy cream, and vanilla.

5. Add the flour mixture to the butter mixture in three additions, beginning and ending with the flour and alternating with the buttermilk mixture; beat well on medium speed after each addition. The batter will be thick.

6. Spoon the batter into the prepared pan all the way to the edges without smoothing the surface. Distribute the strawberries evenly on top, pressing them lightly into the batter, skin-side up if cut. Sprinkle the turbinado sugar evenly across the top.

7. Bake for 45 minutes, rotating the pan from front to back halfway through, until golden brown and a toothpick inserted into the center comes out clean. Let cool slightly, then serve directly from the pan, pouring some heavy cream on each portion, if desired.

FARMHOUSE MUFFINS
with Sausage & Jalapeño

We created a monster with these muffins, and customers weren't happy when we left them off our pandemic-era limited menu available through our Marshall bakery's side-door pickup window. Even after the muffins made it back to the menu, I hope those same folks will prepare these at home whenever the craving strikes. The muffins' origin story goes back to when I wanted a savory breakfast treat and so browned some sausage from the Whole Ox Butcher Shop across the street, then folded it into a muffin batter. Pickled jalapeños were a natural partner, along with our pimento cheese for some bite and cream cheese to mellow everything out. The muffins at the bakery are jumbo size, but we've scaled back the recipe here to accommodate standard muffin pans. If you want to make the larger version, use a jumbo or Texas-size muffin pan and increase the baking time to 25 to 30 minutes.

**MAKES 12 TO 15 REGULAR MUFFINS,
OR 8 TO 10 JUMBO MUFFINS**

¾ cup **sugar**

3 cups **unbleached all-purpose flour**, sifted

1 tablespoon **baking powder**

½ teaspoon **kosher salt**

8 tablespoons (1 stick) **unsalted butter**, melted and cooled

3 large **eggs**

¾ cup **whole milk**

1 tablespoon finely chopped **pickled jalapeño pepper**

¾ cup shredded **cheddar cheese**, plus more (optional) for sprinkling

4 ounces **cream cheese**, at room temperature, cut into pieces

2 cups coarsely crumbled **cooked breakfast sausage** (from 1 pound raw, no casings; some crispy bits are nice)

1. Preheat the oven to 375°F. Grease the wells of a standard muffin pan (or two) with vegetable oil spray, line with paper liners, and spray the inside of the liners.

2. In a large bowl, whisk together the sugar, flour, baking powder, and salt.

3. In a medium bowl, use a fork to whisk together the melted butter, eggs, and milk. Pour into the flour mixture and stir just to combine. Do not overmix. Gently fold in the pickled jalapeño, cheddar, cream cheese, and sausage just until evenly distributed. The batter will be thick.

4. Scoop the batter evenly into the prepared muffin pan(s), filling each well to the top. Sprinkle more cheese on top of each portion, if desired. Bake for 20 to 25 minutes, until light golden brown and a toothpick inserted into the center of a muffin comes out clean.

5. Let cool slightly in the pan, then transfer the muffins to a wire rack to cool completely. Serve within a few hours, or store in an airtight container and refrigerate for up to 3 days or freeze for up to 1 month.

PEACH HAND PIES

Hand pies have come a long way—or perhaps circled around back to what they used to be—since I was at Cal State Fullerton and stumbled into a 7-Eleven for a Hostess apple turnover after a night out with buddies. At the bakery, we use our Classic Piecrust recipe (page 169) and fill these little pockets with whatever is in season. Apple was my go-to until I started playing with bolder flavors built just for these little guys, including the Savory Hand Pies with Butternut Squash & Country Ham (page 86). The pairing of strawberry and guava is a summer treat and a good filling option, as is peach, as you'll soon discover. This recipe could easily be included in the dessert chapter, but there's something fun about pie for breakfast at home or on the run, especially when made ahead and quickly warmed up.

MAKES 12 TO 16 HAND PIES

FOR THE GLAZE:

1 large ripe **peach**, peeled, pitted, and halved

1½ cups **confectioners' sugar**

1 teaspoon **pure vanilla extract**

FOR THE HAND PIES:

1 cup **Grand Champion Peach Jam** (page 206) or store-bought peach jam

2 tablespoons **unsalted butter**

2 tablespoons **cornstarch**

2 cups peeled, pitted, and diced ripe **peaches** (2 or 3 large peaches), plus reserved pulp from the glaze recipe

1 to 1½ recipes (2 to 3 disks) **Classic Piecrust** (page 169), or 4 store-bought crusts, chilled

2 large **eggs**

1. **Make the glaze:** Cut each peach half into chunks and place them in a food processor or blender. Add ¼ cup water and purée until smooth. Push the purée through a fine-mesh strainer set over a bowl, using a flexible spatula to extract all the peachy liquid. Reserve the pulp in the strainer (for the filling); if the liquid in the bowl does not total ½ cup, add water as needed. Add the confectioners' sugar and vanilla and whisk with a fork until smooth. Cover and set aside.

2. **Make the hand pies:** In a medium saucepan over low heat, warm the peach jam and the butter until melted. Increase the heat to medium and stir in the cornstarch, whisking with a fork until combined and the mixture is smooth and glossy. Add the reserved peach pulp (from step 1) and the diced peaches and stir to coat. Let cool completely.

3. Preheat the oven to 375°F and position racks in the upper and lower thirds. Line two baking sheets with parchment paper or silicone liners.

4. Working in batches as needed, roll out the chilled pie dough to a thickness of ⅛ inch. Cut the dough into 12 to 16 rounds that are about 6 inches in diameter (use an inverted bowl as a template), rerolling the scraps of dough as needed to create more circles. In a small bowl, combine the eggs with 2 tablespoons water and brush half of each dough round with the egg wash.

5. Place 2 to 3 tablespoons of the fruit mixture in the middle of each egg-brushed half; distribute any remaining filling evenly between the rounds. Fold over the unbrushed half of each dough round and press the edges with the tines of a fork to seal, or crimp them with your fingers. Cut a slit in the top of each hand pie and brush with the egg wash. (At this point, the unbaked peach hand pies can be individually wrapped in plastic, then sealed in freezer storage bags and frozen for up to 1 month. Unwrap and bake from frozen, brushing again with egg wash and baking for an extra 10 to 15 minutes.)

6. Transfer the hand pies to the prepared baking sheets, spacing the hand pies ½ inch apart. Bake for 25 to 30 minutes, rotating the baking sheets from top to bottom and front to back after 15 minutes, until the crusts are golden brown and the filling is bubbling a bit through the top slits. Transfer the hand pies to a wire rack set over paper towels or a newspaper to cool slightly.

7. Whisk the glaze again, adding water as needed to thin it slightly. Brush a light coating of glaze on each hand pie; repeat with any remaining glaze. Let the glaze set before serving. Store in an airtight container for up to 2 days.

FLOVA'S COFFEE CAKE
(Vegan & Gluten-Free)

I met Pam Northam, Virginia's first lady from 2017 to 2021, at the Virginia Welcome Center on northbound I-95. It was Virginia Tourism Day, and the Red Truck Bakery was handing out samples of cake and granola to visitors. I knew the First Lady eats gluten-free, and I had our almond cake, made with almond flour and Virginia-made amaretto, waiting for her. Her advance man swung by first, telling me that she also is vegan, so I yanked back the buttery cake and scrambled for a bag of our gluten-free granola as she walked up. We laughed over the mishap, and I told her I would conjure up a gluten-free *and* vegan coffee cake for her.

Via back-and-forth emails during the pandemic, she and I worked on this cake together, and when things calmed down she stopped by the bakery with her entourage for a taste. I bantered with her staff that "First Lady of Virginia's Coffee Cake (Vegan and Gluten-Free)" is too long a recipe name to fit on a single page. They said to do what they do: just refer to her as FLOVA. Her cake got a thumbs-up from the entire team, and it can be made with nearly any fruit in season.

MAKES ONE 8 × 8-INCH CAKE

FOR THE STREUSEL:

6 tablespoons **King Arthur Gluten-Free All-Purpose Flour** (see Note)

1 cup **sugar**

1 teaspoon **ground cinnamon**

½ teaspoon **freshly grated or ground nutmeg**

½ teaspoon **kosher salt**

¼ cup **canola oil**

FOR THE CAKE:

1 cup **plain almond milk**

1 tablespoon **apple cider vinegar**

¼ cup **canola oil**

2 cups **King Arthur Measure for Measure Flour**, sifted (see Note)

1 tablespoon **baking powder**

½ teaspoon **kosher salt**

¼ teaspoon **ground cardamom**

¼ teaspoon **ground ginger**

¾ cup **sugar** (see Note)

1 cup peeled, pitted, and chopped ripe **peaches** (1 or 2 large peaches), or 1 cup berries

NOTE: We use King Arthur gluten-free and vegan Measure for Measure flour at the bakery. If you have another gluten-free and vegan brand you trust, such as Nature's Promise or Cup4Cup, feel free to adjust as necessary. If you're baking for strict vegans, you'll need to use vegan sugar.

1. **Make the streusel:** In a medium bowl, use a fork to whisk together the flour, sugar, cinnamon, nutmeg, and salt. Stir in the oil, mixing until just combined and no trace of flour remains. The mixture will look like barely wet sand.

2. **Make the cake:** Preheat the oven to 350°F. Grease an 8 × 8-inch pan with vegetable oil spray.

3. In a liquid measuring cup, use a fork to whisk together the almond milk and vinegar. Let sit for 5 minutes (the mixture will bubble a bit), then pour in the oil and stir. In a large bowl, whisk together the flour, baking powder, salt, cardamom, and ginger just until combined. Add the sugar and stir until blended; do not overmix.

4. Gradually pour the almond milk mixture into the flour mixture, stirring with a fork just until combined. Fold in the fruit. Spoon half the batter into the prepared pan, smoothing it to the edges. Sprinkle half of the streusel evenly over the batter. Spread the remaining batter evenly over the streusel, smoothing it again, and sprinkle the remaining streusel evenly over the top.

5. Bake for 40 to 50 minutes, rotating the pan from front to back halfway through, until the top is golden brown, the streusel has set, and a toothpick inserted in the center comes out clean.

6. Transfer the pan to a wire rack and let the cake cool slightly in the pan. Run a knife around the edge and use a spatula to lift the cake out of the pan to cool completely on the rack.

BREADS

55
RISE & SHINE BISCUITS
with Ham

57
ZUCCHINI BREAD
with Walnuts & Cream Cheese

58
KINDRED MILK BREAD

61
FOCACCIA
*with Sun-Dried Tomatoes &
Goat Cheese*

63
PROPER HOT
CROSS BUNS

67
CORNBREAD
with Sorghum Butter

68
GUSSIED-UP HUSHPUPPIES
with Country Ham & Pepper Jelly

71
IRISH SODA BREAD
with Caraway & Currants

OUR
COMMUNITY
OF ARTISANS

Benton's Smoky
Mountain Country
Hams, *page
212*

RISE & SHINE BISCUITS

with Ham

What's behind my love for biscuits? They are quintessentially Southern, can be made relatively quickly, and freeze well for spontaneous enjoyment (and what's a better host for homemade peach jam?). One of the most popular recipes in my first cookbook, biscuits are a vital part of this book, too—only this time I've scaled them down to be smaller, slightly more elegant country ham biscuits, and tweaked the recipe a bit to be even easier to prepare. If you make these ahead and then freeze them, you can pull them out of your freezer and warm them just a bit before sandwiching with the ham—your guests will think you worked all morning on them. However, you can still make the larger biscuits like we do at the bakery, if you prefer (see Variation, page 56). The biscuits by themselves also serve as a loyal accompaniment for plenty of other recipes in these pages.

Biscuits are the foundation of Southern baking, and every chef has his or her own recipe. Mine is based on my grandmother's, though I've added some newer techniques gleaned over the years from several regions of the country, and after giving many biscuit-making lessons on the road during the last book tour, I found several ways to simplify the process and have updated the recipe here. I've always told readers not to be afraid of biscuit making, and I'm happy to say that everyone who's tried these agree this is an easy and superior biscuit recipe.

**MAKES 30 SMALL (2-INCH) BISCUITS,
OR 16 TO 20 LARGE (3-INCH) BISCUITS**

NOTE: Do not use an electric mixer for these. It's all about a light touch and feeling the dough with your fingers, so grab a large bowl, a pastry cutter if you have one (or two butter knives if you don't), and pat some flour on your clean hands. The dough will be wetter than you expect, but please don't add more flour, thinking it will help. It won't—trust me.

5¼ cups **unbleached all-purpose flour**, sifted, plus more as needed

1 tablespoon **baking powder**

1¼ teaspoons **baking soda**

1 tablespoon plus 3 teaspoons **kosher salt**

2 tablespoons **sugar**

1 cup (2 sticks) **unsalted butter**, chilled and cubed, plus 4 tablespoons (½ stick), melted

½ cup **heavy cream**

2¾ cups **full-fat buttermilk**, plus more as needed

Flaky sea salt, for sprinkling (optional)

Thinly sliced **Virginia ham** or other salty country ham, for serving

Grand Champion Peach Jam (page 206), for serving (optional)

Honey mustard, for serving (optional)

1. In a large bowl, whisk together the flour, baking powder, baking soda, 1 tablespoon plus 2 teaspoons of the kosher salt, and the sugar. Cut the chilled cubed butter into the flour mixture with your fingers, two knives, or a pastry cutter (do not use a mixer) until broken down into pea-size pieces. Combine the heavy cream and the buttermilk in a measuring cup and add it to the flour mixture all at once. Using a spatula or a plastic scraper, fold in the buttermilk mixture as quickly and as gently as possible.

2. Flour your hands and reach into the bowl and under the dough, flipping it around. Mix it up without being too tough on the dough. The dough will be very wet but manageable. If it feels a bit dry after a thorough mixing of the dough, add more buttermilk a tablespoon or two at a time, mixing after each addition.

recipe continues

3. Turn out the dough onto a lightly floured surface and, working lightly, use your floured hands to pat it into a roughly 12 × 9-inch rectangle about 1 inch tall. Lightly sprinkle flour across the top of the dough and pat it with your hands until the flour has been absorbed (if you leave it atop the dough, your biscuits will have unwelcome flour pockets).

4. Flour the bottom of the dough and your work surface. With a bench scraper, fold the dough in half lengthwise, and repeat flouring it and patting it out with your hands. Repeat the process a total of four times. The dough will still be wet but much more manageable. Don't add more flour but again pat the dough into a 12 × 9-inch rectangle about 1 inch tall.

5. Preheat the oven to 400°F. Line two baking sheets with parchment paper or have a large cast-iron skillet ready for two or three batches.

6. Dip a 2-inch biscuit cutter into flour and cut as many biscuits as you can from the dough, pressing straight down with the cutter each time; don't twist the cutter or the biscuits won't rise as well. (Or, for cocktail size or brunch pass-around size, use a 1½-inch cutter.) Reroll the scraps as needed, but try to handle them as little as possible. Arrange just enough biscuits on the baking sheet or in the skillet so they are barely touching one another.

7. Bake one batch for 14 minutes (or 12 minutes for the cocktail-size biscuits), rotating the pan from front to back halfway through, or until the tops are golden brown.

8. Meanwhile, line a portion of your workspace with newspaper and set a raised wire rack on top. In a small bowl, mix the 4 tablespoons melted butter with the remaining 1 teaspoon kosher salt. If the ham is not ready to eat and needs to be lightly seared, warm the sliced ham in a skillet over medium heat for 15 seconds on each side.

9. Immediately transfer the biscuits to the wire rack and brush the tops with the salted melted butter. Sprinkle the flaky sea salt across the tops, if desired. Slice the biscuits in half, add slices of ham (allotting 2 or 3 pieces to each biscuit), and, if using, serve with the peach jam and honey mustard. The biscuits (without the ham) will keep in an airtight container at room temperature for up to 1 day or in the freezer for up to 6 months.

VARIATION: To make larger biscuits, line a single baking sheet with parchment paper and use a 3-inch cutter to cut out the biscuits. Serve warm, slathered with butter, ham, honey mustard, and/or jam, as desired.

ZUCCHINI BREAD
with Walnuts & Cream Cheese

I'll take any zucchini that my vegetable-growing neighbor Alan Davidson wants to leave on my porch. He and his late wife, Joan, liked that notion, too, knowing a loaf of my hearty zucchini bread would arrive as payback. Inspired by our popular cranberry, orange, and walnut muffins, this bread packs in a slightly more robust flavor with the zucchini and gets a nice tang from cream cheese as well, making it a welcome treat for the morning. However, it is still sweet enough to enjoy later with tea or coffee—or even as dessert—with a smear of softened butter or cream cheese. The rich, bold, distinctive taste of black walnuts works especially well here, but they can be substituted with the more subtle, ubiquitous English walnuts. **MAKES ONE 9 × 5-INCH LOAF**

¾ cup (packed) **light brown sugar**

1 teaspoon **freshly grated orange zest**

2 tablespoons **fresh orange juice**

½ cup **canola oil**

2 ounces (¼ cup) **cream cheese**, at room temperature

2 large **eggs**

1 teaspoon **pure vanilla extract**

2 cups **unbleached all-purpose flour**, sifted

½ teaspoon **baking soda**

½ teaspoon **baking powder**

1 teaspoon **kosher salt**

1 teaspoon **ground cinnamon**

1 teaspoon **ground allspice**

2 cups shredded **zucchini** (from 1 large zucchini)

1 cup **walnuts**, coarsely chopped

¾ cup **dried cranberries**

¼ cup **turbinado sugar**, for sprinkling

1. Preheat the oven to 350°F. Grease a 9 × 5-inch loaf pan with vegetable oil spray.

2. In a medium bowl, stir together the brown sugar and orange zest until well blended. Add the orange juice, oil, cream cheese, eggs, and vanilla and stir or whisk until the cream cheese is well incorporated and the mixture is smooth.

3. In a separate bowl, whisk together the flour, baking soda, baking powder, salt, cinnamon, and allspice. Add this to the cream cheese mixture and beat or whisk until smooth (be careful not to overmix). Stir in the zucchini, walnuts, and dried cranberries.

4. Transfer the batter to the prepared pan and smooth the top. Sprinkle with the turbinado sugar. Bake for 1 hour, or until the top is a deep golden brown and a toothpick inserted into the center comes out clean.

5. Let cool in the pan for 10 minutes, then use a knife to loosen the loaf around the edges. Turn out onto a wire rack to cool completely.

KINDRED MILK BREAD

Moments after being seated during the Saturday night bustle at Kindred restaurant in Davidson, North Carolina, a warm greeting arrived on our table: a speckled enamel pot overflowing with four peaks of just-baked milk bread, sprinkled with fleur du sel and partnered with a crock of house-made butter. Katy Kindred, co-owner of the restaurant with her husband, Joe, sidled up next to me on the banquette seat as I mentioned that the bread had arrived even before we had settled in. Katy laughed: "We want guests to feel comfortable as soon as they arrive, and we present this over-the-top welcome even before the water glasses are filled." Their bread is so popular that they've launched two cafés based on this airy nugget named, reverently, "milkbread."

Milk bread is light, buttery, and incredibly versatile. This recipe can make a full loaf, which is great for toast and sandwiches—including Fried Green Tomato Sandwiches with Pimento Cheese (page 77) and Tarragon Chicken Salad (page 85)—or you can shape the dough into individual rolls, so that everyone at the table gets their own. **MAKES ONE 9 × 5-INCH LOAF, OR 6 ROLLS**

2½ cups plus 3 tablespoons **bread flour**, sifted

¾ cup **half-and-half**

¼ cup **honey**

2 tablespoons **nonfat dry milk powder**

1 tablespoon **active dry yeast**

1 teaspoon **kosher salt**

2 large **eggs**

4 tablespoons (½ stick) **unsalted butter**, cut into pieces, at room temperature

Flaky sea salt, for sprinkling

1. In a small saucepan over medium heat, combine 3 tablespoons of the flour, 2 tablespoons of the half-and-half, and 3 tablespoons water and whisk until the mixture thickens, 1 to 2 minutes. Gradually add the remaining half-and-half and then the honey, whisking until the honey dissolves and there are no large lumps.

2. Transfer the mixture to the bowl of a stand mixer fitted with the dough hook. Add the milk powder, yeast, kosher salt, 1 of the eggs, and the remaining 2½ cups flour. Let sit until the mixture starts to foam and bubble, about 10 minutes. Mix on medium speed until the dough comes together and is smooth, about 6 minutes. Add the butter, a piece at a time, waiting until each piece is fully incorporated into the dough before adding more. Continue mixing until the dough is very smooth and shiny, about 5 minutes.

3. Grease a large bowl with vegetable oil spray and transfer the dough to the bowl, flipping it to coat completely. Grease a piece of plastic wrap with the spray and place it lightly atop the dough. Let the dough rise in a warm, draft-free area until doubled in size, about 1 hour.

4. **If making a loaf:** Grease a 9 × 5-inch loaf pan with vegetable oil spray. Punch down the proofed dough in the bowl, then use your hands to shape it into a loaf and place in the prepared pan, with any seam on the bottom. Re-cover it lightly with the same greased plastic wrap and let the loaf rise in a warm, draft-free area until doubled in size, about 1 hour.

5. **If making rolls:** Grease a 9 × 5-inch loaf pan or sheet pan with vegetable oil spray. Punch down the proofed dough in the bowl, then divide it into 6 equal pieces using a knife or bench scraper. Roll each piece into a ball and place almost touching in the pan, with any seams on the bottom. Re-cover them lightly with the same greased plastic wrap and let them rise in a warm, draft-free space until doubled in size, about 1 hour.

6. Preheat the oven to 350°F.

7. In a small bowl, beat the remaining egg with 1 tablespoon water. Carefully remove the plastic wrap from the dough. Brush the top of the dough with the egg wash and sprinkle with flaky salt. Bake for 25 to 30 minutes, rotating the pan from front to back halfway through, until the top is golden brown. Transfer the pan to a wire rack and let the bread cool slightly in the pan before turning it out right-side up on the rack to cool completely.

FOCACCIA
with Sun-Dried Tomatoes & Goat Cheese

Our focaccia is the most addictive item we bake. Back in the earliest days of the Red Truck Bakery, when I was delivering to country stores out of the old red truck, I heard customers say time and time again, "I buy one loaf for home and one for the trip home." And they always used plenty of napkins to catch the olive oil dripping down their chins. We've lately been making several versions of the original rosemary and sea salt loaf, including this one with sun-dried tomatoes, sautéed onion, and goat cheese. (To make plain focaccia like the one we use for the bakery's meatloaf sandwiches, simply omit these three toppings.) It's also a great blank canvas for seasonal variations—in the fall and winter, I sweeten the focaccia by adding dried cranberries and golden raisins to the dough and topping it with aniseed and turbinado sugar, instead of fresh rosemary and salt.

Knead the dough with a stand mixer, if you like, but we find it more satisfying to knead it by hand.

MAKES ONE 9-INCH ROUND LOAF

FOR THE DOUGH:

1 (0.25-ounce) packet (2¼ teaspoons) **active dry yeast**

1 cup **warm (not hot) water**

1½ cups **bread flour**, sifted, plus more as needed

Extra-virgin olive oil

½ teaspoon **kosher salt**, plus more as needed

1½ cups **unbleached all-purpose flour**, sifted, plus more as needed

FOR THE TOPPING:

Extra-virgin olive oil

1 medium **yellow onion**, thinly sliced

Kosher salt and **freshly ground black pepper**

¼ cup chopped **oil-packed sun-dried tomatoes**

4 tablespoons **goat cheese**, at room temperature

2 tablespoons minced **fresh rosemary**

Flaky sea salt

1. **Make the dough:** In the bowl of a stand mixer fitted with the paddle attachment, dissolve the yeast in the warm water. Add 2 tablespoons of the bread flour, whisk well, and let stand until foamy, about 10 minutes.

2. Add 1 tablespoon of the olive oil, the kosher salt, and the remaining bread flour. Start mixing on medium-low speed, adding the all-purpose flour ½ cup at a time, until the dough starts to pull away from the sides of the bowl and is smooth (you may not need to add all of the all-purpose flour, although if it's a humid day, you may need to add a bit more).

3. Switch to the dough-hook attachment and continue mixing the dough on medium speed for about 10 minutes, adding more bread flour as necessary, until it looks very smooth. (Alternatively, turn out the dough onto a lightly floured work surface and knead it by hand, adding more flour as necessary, until the dough feels very smooth, about 15 minutes.)

4. Coat a large bowl with some olive oil, form the dough into a ball, and place it in the bowl. Gently turn the dough to coat all sides. Cover the bowl with plastic wrap or a damp dish towel and let it rise in a warm, draft-free space for 1 hour, or until doubled in size.

5. Preheat the oven to 425°F. Grease a 9-inch round cake pan with vegetable oil spray.

6. Punch down the dough and turn it out onto a lightly floured work surface. Pat the dough into a round about 7 inches in diameter and place it in the prepared pan. Brush the top generously with olive oil. Cover the pan with plastic wrap or a damp dish towel and let the dough rise in a warm, draft-free spot for 30 minutes, or until doubled in size.

7. **Meanwhile, prepare the topping:** In a large skillet, heat 1 tablespoon olive oil over medium heat. Add the onion and stir to coat, seasoning lightly with kosher salt and pepper, and reduce

recipe continues

the heat to low. Cook for 15 minutes, stirring occasionally, until the onion is translucent and just barely turning golden brown. Use a fork or tongs to transfer the onion to a plate to cool.

8. Use your fingers to dimple the uncovered, proofed dough all over (still in the pan). Scatter the sun-dried tomatoes (pushing them gently into the dimples) and the cooled onion across the top. Dot with chunks of the goat cheese.

9. Place the pan on a rimmed baking sheet (to catch any toppings that may spill over) and bake for 25 to 35 minutes, rotating the baking sheet from front to back halfway through, until the focaccia is puffed and lightly browned. Immediately drizzle the top with a thin layer of olive oil and sprinkle it with the fresh rosemary and flaky salt.

10. Use a knife to loosen the focaccia around the edges of the pan. Slide a fork underneath to ease it out of the pan and onto a wire rack to cool. Store leftovers (if there are any) in an airtight container at room temperature for up to 3 days or in the freezer for up to 1 month.

VARIATION: To make a sweet version of this focaccia, omit the onion, sun-dried tomatoes, goat cheese, and rosemary. In step 3, knead ½ cup dried cranberries and ½ cup golden raisins into the dough. Brush a thin layer of olive oil onto the proofed loaf in the pan and top with 1 tablespoon aniseed. Sprinkle generously with turbinado sugar for a crackly finish. Bake as directed above.

PROPER HOT CROSS BUNS

I'm on a one-man mission to teach the world that traditional hot cross buns don't have cloying white frosting crisscrossing their tops—that's "grocery store cheating." We make them the old-world way: piping a sweetened pastry dough onto the buns *before* baking, which creates a golden sweet topping baked right into the bread. These are truly delicious, and at home I will freeze as many seconds as I can grab from the bakery—usually the buns that got too brown or any that got smashed—to eat when we need a snack with tea or as a late-day pick-me-up. At the bakery, we're rolling out 1,200 or so from Good Friday up to Easter, and they still sell out. But let's start with just a dozen at your place. The buns can be baked a day ahead; wrapped in plastic overnight, they'll be great the next morning with the quickest little warm-up in the oven. They also freeze well: bring them to room temperature and then microwave for just 3 or 4 seconds—no longer. (Just don't refrigerate the buns or they'll dry out.)

MAKES 12 BUNS

NOTE: While it might seem unusual to use a small rather than large egg for the pastry dough, it makes a significant difference in this case—a large egg will bring too much moisture to the dough and make it soggy. If you don't have a small egg, you really do need to whisk a large egg and then measure it so that you're using only 3 tablespoons plus ½ teaspoon's worth.

FOR THE PASTRY DOUGH (CROSSES):

½ cup **unbleached all-purpose flour**, sifted

2 tablespoons **sugar**

2 tablespoons **unsalted butter**, melted and cooled

1 small **egg**, or 3 tablespoons plus ½ teaspoon of 1 large egg, whisked with a fork (see Note)

1 tablespoon plus 1½ teaspoons **whole milk**

¼ teaspoon **pure vanilla extract**

½ teaspoon **freshly grated lemon zest**

½ teaspoon **freshly grated orange zest**

FOR THE SPONGE:

½ cup **bread flour**, sifted

1 cup **whole milk**, warmed to no more than 110°F

2 teaspoons **sugar**

1 tablespoon **active dry yeast**

FOR THE BUNS:

2¾ cups **bread flour**, sifted, plus more as needed

1 large **egg**

1 tablespoon **freshly grated lemon zest**

6 tablespoons (¾ stick) **unsalted butter**, at room temperature

½ cup plus 1 tablespoon **whole milk**

2 teaspoons **honey**

1 tablespoon **canola oil**

¼ cup **sugar**

¼ teaspoon **ground cinnamon**

1 teaspoon **ground cardamom**

¼ teaspoon **freshly grated or ground nutmeg**

1 teaspoon **kosher salt**

½ cup (packed) **dried currants** (2½ ounces)

½ cup (packed) chopped **candied orange peel** (3 ounces)

1 large **egg yolk**

1. **Make the pastry dough:** In a medium bowl, stir together the all-purpose flour, sugar, butter, egg, milk, vanilla, and lemon and orange zests until smooth. The dough should be elastic. Cover the surface directly with lightly greased plastic wrap and refrigerate for at least 30 minutes and up to 1 day in advance. Bring the dough to room temperature for 30 minutes to 1 hour before baking the buns.

2. **Make the sponge:** In the bowl of a stand mixer fitted with the paddle attachment, combine the bread flour, milk, sugar, and yeast. Beat on low speed for 2 minutes, then stop to scrape down the paddle and sides of the bowl with a rubber

recipe continues

spatula. Increase the speed to medium-low and beat for 2 minutes more, until smooth. Remove the bowl from the stand mixer; cover with a dish towel and let the sponge rise in a warm, draft-free area for 30 minutes.

3. **Make the buns:** Add the bread flour, 1 large egg, lemon zest, butter, milk, honey, oil, sugar, cinnamon, cardamom, nutmeg, and salt to the risen sponge dough, stirring it with a spatula just until combined. Replace the stand mixer's paddle attachment with a dough hook and beat the mixture on medium-low speed for 5 minutes, then stop to scrape down the sides of the bowl. Increase the speed to medium and continue to beat for 8 minutes more, until the dough is smooth.

4. Add the currants and candied orange peel; scrape down the bowl again and then beat on low speed for 1 minute, or until the dried fruits are well distributed (don't use a higher speed, which will shred the fruit). If needed, gently press any unincorporated fruit into the dough. Remove the bowl from the stand mixer, cover with a dish towel, and transfer to a warm, draft-free area to let the dough rise for 1 hour.

5. Lightly grease a rimmed baking sheet with vegetable oil spray. Lightly flour a work surface. Uncover the proofed bun dough, which should be softer than before and a little sticky. Use a flexible bowl scraper or spatula to dislodge it onto the floured surface and divide the dough into 12 equal portions. Lightly flour your hands and form the portions into balls about 2 inches in diameter, tucking any seams underneath. Roll the balls tight, gently dragging them across the work surface to seal the seams on the bottom, keeping the tops smooth and re-flouring your hands and/or the work surface as needed. Place the buns on the prepared baking sheet in a three-by-four grid, leaving a little space between them.

6. In a small bowl, use a fork to whisk together the egg yolk and 1 tablespoon water. Lightly brush about half of the egg wash over the buns. Let the buns rise, uncovered, in a warm, draft-free area for 45 minutes to 1 hour until doubled (do not overproof). Reserve the leftover egg wash.

7. Preheat the oven to 375°F.

8. Use the remaining egg wash to once more brush the buns, which will have risen enough to now be touching each other. Let them sit, uncovered, for 10 minutes before piping the pastry dough (otherwise the crosses will slip off the buns during baking).

9. Transfer the room-temperature pastry dough to a pastry bag fitted with a small tip (or to a freezer storage bag with a small bit of one bottom corner snipped off). Pipe an X shape (the lines should be slightly thinner than a pencil) on top of each bun.

10. Bake the buns for 16 minutes, rotating the pan from front to back halfway through, or until the buns are fragrant, golden, and the crosses are lightly browned. Do not overbake. Let the buns cool slightly in the pan, then transfer them to a plate and serve. Store the completely cooled buns wrapped in plastic at room temperature for up to 2 days or freeze for up to 1 month.

CORNBREAD
with Sorghum Butter

Our pimento-cheese-and-bacon-topped cornbread recipe in the *Red Truck Bakery Cookbook* included a little sugar, going against all Southern tradition while making one incredible side dish. Here's our true Southern cornbread—unsweetened, but with a helping of whipped sorghum butter ready to spread on a slice for a touch of sweetness. Chef Jeremiah Langhorne serves up a side of sorghum butter for the bread service at his restaurant The Dabney in Washington, D.C.'s Blagden Alley, and we've enjoyed our cornbread this way ever since our first meal there. Try baking the batter in a couple of cast-iron corn-stick skillets, shaped just like a cob of corn, for a little whimsy. Serve the cornbread with Aunt Molly's Brunswick Stew (page 92), Corn Chowder with Bacon (page 101), or Pork Stew with Sweet Potatoes (page 96). If you come across heirloom cornmeal, such as Geechie Boy Mill's Jimmy Red, by all means use it.

MAKES ONE 8- OR 9-INCH CORNBREAD

FOR THE SORGHUM BUTTER:

8 tablespoons (1 stick) **unsalted butter**, at room temperature

¼ cup **sorghum syrup**

FOR THE CORNBREAD:

2 cups **coarse yellow cornmeal**

½ cup **unbleached all-purpose flour**

1 teaspoon **baking soda**

1 teaspoon **baking powder**

¾ teaspoon **kosher salt**

¾ cup **whole milk**

¾ cup **full-fat buttermilk**

1 large **egg**, lightly beaten

½ cup **rendered bacon fat** or **vegetable oil**

1 cup **fresh or frozen corn kernels** (thawed and drained if frozen) (optional)

1. **Make the sorghum butter:** In a food processor, combine the softened butter and sorghum and blend until whipped and airy, about 1 minute. Serve at room temperature. The sorghum butter can be refrigerated, covered, for up to 1 week.

2. **Make the cornbread:** Preheat the oven to 450°F and place an 8- or 9-inch cast-iron skillet on the center rack.

3. In a mixing bowl, whisk together the cornmeal, flour, baking soda, baking powder, and salt. In a separate bowl, stir together the whole milk, buttermilk, and egg.

4. Carefully remove the hot skillet from the oven and add the bacon fat. Return the skillet to the oven for no more than 5 minutes (don't overheat it or you'll burn the fat).

5. Meanwhile, stir the milk mixture into the flour mixture with a rubber spatula, scraping the sides and bottom, until combined. Add the corn, if using, and stir until incorporated, again scraping the sides and bottom of the bowl.

6. Remove the skillet from the oven and pour the batter into the hot skillet, being careful to avoid fat splatters and quickly spreading the batter in an even layer. Return the skillet to the oven and bake on the center rack for 20 to 25 minutes, rotating it from front to back halfway through, until the top of the cornbread is browned and the sides have started to pull away from the edges of the skillet. (You can also test for doneness by inserting a knife in the center, which should come out clean.) Remove from the oven and let cool for 5 minutes. Run a knife around the edges to loosen the cornbread, and then slip a thin spatula underneath to lift it from the skillet.

7. Cut the cornbread into wedges and serve hot, with a dollop of the sorghum butter on top or spread on each slice.

GUSSIED-UP HUSHPUPPIES

with Country Ham & Pepper Jelly

I'm leaving the main event of barbecues to other chefs, but all the sides (except for fried okra) that make up the best part of a North Carolina barbecue dinner are, somewhat accidentally but nonetheless serendipitously, within these pages: minced coleslaw (page 151), baked beans (page 148), cornbread (page 67), banana pudding and vanilla wafers (page 175), plenty of pies for dessert (see pages 162–198), and arguably the best part: hot, addictive hushpuppies. They're traditionally known as sweet little nuggets of fried cornmeal dough, but here I take them beyond traditional—sweetened with a hint of pepper jelly and buttressed with finely chopped country ham. I once made them this way for my Aunt Darla, who thought they were a little fancy ("these hushpuppies are loud," quipped my Uncle Stan). But she won't know until she reads this that I saw her swipe the last two hushpuppies from my plate while I cleared the table. Serve these with Pork Stew with Sweet Potatoes (page 96), Baked Chicken with Oaxacan Mole Sauce (page 136), or Roast Chicken with Guava and Pineapple (page 139). Truthfully, though, they're hard to resist on their own.

MAKES ABOUT 48 HUSHPUPPIES

2½ cups **finely ground yellow cornmeal**

½ cup plus 1 tablespoon **unbleached all-purpose flour**, sifted

¼ teaspoon **sugar**

2 teaspoons **baking soda**

1 tablespoon **baking powder**

1 teaspoon **ground cayenne pepper**

1½ teaspoons **freshly ground black pepper**

1½ teaspoons **kosher salt**

1 tablespoon **hot pepper jelly**, plus more for serving

1½ cups **full-fat buttermilk**

3 large **eggs**

2 tablespoons finely chopped **cooked country ham**

½ cup minced **scallions**, white and green parts (from 5 or 6 scallions)

Peanut oil, for frying (at least 4 cups)

1. In a large bowl, whisk together the cornmeal, flour, sugar, baking soda, baking powder, cayenne, black pepper, and salt.

2. In a large liquid measuring cup, use a fork to whisk the pepper jelly into the buttermilk. Whisk in the eggs and mix thoroughly until smooth. Stir in the ham and scallions and mix well. Pour the buttermilk mixture into the flour mixture, using a rubber spatula to fold it in just until there's no trace of dry ingredients and the mixture is smooth (be careful not to overmix or the hushpuppies will be tough). Let it sit for 10 minutes. The batter should be spongy and light.

3. Place a large wire rack over a rimmed baking sheet. In a large heavy pot, pour in enough oil to reach a depth of at least 2 inches. Set the pot over medium-high heat until it reaches 370°F.

4. Carefully drop heaping tablespoons of the batter into the hot oil, cooking no more than 6 to 8 at a time (don't crowd the pot). The hushpuppies will sink and then rise to the surface; once that happens, gently poke them back down with a wooden spoon so that they cook evenly. Within 90 seconds, the hushpuppies will be golden brown. Use a slotted spoon to transfer them to the wire rack over the baking sheet. Wait to fry subsequent batches until the oil temperature again reaches 370°F, adjusting the heat again as needed.

5. Transfer the hushpuppies from the wire rack to a plate and serve hot with more jelly.

IRISH SODA BREAD

with Caraway & Currants

Why do we have to wait until March to make this bread? I'm kind of crazy about Irish soda bread all year. At the bakery we sell it only around St. Patrick's Day, but I make it at home in the fall and winter when there's a big stew with carrots cooking, or in smaller muffin sizes to go with a cup of Earl Grey tea. My tip: Soak the currants in orange juice overnight, then drain them—they'll reach their ideal level of plumpness that way. Serve with softened butter (the Irish Kerrygold brand, available in most supermarkets, is worth every penny). Even better, make a sandwich with this bread and Tarragon Chicken Salad (page 85).

MAKES TWO 8-INCH ROUND LOAVES

---

8 ounces **dried currants** (about 2 cups)

1 cup **fresh orange juice**

6 cups **unbleached all-purpose flour**, plus more as needed

¾ cup **sugar**

2 teaspoons **baking soda**

1 tablespoon **baking powder**

1½ teaspoons **kosher salt**

3 tablespoons **caraway seeds**

8 tablespoons (1 stick) **unsalted butter**, melted and cooled

1 tablespoon **canola oil**

2 cups **full-fat buttermilk**

½ cup **heavy cream**

2 large **eggs**

1. Soak the currants in the orange juice overnight if possible or for at least 2 hours.

2. Preheat the oven to 375°F. Line a baking sheet with parchment paper or a silicone liner.

3. Drain the plumped currants, discarding the orange juice. Spread the fruit on paper towels to soak up any excess liquid and pat them dry.

4. In a very large bowl, stir together the flour, sugar, baking soda, baking powder, salt, and caraway seeds. Scatter the rehydrated currants into the flour and stir with your fingers to mix. Generously flour a work surface and place a small pile of extra flour nearby.

5. In a medium bowl, whisk together the melted butter, oil, buttermilk, cream, and 1 of the eggs. Pour into the flour mixture.

6. Bring the dough together with your well-floured hands (do not use an electric mixer). Reach in and around the dough, turning it over and over until combined. The dough should be slightly wet but not gloppy. Add a bit more flour, a tablespoon at a time, if the dough feels too wet and is spreading.

7. Turn out the dough onto the floured work surface. Flour your hands again and gently knead the dough, sprinkling more flour as needed (from the extra pile), just until it is somewhat firmer. If any currants pop out, just poke them back in. Divide the dough in half, shaping each portion into a round loaf with any seams on the bottom.

8. Place the loaves several inches apart from one another on the prepared baking sheet (they may spread a little) but not up against the rim. Combine the remaining egg with a spoonful of water. Brush the egg wash on the top and sides of each loaf. Use a wet serrated knife to slightly score an X into the top of each loaf. Bake for 50 to 60 minutes, rotating the baking sheet from front to back halfway through, until the loaves are nicely browned and a knife inserted in the center comes out clean. The loaves should also sound hollow when tapped on the bottom. Cool completely on a wire rack and rub off and discard any burnt currants before serving.

LUNCH

74
BLTS
with Avocado & Pesto Mayonnaise

77
**FRIED GREEN
TOMATO SANDWICHES**
with Pimento Cheese

79
BEETLOAF SANDWICHES

80
**GRILLED CHICKEN
SANDWICHES**
with Sage Leaves & Pancetta

82
**JIMTOWN EGG SALAD
SANDWICHES**

83
**POTATO & PESTO
FLATBREAD**

85
**TARRAGON
CHICKEN SALAD**
on Irish Soda Bread

86
SAVORY HAND PIES
*with Butternut Squash &
Country Ham*

89
**WILD MUSHROOM
TARTINES**
with Black Pepper Ricotta

BLTS

with Avocado & Pesto Mayonnaise

There isn't much that gets me more fired up at the peak of summer than crafting and eating a proper bacon, lettuce, and tomato sandwich. I've made hundreds and, well, I know what I like (and what I don't like). Terri Lehman at the much-missed Epicurious Cow in Rappahannock County, not far from the original Warrenton bakery location, showed me the value of adding avocado (it became a BLAT) and a little bit of chipotle peppers to the mayo (always Duke's). I do that on occasion, although pesto is more often my go-to swipe on the bottom slice of bread. Big puffy leaves of Bibb lettuce finish it off.

I don't bend on one important component: I insist on Allan Benton's smoked bacon from Madisonville, Tennessee. And the tomato? Make sure it's fresh from a farmer or your garden. Aim for a big, fat heirloom variety (grab some Cherokee Purples if you find them) and slice them thick. I feel a bit sheepish to mention this, but I like to add just a couple drops of ketchup to the tomato slices before adding the bacon. You okay with that? As for the bread, nothing beats our focaccia, especially when you grill it in a stovetop grill pan, but you can simply toast the bread if you prefer. Wipe your chin.

SERVES 4

NOTE: If you're using ciabatta rolls, halve each roll crosswise and toast or grill the inside of each half in the grill pan. If you're using country bread, simply toast each slice.

1 plain **focaccia loaf** (page 61), 4 ciabatta rolls, or 8 hefty country bread slices (see Note)

12 thick slices **best-quality smoky bacon**

3 or 4 large ripe **heirloom tomatoes**, such as Cherokee Purple or beefsteak, or enough for 8 thick slices

Kosher salt (optional)

½ cup **mayonnaise**, plus more as needed

¼ cup **pesto**, homemade (page 83) or store-bought

Lettuce leaves, such as Bibb, or other greens

Ketchup (optional)

½ ripe **avocado**, cut lengthwise into 4 slices

1. Slice the focaccia into quarters and halve each slice horizontally. Spray a stovetop grill pan with vegetable oil spray and heat it over medium heat. Add the focaccia, cut-side down, to the pan and grill until crisp and slightly charred, about 4 minutes. Set aside.

2. Wrap the bacon in paper towels, put it on a microwave-safe dinner plate, and microwave until the bacon is crispy, 3 to 5 minutes. Let cool slightly and then pat the bacon with fresh paper towels to soak up any excess grease.

3. Thickly slice the tomatoes. Season with salt, if desired. Use your finger to poke out the juices and the gel inside each slice. Set the slices on paper towels and use additional paper towels to blot the tomatoes dry.

4. To assemble the sandwiches, arrange the bottom pieces of focaccia in a row in front of you, grilled-sides up. Line the tops in the row above them, grilled-sides up. Smear a good amount of mayonnaise on each piece (use more on the bottoms than the tops). Divide the pesto among the 4 sandwich bottoms and smear it into the mayo. Add lettuce to each bottom half, then overlap 2 tomato slices on each portion of lettuce. Top the tomato with some ketchup, if desired. Add an avocado slice on each half, then add 3 bacon slices (folding over or tearing the bacon as needed to fit). Place the top pieces of focaccia, grilled-sides down, and dig in.

OUR
COMMUNITY
OF ARTISANS

Benton's Smoky
Mountain Country
Hams, *page
212*

FRIED GREEN TOMATO SANDWICHES

with Pimento Cheese

Growing up in California, I had never heard of pimento cheese until I visited my relatives in the Southern states, where the bright orange mixture would be spread on the likes of Wonder Bread, in the groove of a celery stick, on cornbread, and in fried green tomato sandwiches. When I headed back to the West Coast, it was pimento cheese I craved most, and when I'd find it or make it myself, I'd slather it between two flour tortillas (hey, I'm a Californian) and grill each side until the pimento cheese was golden brown and oozing out of the center. Now that I've been in the South for forty years, this is the pimento cheese sandwich I hanker after, using my Aunt Darla's smoky pimento cheese recipe that gets a kick from pickled red onions. Use green tomatoes throughout the season—just find them before they ripen. Sneak in a couple of slices of cooked bacon if you'd like.

MAKES 6 SANDWICHES

NOTE: If you've already made the Pickled Red Onions (page 209) and have them on hand, you only need ¼ cup (plus 1 teaspoon of the pickling brine) for the pimento cheese recipe here, and you can skip step 1.

FOR THE PIMENTO CHEESE:

3 tablespoons **apple cider vinegar**

2 teaspoons **sugar**

½ teaspoon **kosher salt**

½ teaspoon **pickling spice**

¼ cup chopped **red onion**

½ cup coarsely chopped drained **roasted red peppers** from a jar

½ cup (4 ounces) **cream cheese**, at room temperature

¼ teaspoon **ground cayenne pepper**

1 teaspoon **smoked paprika**

½ teaspoon crushed **red pepper flakes**

2 cups (8 ounces) grated **cheddar cheese**, at room temperature

1 cup (4 ounces) grated **pepper Jack cheese**, at room temperature

1 teaspoon **dried chives**

½ cup **mayonnaise**

FOR THE FRIED GREEN TOMATOES:

6 medium **green tomatoes**

2 cups **full-fat buttermilk**

2 large **eggs**

2 cups **self-rising flour**

1 cup **cornmeal**

1 teaspoon **garlic powder**

Kosher salt and **freshly ground black pepper**

2 cups **canola oil**, for frying

1 cup (2 sticks) clarified **unsalted butter**, for frying

FOR THE SANDWICHES:

12 slices **white bread**, such as Kindred Milk Bread (page 58), Focaccia with Sun-Dried Tomatoes & Goat Cheese (page 61), or store-bought bread

Mayonnaise

Watercress greens

1. **Make the pimento cheese:** In a small saucepan, combine the vinegar, sugar, salt, pickling spice, and red onion and bring to a low boil over medium to medium-high heat. Cook for 5 minutes to allow the flavors to infuse, then transfer to a heatproof container and refrigerate for 10 minutes.

2. In a food processor, pulse the roasted red peppers until they are almost reduced to a paste but still a bit chunky, then scrape them into a large bowl (no need to wash the processor bowl). Combine the pickled red onion and its brine,

recipe continues

the cream cheese, cayenne, smoked paprika, and red pepper flakes in the food processor and purée until smooth.

3. Add the cream cheese mixture to the bowl with the red peppers, along with the cheddar, pepper Jack, dried chives, and mayonnaise and stir until well combined. You should have about 3½ cups. Set aside or transfer to a lidded container and refrigerate for up to 10 days.

4. **Make the fried green tomatoes:** Slice off and discard the tops and bottoms from the tomatoes. Cut the tomatoes horizontally into ⅓-inch-thick slices. On a platter or baking sheet covered with paper towels, lay out the tomato slices. Let them sit for 5 minutes to draw out their moisture, then pat them dry with additional paper towels.

5. In a shallow bowl, whisk together the buttermilk and eggs. In a separate bowl, combine the flour, cornmeal, garlic powder, and a generous amount of salt and black pepper.

6. Heat the oil and clarified butter in a large cast-iron skillet until it registers 350°F on an instant-read thermometer, adjusting the heat as needed to maintain that temperature.

7. Working with 3 tomato slices at a time, dip each slice into the buttermilk mixture and then into the flour mixture. Fry the tomato slices for 2 minutes on each side, until golden brown, then remove them with a slotted spatula to drain on a brown paper bag or paper towels. Repeat with the remaining tomato slices. Discard any of the remaining buttermilk and flour mixtures.

8. **Assemble the sandwiches:** Toast or grill the bread, if desired. Slather one side of each slice with mayonnaise and add the watercress to half of the slices. Divide the fried tomatoes evenly among those 6 halves, then spread with generous portions of pimento cheese. Cover the sandwiches with the remaining 6 bread slices, slice each sandwich in half, and serve.

BEETLOAF SANDWICHES

This is the most requested lunch recipe that did *not* appear in our first cookbook. I forgot about including it then, but scores of customers were very eager to remind me this time around. Our lead baker, Kevin Powers, pulled it together when I asked him for a veggie option to serve at the bakery; we're both beet lovers and this is a winner (and if you don't like beets, you'll still enjoy these; there are many other flavors going on in the patties). The spread of goat cheese on the buns makes these sandwiches sing. We use our whole-wheat focaccia in keeping with the healthy veggie aspect of the beetloaf. Adding a pickle, or Pickled Red Onions (page 209), would be a treat.

MAKES 6 SANDWICHES

FOR THE BEETLOAF PATTIES:

3 medium **red beets** (about 1 pound), peeled

1 medium **sweet potato** (about 9 ounces), peeled

3 tablespoons chopped **walnuts**

¼ cup chopped **yellow onion**

2 tablespoons **apple cider vinegar**

1 tablespoon **extra-virgin olive oil**

½ teaspoon **soy sauce**

1 tablespoon plus 1½ teaspoons **white sesame seeds**

1 tablespoon plus 1½ teaspoons **black sesame seeds**

1 large **egg** plus 1 large **egg yolk**

1 teaspoon chopped **fresh rosemary**

½ teaspoon chopped **fresh thyme**

2 tablespoons finely chopped **fresh parsley**

¼ cup **whole-wheat flour**

¾ cup **quick-cooking oats**

2 cups **cooked quinoa**

1 teaspoon **kosher salt**

1 teaspoon **freshly ground black pepper**

FOR THE SANDWICHES:

6 **whole-wheat buns**

Goat cheese, at room temperature, for spreading

Bibb lettuce leaves

1 cup **Pickled Red Onions** (page 209) (optional)

1. **Make the patties:** In a food processor using the grating-disk attachment, shred the beets and the sweet potato (this could get messy, so wear an apron). Transfer to a large stainproof bowl. Replace the grating attachment with the regular blade and pulse the walnuts and onion until finely ground.

2. Preheat the oven to 375°F. Line a rimmed baking sheet with parchment paper or a silicone liner.

3. In a small bowl, combine the vinegar, oil, soy sauce, white and black sesame seeds, and the egg and egg yolk and whisk with a fork until smooth. Add the rosemary, thyme, parsley, flour, and oats and stir until incorporated.

4. To the grated beets and sweet potato, add 1½ cups of the cooked quinoa, the walnut-onion mixture, and the vinegar-egg mixture. Stir in the salt and pepper until well combined. If the mixture seems too wet, add the remaining ½ cup cooked quinoa. Shape the mixture into 6 thick patties of equal size and flatten the patties on the prepared baking sheet. Bake for 20 minutes, or until browned and firm. Let cool completely on the baking sheet.

5. **Assemble the sandwiches:** Dress the top and bottom of each sandwich bun with a decent spread of the goat cheese. Add the lettuce leaves and the pickled onions (if using). Use a metal spatula to transfer a beetloaf patty to each bottom bun; finish off with the top buns and serve.

GRILLED CHICKEN SANDWICHES

with Sage Leaves & Pancetta

It was Bastille Day at Alice Waters's Café Fanny in Berkeley about thirty years ago, and we were lined up with the masses for a celebratory lunch outside. I remember a watermelon punch that was handed out to each of us, and I haven't forgotten the grilled chicken sandwich wrapped in sage leaves and pancetta, with the bite of a garlicky aioli and watercress. The café eventually provided the recipe, and I have been making it for summer meals at the farm and at the bakery for special catering events ever since. Plan ahead: the chicken and the aioli both need to sit for at least 3 hours.

MAKES 4 LARGE SANDWICHES

FOR THE AIOLI:

¾ cup **mayonnaise**

2 **garlic cloves**, crushed to a pulp

FOR THE MARINADE:

2 tablespoons **extra-virgin olive oil**

Juice of 1 **lemon**

3 **fresh thyme sprigs**

Pinch of **kosher salt**

¼ teaspoon **freshly ground black pepper**

2 **boneless, skinless chicken breasts**, trimmed of excess fat

FOR THE SANDWICHES:

16 **fresh sage leaves**

12 generous slices of **pancetta** (not too thin or short; they need to wrap around the chicken breasts)

1 **Focaccia with Sun-Dried Tomatoes and Goat Cheese round loaf** (page 61), or 4 sandwich rolls

Watercress greens or **arugula**

1. **Make the aioli:** In a medium bowl, use a fork to stir together the mayonnaise and garlic until well blended. Cover and refrigerate for at least 3 hours and up to overnight.

2. **Make the marinade:** In a liquid measuring cup, whisk together the oil, lemon juice, thyme sprigs, salt, and pepper. Pour the marinade into a zip-top food storage bag, add the chicken, and seal, pressing out as much air as possible. With the bag closed, massage the marinade into the chicken and then refrigerate for at least 3 hours and up to overnight.

3. Transfer the chicken from the bag to a cutting board, discarding the marinade. Lay 4 sage leaves diagonally across each chicken breast, then wrap each one with 3 slices of pancetta to hold the sage in place.

4. Heat an outdoor grill or an oiled grill pan on the stovetop over medium heat. Grill the chicken for 5 to 7 minutes on each side, until the chicken is charred and cooked through and the juices run clear. Let cool, then slice crosswise into ½-inch pieces, keeping the crisped pancetta in place.

5. **Assemble the sandwiches:** Use a bread knife to cut the focaccia in half horizontally; then cut the round loaf into quarters. Lay the 4 tops on your work surface, cut-sides up. Arrange the 4 bottom quarters below them, cut-sides up. Spread the aioli generously on all the cut sides. Lay a quarter of the watercress on each bottom half, and then a quarter of the chicken slices. Complete the sandwiches with the focaccia tops and serve.

JIMTOWN EGG SALAD SANDWICHES

One of the saddest things to happen in years was the closing of the beloved Jimtown Store in Alexander Valley, California. I wouldn't have my rural bakery if Carrie Brown and John Werner hadn't stumbled upon the little hamlet of Jimtown themselves years earlier and poured their lives into their roadside gem, which I discovered on a road trip there in 2002. The Jimtown Store greatly influenced my decision to leave publishing and open a rural bakery in Virginia. I blatantly stole Carrie's egg salad sandwich recipe (which she has since handed over to me with a hug and a kiss) and used it for years—until it became too popular with our customers, leading my staff to complain about all the boiled eggs that they had to peel. Thank you, Carrie, for changing my life, influencing my new passion, and giving my home state a beloved jewel. We miss you and Jimtown Store immensely.

Carrie mentions that her egg salad, while perfectly delicious the next day, is most exquisite if never refrigerated. We agree and cherish its room-temp fluffiness. Adding tomato and bacon to the sandwich is an idea we both love, and I've been known to add a tablespoon of chopped homemade sweet pickles along with the mayonnaise.

MAKES 4 SANDWICHES

8 large **eggs**

½ cup **mayonnaise**, plus more for spreading

½ teaspoon **dry mustard**, preferably Colman's, plus more as needed

½ teaspoon **kosher salt**, plus more as needed

¼ teaspoon **hot pepper sauce**, preferably Tabasco, plus more as needed

¼ teaspoon **freshly ground black pepper**, plus more as needed

8 slices **whole-wheat sandwich bread**, lightly toasted

Thinly sliced ripe **red tomato** (optional)

Watercress greens

1. In a medium pan large enough to accommodate the eggs in a single layer, cover the eggs with cold water. Bring just to a boil over medium-high heat, then remove from the heat, quickly cover with a lid, and let stand for exactly 12 minutes. Drain, cover the eggs with cold water, and let stand until cool. Peel the eggs when cool enough to handle.

2. In a small bowl, whisk together the mayonnaise, mustard, salt, hot pepper sauce, and black pepper.

3. Chop the eggs with a pastry cutter (the kind with curved blades) or with two knives and place them in a large bowl. Add the mayo mixture and stir until well combined. Taste and adjust the seasoning as needed.

4. Lay half of the toasted bread slices on a work surface. Spread each one with a thin layer of mayo, then distribute the egg salad evenly among them (you should absolutely use all of it). Arrange the tomato slices, if using, on top of the egg salad. Lay the watercress on top, making sure some leaves extend past the bread's edges. Complete the sandwiches by topping each with a remaining slice of toasted bread. Use a serrated knife to cut each sandwich in half, on the diagonal, and serve.

POTATO & PESTO FLATBREAD

There should be much to reminisce over after a trip to Italy, but when we returned home the thing I couldn't forget was a simple pizza we had enjoyed in Florence. Our pal Nica Lalli had told us we needed to try the potato pizza at a little *forno* (bakery) she loved. It was glorious, with thin slices of potato so translucent we could clearly see the fresh mozzarella underneath. We ate it overlooking the Arno River and found its equal a few days later in Rome, where we enjoyed it on the Spanish Steps. This is our flatbread version, created on our popular focaccia dough, finished off with a swipe of fresh pesto, melted cheese, pine nuts, and caramelized onions. We stack slices on the bakery counter on Saturdays, and they barely last through the lunch hour. Allow an hour or two for the dough to rise and proof properly and to build the flavor. To make things easy at home, you can make the dough, pesto, and onions ahead of time and refrigerate everything for up to 2 days. If you want to use store-bought pesto, that's fine, too, though it's hard to resist homemade, especially if you find yourself with a large supply of fresh basil.

MAKES ONE 13 × 9-INCH FLATBREAD

NOTE: The dough here is identical to the one we use for the Focaccia with Sun-Dried Tomatoes & Goat Cheese (page 61), so you'll be using the same base recipe, only in this case you'll be shaping it differently and incorporating different toppings. For the flatbread, follow steps 1 through 4 of the focaccia recipe to prepare the dough, then proceed with the steps listed at right.

FOR THE FLATBREAD:

1 recipe **plain Focaccia dough** (page 61) (see Note)

Unbleached All-purpose flour, for dusting

FOR THE PESTO:

2 cups **fresh basil leaves** (about 1½ ounces— no stems)

2 tablespoons **pine nuts**

2 large **garlic cloves**

½ cup **extra-virgin olive oil**, plus more as needed

2 ounces **Parmigiano-Reggiano** or **pecorino cheese**, freshly grated (½ cup)

FOR THE TOPPINGS:

1 large **Yukon Gold potato**, well scrubbed

2 tablespoons **extra-virgin olive oil**, plus more as needed

2 medium **yellow onions**, thinly sliced

Flaky sea salt and **freshly ground black pepper**

About 12 ounces **fresh whole-milk mozzarella**, sliced, or 2 cups store-bought shredded mozzarella

¼ cup minced **fresh rosemary**

¼ cup **pine nuts**

Freshly grated **Parmigiano-Reggiano** or **pecorino cheese**

1. **Make the flatbread:** After the dough has completed its first rise and doubled in size, punch it down in the bowl, re-cover the bowl loosely with plastic wrap or a dish towel, and refrigerate overnight or for up to 2 days. (If you're in a hurry, you can skip the refrigeration and let the dough rest at room temperature for 1 hour, but you'll lose the aging quality that develops flavor and characteristics similar to a sourdough.)

2. **Make the pesto:** Combine the basil, pine nuts, and garlic in a food processor. Pulse repeatedly until finely minced. While the machine is running, slowly pour in ½ cup olive oil and continue to pulse until the pesto is smooth, scraping down the bowl with a flexible spatula as needed. Add the cheese and pulse just until combined. You should have about 1 cup. Transfer to an airtight container and pour a thin layer of oil on top of the pesto. Seal and refrigerate for up to 2 days or freeze for up to 3 months.

recipe continues

3. **Prepare the toppings:** In a food processor outfitted with a very thin slicing-blade attachment, or using a mandoline's thinnest blade, slice the potato as thinly as possible. Place the slices in a bowl with enough cold water to cover.

4. In a medium skillet, heat 2 tablespoons oil over medium heat. Add the onions and stir to coat with the oil. Season lightly with salt and pepper and reduce the heat to low. Cook for 15 minutes, stirring occasionally, until the onions are translucent and just barely turning golden brown. Use a fork or tongs to transfer the onions to a plate or bowl. Have the rest of the toppings ready.

5. **For assembly:** Remove the dough from the refrigerator at least 45 minutes before you begin to shape it.

6. Preheat the oven to 450°F. Pour two quarter-size spots of oil into a 13 × 9-inch baking sheet with 2-inch sides. Use your hand to wipe the oil around the bottom and sides so the pan is evenly coated.

7. Punch down the dough and turn it out onto a lightly floured surface. Pat it out into a large, thin rectangle about 13 × 9 inches, place it in the prepared baking sheet, and let it rest for 5 minutes. Lightly coat your hands with oil and smooth out the dough to the edges, filling the pan's corners.

8. Scoop out ¾ cup of the pesto from its container; refrigerate or freeze the remaining ¼ cup for another use. Gently spread a thin layer of the pesto across the dough, leaving about a ½-inch border on all sides. Distribute the mozzarella evenly over the pesto and scatter about three-quarters of the minced rosemary evenly across the cheese. Drain the potato, placing the slices on paper towels and blotting them until dry. Evenly distribute the potato slices across the flatbread; some overlapping is okay. Sprinkle with the remaining rosemary and season with salt and pepper. Spread the cooked onions evenly over everything and scatter the pine nuts on top.

9. Bake for 30 to 40 minutes, until the flatbread is puffed and browned at the edges, the potatoes are tender, and the onions are browned. Use a fork to lift a corner and check that the crust is browned underneath. Transfer the pan to a wire rack and immediately sprinkle with the grated Parmesan. Let the flatbread sit for 5 to 10 minutes before slicing it with a pizza cutter.

TARRAGON CHICKEN SALAD

on Irish Soda Bread

Bonnie Benwick, one of my old *Washington Post* colleagues and now my recipe tester, fondly remembers D.C.'s much missed American Café and their chicken salad loaded with fresh tarragon, and we thought our Irish Soda Bread, tasty in its own right, would be a perfect match for it. Our bakery's original chicken salad, featured in the first cookbook, uses curry powder and gets texture from the apples, grapes, raisins, and walnuts, which might overwhelm the dense soda bread, which is already sprinkled with currants. This simpler, creamy chicken salad partners just as superbly with Kindred Milk Bread (page 58) as it does with the soda bread.

MAKES 4 SANDWICHES

1½ pounds **boneless, skinless chicken breast halves**, trimmed of excess fat

2 teaspoons **chicken stock base**, such as Better Than Bouillon Roasted Chicken Base

1 teaspoon **whole black peppercorns**

1 **celery stalk** (with leaves), cut into a few pieces

1 large or 2 small **shallots**, finely chopped (about ¼ cup)

1 tablespoon **coarse-grain mustard**

2 teaspoons **honey**

3 tablespoons **fresh lime juice** (from 1 or 2 limes)

1 tablespoon **unseasoned rice vinegar**

¼ teaspoon **granulated garlic** or **garlic powder**

½ teaspoon **freshly ground black pepper**

½ cup **mayonnaise**

⅓ cup finely chopped **tarragon leaves** (about ½ ounce or 1 small bunch, stems discarded)

½ teaspoon **kosher salt**, plus more to taste

8 slices **Irish Soda Bread** (page 71) or **Kindred Milk Bread** (page 58), toasted if desired, for serving

1. Fill a large saucepan two-thirds full with water. Add the chicken, chicken stock base, whole black peppercorns, and celery. Bring to barely a boil over medium-high heat, then reduce the heat to low and cook for 20 minutes, stirring a few times, until the chicken is just cooked through and no longer pink on the inside. Drain and discard the cooking liquid and solids, transferring the chicken to a cutting board to cool.

2. Meanwhile, in a large liquid measuring cup, use a fork to whisk together the shallot, mustard, honey, lime juice, vinegar, granulated garlic, ground pepper, and mayo until well blended.

3. Chop the cooled chicken into bite-size pieces and place it in a mixing bowl. Add the tarragon and ½ teaspoon salt, tossing until evenly distributed. Let sit for 5 minutes and taste, seasoning with additional salt if desired. Pour in the shallot-lime dressing and stir gently until the chicken is evenly coated.

4. Cover and refrigerate in an airtight container for at least 1 hour and up to 3 days to allow the chicken to soak up some of the dressing. Serve on top of sliced bread, toasted if you like.

SAVORY HAND PIES
with Butternut Squash & Country Ham

The Dabney restaurant in Washington, D.C.'s Blagden Alley is our place for a celebratory meal. One autumn night, owner Jeremiah Langhorne prepared for us a side dish of butternut squash, walnuts, smoked feta, cooked greens, and Virginia maple syrup, and I thought that mix might prove to be a hearty filling for savory hand pies. I've added Virginia country ham, but you can omit it for a vegetarian version. Extra points for pulling these out of a knapsack in the middle of a crisp fall hike.

We use our Savory Pie & Quiche Crust recipe for these hand pies—go ahead and make the full recipe, which will give you two disks of dough to work with. For the hand pies, you'll just need one and a half of those disks, but you can freeze the remaining half for later. Alternatively, any unsweetened pie dough would work.

MAKES 12 TO 16 HAND PIES

---

1 pound **butternut squash**, peeled, seeded, and cut into ½-inch dice (3 to 3½ packed cups)

2 tablespoons **unsalted butter**, melted

5 ounces **country ham**, cut into small dice (about 1 cup)

3 cups (packed) stemmed and coarsely chopped **fresh greens**, such as collards, Swiss chard, kale, and/or beet greens

1 cup **walnut pieces**

1 tablespoon **maple syrup**

1 teaspoon **smoked paprika**

½ teaspoon crushed **red pepper flakes**

8 ounces **feta cheese**, crumbled (about 2 cups)

Unbleached all-purpose flour, for dusting

1½ recipes (3 disks) **Savory Pie & Quiche Crust** (page 128)

1 large **egg**

Flaky sea salt, for sprinkling

1. Preheat the oven to 375°F. Line a baking sheet with parchment paper or aluminum foil.

2. Spread the squash on the baking sheet in a single layer and drizzle with the melted butter, tossing to coat completely. Roast for 20 to 25 minutes, or until the squash is tender but still holding its shape. Transfer the squash to a large bowl to cool.

3. Meanwhile, in a large skillet over medium heat, sauté the ham just until it sizzles and some fat has rendered, about 1 minute. Add the greens and ¼ cup water and continue to cook until the greens are wilted, 5 to 8 minutes. Let the mixture cool in the pan, then transfer everything to the bowl with the squash. Add the walnuts, maple syrup, smoked paprika, and red pepper flakes and stir gently with a flexible spatula. Fold in the feta. You should have about 5 packed cups of the mixture. The filling should hold together when pressed between your fingers.

4. Dust a work surface with flour and, working in batches, roll out the pie dough to a thickness of ⅛ inch. Cut 12 to 16 rounds that are about 6 inches in diameter (use an inverted bowl as a template), rerolling the scraps of dough as needed to create more circles.

5. In a small bowl, use a fork to whisk the egg with 1 tablespoon water. Brush half of each dough round with the egg wash. Spoon about 2 tablespoons of the squash mixture in the middle of each egg-brushed half. Fold over the unbrushed side of each dough round and press the edges with the tines of a fork to seal. Pierce the tops of the hand pies once with the tines of a fork. Brush the tops with more egg wash and sprinkle with the flaky salt. Cover loosely and refrigerate for 30 minutes.

6. Preheat the oven to 375°F. Line two or three baking sheets with parchment or foil.

7. Transfer the hand pies to the prepared baking sheets, spacing the pies an inch apart. Bake one sheet at a time for 30 to 40 minutes, rotating it from front to back after 15 minutes, until the crusts are golden brown. Transfer the hand pies to a wire rack to cool before serving. The pies can be refrigerated in an airtight container for up to 4 days, or individually wrapped and frozen for up to 3 months.

TIP: Any leftover filling would be great as a last-minute addition to an omelet or stirred into pasta.

WILD MUSHROOM TARTINES
with Black Pepper Ricotta

Bon vivant William Dissen, raised in the hills of Appalachia, brings together a cadre of local farmers and artisan producers to produce award-winning food at his Charlotte restaurant, Haymaker. I asked him for a unique addition to our bakery's lunch lineup, and he suggested making his favorite tartine—an open-faced sandwich with wild mushrooms and homemade ricotta. True wild mushrooms—such as morels and maitakes—are foraged, and you may be able to find them at farmers' markets or gourmet grocers, but a mix of porcinis, shiitakes, oysters, and/or creminis works here. The homemade Black Pepper Ricotta is far superior to what you can buy in supermarkets. I also urge you to make Will's Pickled Ramps, but the Pickled Red Onions (page 209) are a good acidic punch for this recipe, too. (Just remember to make those ahead of time.)

MAKES 4 TARTINES

FOR THE MUSHROOMS:

3 tablespoons **extra-virgin olive oil**

2 pounds **wild or mixed mushrooms**, stemmed as needed, cleaned well, and cut into ½-inch dice

4 **shallots**, cut into quarters

6 **garlic cloves**, thinly sliced

½ teaspoon crushed **red pepper flakes**

½ cup **bourbon**

½ cup **Mushroom Stock** (page 211) or store-bought vegetable broth

8 tablespoons (1 stick) **unsalted butter**, cut into chunks

¼ cup mixed, chopped **fresh herbs**, such as parsley, chives, and/or basil, plus more for serving

Kosher salt and **freshly ground black pepper**

FOR THE TARTINES:

½ cup **Black Pepper Ricotta** (page 209) or store-bought whole-milk ricotta

1 teaspoon **coarsely ground black pepper** (if using store-bought ricotta), or as needed

4 slices (1-inch-thick) **sourdough bread**

Extra-virgin olive oil

Kosher salt

½ cup sliced **Pickled Ramps** (page 210) or **Pickled Red Onions** (page 209)

½ cup thinly sliced **red radishes**

¼ cup (packed) **flat-leaf parsley leaves**

¼ cup chopped **fresh chives**

¼ cup (packed) **basil leaves**, stacked, rolled, and cut into ribbons

1. **Prepare the mushrooms:** In a large skillet, heat the olive oil over medium-high heat until shimmering. Add the mushrooms and the shallots and toss to coat. Cook for 4 minutes, or until the mushrooms begin to brown and the shallots break up a bit (you may need to do this in two batches, depending on the size of your skillet). Stir in the garlic and red pepper flakes and cook, stirring until the garlic is fragrant and just begins to brown, about 30 seconds.

2. Return any batches of the mushroom mixture to the skillet. Carefully pour the bourbon into the center of the skillet, using a wooden spoon to dislodge any browned bits. Cook over medium-high heat, stirring frequently, until the liquid has reduced by half and the shallots have further broken up, 8 to 10 minutes. Pour in the mushroom stock and continue to cook, stirring occasionally, until it has reduced by three-quarters (there should be barely any liquid in the skillet, just enough to keep the mixture moist), 10 to 15 minutes.

3. Stir in the butter and chopped herbs. When the butter has melted, taste and season the mushrooms with salt and black pepper, as needed. Reduce the heat to low and cover loosely to keep warm.

4. **Make the tartines:** Place the ricotta in a medium bowl. If you are using store-bought ricotta, stir in the teaspoon of coarsely ground black pepper.

5. Generously brush one side of each slice of bread with olive oil and sprinkle lightly with salt. Heat a cast-iron skillet over medium-low heat. Add the bread slices, oiled-sides down, and toast for a few minutes until the undersides are golden brown. Transfer to a platter, toasted-sides up.

6. Spread 2 tablespoons of the ricotta evenly over each toasted slice. Spoon a quarter of the mushroom ragout on each ricotta toast. Layer on the pickled ramps, then the sliced radishes, and finish with the herbs. Lightly drizzle the top of each tartine with olive oil and serve immediately.

SOUPS & STEWS

92
AUNT MOLLY'S BRUNSWICK STEW

94
OLD-SCHOOL CHICKEN SOUP

95
HEIRLOOM TOMATO BISQUE
with Fresh Basil

96
PORK STEW
with Sweet Potatoes

97
CONDE ROAD CHILI
with Oaxacan Mole Sauce

99
BUTTERNUT SQUASH SOUP
with Apples, Pears & Pecan Butter

100
CREAMY POTATO SOUP
with Bacon & Rosemary

101
CORN CHOWDER
with Bacon

102
SHRIMP STEW
with Okra & Tomatoes

105
SUMMER GAZPACHO

AUNT MOLLY'S BRUNSWICK STEW

The states of Virginia, North Carolina, and Georgia each lay claim to originating and naming Brunswick stew, sometimes made back in the day with rabbit or even squirrel meat. My grandmother in Hendersonville, North Carolina, made a hearty chicken Brunswick stew (I always thought hers originated in Brunswick County, North Carolina), but she never wrote down her recipe. I told my ninety-seven-year-old Aunt Molly from Enfield, on the other side of the state, that I was searching for a version that came close to my grandmother's, and she described how she used to make Brunswick stew for her church. Hers comes close to what I grew up with (although I've added ketchup, as my grandmother did), with hearty chunks of ham—nearly mandatory for her region near Smithfield, North Carolina, home of the famous Smithfield hams made from peanut-fed hogs. However, since Smithfield, Virginia, also takes credit for Smithfield hams and for peanut-fed Smithfield hogs, I'll just move right on to the recipe before I get the locals upset. Food history ain't easy.

SERVES 4 TO 6

1. **Cook the chicken:** Place the chicken breast-side down in a large Dutch oven or other heavy-bottomed pot. Add the salt and enough water to cover the chicken completely. Bring to a boil, skimming off any foam. Reduce the heat to medium-low, cover, and simmer for 1 hour, using tongs to turn the chicken breast-side up halfway through. Continue to skim off any foam as needed while it cooks.

2. Transfer the chicken to a wire rack set over a rimmed baking sheet, leaving the broth inside the pot. Let the chicken cool; discard the skin, bones, and cartilage. (Return any juices that have collected in the baking sheet back to the pot with the broth.) Transfer the chicken to a cutting board and coarsely chop the meat. You should have 2½ to 3 cups. Skim or remove any stray bits left in the broth.

3. **Make the stew:** To the pot of broth, add the chopped chicken, ham, onion, bell pepper, parsley, tomatoes and their juices, corn, lima beans, okra, salt, black pepper, bay leaf, thyme, and ketchup. Cover and simmer over low heat for 2 hours, stirring often, until slightly thickened.

4. Discard the bay leaf. Taste the stew, adjust the seasoning as needed, and serve. The stew can be covered and refrigerated for up to 3 days or frozen in an airtight container for up to 1 month.

FOR THE CHICKEN:

1 **whole chicken** (about 3 pounds), giblets removed

1 tablespoon **kosher salt**

FOR THE STEW:

1 (8-ounce) **ham slice**, skin removed and discarded, cut into ½-inch cubes

1 large **yellow onion**, chopped

1 **green bell pepper**, seeded and chopped

2 tablespoons chopped **fresh parsley**

1 (14.5-ounce) can peeled **whole tomatoes**, chopped, with their juices

1 (15-ounce) can **corn**, drained

10 ounces frozen **lima beans**

10 ounces frozen sliced **okra**

1 teaspoon **kosher salt**

½ teaspoon **freshly ground black pepper**

1 **bay leaf**

½ teaspoon **ground thyme**

1 cup **ketchup**

OUR
COMMUNITY
OF ARTISANS

Smithey Ironware,
page 213

OLD-SCHOOL CHICKEN SOUP

Normally I'm a shortcut chicken-soup maker, using boneless thighs and breasts. But when I have the time, I much prefer to slowly cook a whole chicken with root vegetables for incredible flavor—letting everything simmer long enough to coax additional depth from the bones and veggies. I'm a purist, letting the chicken and vegetables share the spotlight, so I don't add noodles, rice, or pasta. You could cook the chicken a day ahead and let the strained broth's fat solidify in the fridge so it can be spooned off for simple removal, then make the soup the next day.

SERVES 6

4 medium **carrots**, trimmed and scrubbed well

1 **whole chicken** (3 to 4 pounds), giblets removed

12 cups **water**

2 medium **parsnips**, peeled and cut into thirds

2 **celery stalks**, cut into thirds

1 large **yellow onion**, quartered

1 **head of garlic**, halved horizontally

2 medium **fresh rosemary sprigs**

Small bunch of **fresh dill**, stems and fronds

1 tablespoon **whole black peppercorns**

1 tablespoon **kosher salt**, plus more as needed

1 teaspoon **chicken broth base**, such as Better Than Bouillon (optional)

1½ cups **fresh corn kernels** (from 2 ears) or frozen

2 tablespoons chopped **fresh parsley**

1. Cut 2 of the carrots into three equal pieces each. Reserve the remaining 2 carrots.

2. In a Dutch oven or other heavy-bottomed pot, place the chicken breast-side down. Pour in the water. Around the sides of the chicken, add the cut carrots, parsnips, celery, onion, garlic, rosemary, and half of the dill. Sprinkle in the peppercorns and 1 tablespoon salt. Bring just to a boil, then reduce the heat to a simmer and partially cover the pot. Cook for 20 minutes, skimming off any foam. Turn off the heat; the chicken will not be cooked through.

3. Use tongs or two large forks to carefully transfer the chicken to a cutting board. Once it's cool enough to handle, tear or cut away the wings and then detach the legs and thighs. Return the wings, legs, and thighs (all with skin) to the pot. Cut through the center of the breasts and remove most of the meat. Chop the breasts and tenderloins, place on a plate, cover with plastic wrap, and refrigerate. Return the carcass to the pot.

4. Bring the broth back to a simmer over medium-low heat and cook, uncovered, for 40 to 50 minutes, until the broth has reduced by an inch. Transfer the legs, thighs, and wings to a clean cutting board. Discard the bones and skin (including any that might still be in the pot). Chop the cooked meat and add it to the plate of chopped breast meat. Cover again and return to the refrigerator.

5. To the pot, stir in the chicken broth base, if using. Reduce the heat to low, partially cover, and continue to gently simmer for 1 hour. Turn off the heat and let the broth cool slightly.

6. In a clean sink, place a colander over a large heatproof bowl. Working in batches, carefully transfer the vegetables and herbs to the colander, letting them drain into the bowl, and use a wooden spoon to press down on them. Discard all the solids and remove the colander. Place a fine-mesh strainer over the bowl. Pour in the broth from the pot, discarding any remaining solids. Cover the bowl with plastic wrap and refrigerate for several hours. Skim off any fat with a large spoon and discard it.

7. Add the chilled, skimmed broth back to the pot and bring it to a simmer over medium heat. Slice the remaining 2 carrots into very thin rounds and add them to the broth, along with all of the cooked chicken, the remaining half bunch of dill, and the corn. Reduce the heat to medium-low and cook for 15 minutes, stirring once or twice, then discard the dill.

8. Right before serving, stir in the parsley and taste the soup, seasoning with more salt as needed. Serve hot. The soup can be covered and refrigerated for up to 3 days or frozen in an airtight container for up to 3 months.

HEIRLOOM TOMATO BISQUE
with Fresh Basil

"Can you make a tomato soup that rivals Safeway's Signature brand?" That request came not from a bakery customer but from within my own household after I loaded our shopping cart—and then our freezer—with little soup tubs from the grocery store's prepared foods aisle. I took on the challenge at the height of tomato season, opting to use heirloom varieties, because they looked and tasted so darned good, and think that we came close (but go ahead and make it in the winter with whatever is available fresh at the grocery store). This soup is good hot or chilled, and nothing partners with it like Fried Green Tomato Sandwiches with Pimento Cheese (page 77).

SERVES 8 TO 10

---

4 pounds ripe **heirloom tomatoes**, such as Cherokee Purple, Brandywine, or Mortgage Lifter, or regular tomatoes, cored and cut into quarters

¼ cup **extra-virgin olive oil**

1 tablespoon **kosher salt**

1½ teaspoons **freshly ground black pepper**

3 tablespoons **unsalted butter**

1½ cups chopped **red onions** (from 1 large onion)

2 medium **carrots**, trimmed, scrubbed well, and diced

2 tablespoons **minced garlic** (about 6 cloves)

1 teaspoon **adobo sauce** from canned chipotle peppers

1 tablespoon **tomato paste**

1 (28-ounce) can **whole peeled tomatoes**, plus their juices

½ teaspoon **ground thyme**

1 cup (packed) **fresh basil leaves**

3 cups **chicken stock**

1 cup **heavy cream**

1. Preheat the oven to 425°F. Line a rimmed baking sheet with parchment paper.

2. Remove the seeds from the quartered tomatoes and pat with paper towels to drain the tomatoes.

3. Drizzle the drained tomatoes with the oil, salt, and pepper, then spread the mixture evenly on the prepared baking sheet. Roast for 30 minutes, stirring halfway through.

4. Meanwhile, in a Dutch oven or other heavy-bottomed pot, melt the butter over medium heat. Add the red onion, carrots, and garlic and cook uncovered for 6 minutes, or until the onions have lightly browned and the carrots have started to soften. Add the adobo, tomato paste, canned tomatoes and their juices, thyme, and basil. Stir well and continue to cook, uncovered, over medium heat for 5 minutes more.

5. Remove the roasted tomatoes from the oven and add them, along with any accumulated juices, to the pot and stir in the chicken stock. Increase the heat to medium-high and bring to a boil, then reduce the heat to a simmer and cook, uncovered, for 1 hour, or until thickened, stirring occasionally and scraping the sides and bottom of the pot. Remove from the heat and let cool slightly.

6. Working in batches if needed, transfer the mixture to a food processor or blender and purée until smooth.

7. Return the puréed mixture to the pot and cook over low heat until it has reduced by one-quarter, about 25 minutes. Whisk in the heavy cream and cook for 4 minutes more. Serve hot or cover and refrigerate until chilled. The soup can be refrigerated for up to 3 days or frozen in an airtight container for up to 1 month.

PORK STEW

with Sweet Potatoes

One of the old-timers in my stockpile, this hearty stew was what I first made in the 1980s for a group gathered in our D.C. apartment to watch the president's State of the Union address. It was a fun night and, for a while, an annual event—this recipe had a lot to do with bringing the guests back each year. There's a tiny bit of heat—chipotle adds depth—and the apple cider and orange zest complement the pork and mellow everything out. By the time the address was over that first night I made the stew, the splash of bourbon had mellowed us all out.

SERVES 8

3 pounds **boneless pork shoulder**, trimmed of excess fat and cut into 1½-inch chunks

Kosher salt and **freshly ground black pepper**

2½ tablespoons **masa harina** (corn masa flour mix), such as Maseca brand (see Note)

¼ cup **extra-virgin olive oil**

2 pounds **sweet potatoes**, peeled and cut into 1-inch chunks

1½ cups **dry red wine**

1½ cups **apple cider** or **unsweetened apple juice**

½ cup **red wine vinegar**

2 medium **red onions**, chopped (about 2 cups)

½ canned **chipotle pepper**, plus 2 teaspoons adobo sauce from the can

1 **red bell pepper**, seeded and coarsely chopped

1 **poblano pepper**, seeded and coarsely chopped

7 **garlic cloves**, minced

2 tablespoons **cumin seeds**, toasted in a skillet and freshly ground

1 tablespoon **freshly grated orange zest** (from 2 large oranges)

3 cups cooked **black beans**, rinsed and drained (from two 15-ounce cans)

1 cup chopped **fresh cilantro**

1 to 2 tablespoons **good-quality bourbon** (optional)

Warm flour tortillas or **Cornbread with Sorghum Butter** (page 67), for serving

NOTE: You'll see masa harina listed in some other recipes throughout this chapter, too; it's the instant corn flour mix found in Latin markets as well as in the baking or international aisle in many grocery stores (and online). In this recipe as in others, it helps thicken the soup with the benefit of a little extra corn flavor, but you can substitute an equal amount of regular all-purpose flour if you can't get ahold of it.

1. Preheat the oven to 350°F.

2. Season the pork lightly with salt and black pepper and sprinkle the masa harina over the pork, tossing to evenly coat the pork. In a Dutch oven or other heavy-bottomed pot, heat 2 tablespoons of the oil over medium-high heat until shimmering. Add half of the pork and cook, flipping it frequently to ensure it browns on all sides, then use a slotted spoon to transfer the pork to a plate. Repeat with the remaining oil and pork.

3. To the pot, add the sweet potatoes, wine, apple cider, and vinegar, stirring with a wooden spoon to dislodge any browned bits from the bottom of the pot. Add the red onions, chipotle pepper and adobo sauce, red bell pepper, poblano, garlic, and ground cumin and stir to combine. Return the pork to the pot, cover, transfer to the oven, and cook for 1 hour.

4. Remove the pot from the oven, uncover, and gently stir in the orange zest and black beans until evenly distributed. Return to the oven, uncovered, and bake for 15 minutes, just until the beans are heated through. Remove from the oven, taste, and season with salt and black pepper as needed. Stir in the cilantro and the bourbon (if using) and return to the oven, uncovered, to bake for 5 minutes more.

5. Serve the stew hot, with warm tortillas or cornbread. The stew can be covered and refrigerated for up to 4 days or frozen in an airtight container for up to 3 months.

CONDE ROAD CHILI
with Oaxacan Mole Sauce

The first year we moved into our Orlean farmhouse on Conde Road, our next-door neighbors Lynne and Scooter Johnson held a chili cook-off for the locals. I brought Key lime pie for dessert, usually a big hit, but that year it was surprisingly overshadowed by the chili I threw together. I made my standard sirloin–black bean version, inspired by a chili we enjoyed at San Francisco's Fog City Diner. While cooking, I thought I had some chili spices on hand, but when I found none, I added a cup of my homemade Oaxacan Mole Sauce, discovered way in the back of the freezer. I think that's what clinched my first chili cook-off championship. Top this off with the usual fixins: sour cream, shredded cheese, onions, and a handful of Fritos. And, if you like, serve the Cornbread with Sorghum Butter alongside—kind of a no-brainer with chili.

SERVES 8

FOR THE CHILI:

½ cup **extra-virgin olive oil**

2 pounds **boneless sirloin**, cut into ½-inch cubes

2 medium **yellow onions**, chopped (about 2 cups)

2 tablespoons minced **garlic** (about 6 cloves)

2 **jalapeño peppers**, seeded and finely chopped

2 cups diced **tomatoes** (from about 3 medium tomatoes or 6 plum tomatoes)

½ cup **masa harina** (corn masa flour mix), such as Maseca brand (see Note on page 96)

1 teaspoon **ground cumin**

1 teaspoon **freshly ground black pepper**

1 tablespoon **kosher salt**

1 cup **Oaxacan Mole Sauce** (page 137)

4 cups **beef broth**

2 cups cooked **black beans**, rinsed and drained (from two 15-ounce cans)

FOR SERVING (OPTIONAL):

Sour cream

Grated or shredded **cheddar cheese**

Minced **red onion**

Fritos corn chips

Cornbread with Sorghum Butter (page 67)

1. In a Dutch oven or other heavy-bottomed pot, heat the oil over high heat just until it shimmers. Add the sirloin in batches to avoid crowding the pot, flipping the pieces frequently so that the cubes brown on all sides, and use a slotted spoon to transfer the browned meat to a plate, leaving the rendered fat behind.

2. Reduce the heat to medium-low and stir in the onions, garlic, jalapeños, and tomatoes. Cook, stirring occasionally, until everything has softened, about 10 minutes. Add the masa harina, cumin, black pepper, salt, and 1 cup mole sauce, stirring until blended. Continue to cook for 5 minutes, stirring frequently to avoid scorching. Pour in the broth and use a wooden spoon to dislodge any browned bits at the bottom, then return the browned sirloin to the pot. Cook, uncovered, for 45 minutes, or until the meat is tender. Add the drained beans and cook for 20 minutes more, stirring occasionally.

3. To serve, portion the chili into bowls and top with some of the sour cream, cheddar cheese, red onion, and corn chips, as desired. Serve with cornbread (if using). The chili can be covered and refrigerated for up to 4 days or frozen in an airtight container for up to 3 months.

BUTTERNUT SQUASH SOUP
with Apples, Pears & Pecan Butter

Our contribution to a Thanksgiving get-together? This soup, which tastes like autumn in a bowl. Two of our Washington buddies—former US representative Steve Gunderson and his partner, Rob Morris—used to host a holiday meal every November, and I made the soup while Dwight carved out mini pumpkins as the serving bowls. It was easy when the head count was eight, but as the guest list climbed to fifty over the years, Dwight said, "Enough!" and we bought glass soup bowls instead. The puddle of warm butter with toasted pecans is a robust finishing touch. For big dinners, I've learned my lesson and make the soup a day ahead and store it in the fridge, reheating it just before dinner. Add the scallions just before serving, too.

SERVES 8

FOR THE PECAN BUTTER:

2 tablespoons **unsalted butter**, at room temperature

2 tablespoons toasted, chopped **pecans**

1 tablespoon **honey**

Kosher salt and **freshly ground black pepper**

FOR THE SOUP:

2 pounds **butternut squash**, peeled, seeded, and cut into 2-inch chunks

3 large **Granny Smith apples** (about 1¾ pounds), peeled, cored, and cut into 2-inch chunks

1 large **yellow onion**, chopped

½ cup **canola oil**

1 teaspoon **kosher salt**, plus more as needed

½ teaspoon **freshly ground black pepper**, plus more as needed

3 ripe **pears** (about 1½ pounds total), peeled, cored, and cut into 2-inch chunks

1 teaspoon **curry powder**

1 teaspoon **ground mace**

½ teaspoon **ground cardamom**

1 cup **apple cider**

6 cups **chicken stock**

1 cup **half-and-half**

2 **scallions**, white and green parts, trimmed and thinly sliced

1. **Make the pecan butter:** In a small bowl, mash together the softened butter, toasted pecans, honey, and salt and pepper to taste. Using plastic wrap, roll the mixture into a 1-inch-thick log. Twist the ends to close and refrigerate for at least 1 hour.

2. **Make the soup:** Preheat the oven to 400°F. In a Dutch oven or other heavy-bottomed pot, combine the butternut squash, apples, and onion. Add ¼ cup of the oil and stir to completely coat them. With a slotted spoon, transfer the squash, apples, and onion to a large rimmed baking sheet. Spread them out in one layer, season with a little salt and pepper, and roast for 10 to 20 minutes, or until everything is browned but not completely tender.

3. Add the remaining ¼ cup oil to the pot and heat over medium-low. Return the roasted squash, apples, and onion to the pot, along with the pears. Stir to coat everything evenly and cook for 10 minutes, stirring occasionally, until the pears are softened. Stir in the curry, mace, and cardamom and cook for 5 minutes more.

4. Stir in the cider, increase the heat to medium, and bring to a boil. Reduce the heat to low and simmer for 4 minutes. Pour in the stock and reduce the heat to medium-low, partially cover, and cook for 25 minutes more, stirring occasionally. The solids in the pot should be tender. Remove from the heat and uncover to let the mixture cool slightly.

5. Working in batches, ladle the soup into a food processor or blender and purée until smooth. Wipe the pot clean and pour the puréed soup back in. Cook, uncovered, over medium-low heat, stirring often, until the soup has reduced by about a quarter, about 20 minutes.

6. Stir in the half-and-half, season the soup with 1 teaspoon salt and ½ teaspoon pepper, and bring to a simmer. Remove the pecan butter from the refrigerator and slice it into ¼-inch-thick rounds. Divide the soup among bowls and gently place a pecan butter slice on top of each portion. Scatter with chopped scallions and serve. The soup can be covered and refrigerated for up to 4 days or frozen in an airtight container for up to 3 months.

CREAMY POTATO SOUP

with Bacon & Rosemary

This luscious soup is the first dish I made on my own at eighteen, in my new apartment two blocks from Newport Bay in Corona del Mar, California. I was the just-hired art director of the *Newport Ensign* weekly newspaper and tested this recipe (my professional cooking debut!) before we ran it in our Coastal Living section. My clipping is covered with forty years' worth of food splatters and my subsequent notes about ingredient substitutions, and I now can barely unfold it without the pages crumbling. Luckily, I can make this from memory, although I'll be glad to see it in print again with this book. A little dry sherry really makes a big difference, but if you prefer to avoid booze, just omit it.

SERVES 6

3. Working in batches, transfer the mixture to a blender or food processor and purée until smooth. Wipe the pot clean and return the purée to the pot. Stir in the sherry and season with salt and pepper to taste. Continue to cook over low heat for 10 minutes more, just to warm it through. Meanwhile, crumble or finely chop the bacon and set it aside.

4. Whisk the cream into the puréed soup and continue to cook for 1 minute more, or until warmed through. Divide the soup among bowls and garnish with the sliced scallions and crumbled bacon. The soup can be covered and refrigerated for up to 4 days or frozen in an airtight container for up to 3 months.

---

3 thick slices **smoked bacon**

4 large **Yukon Gold potatoes** (about 2 pounds), peeled and thinly sliced

1 large **leek**, white and green parts, cut crosswise in chunks and rinsed well

2 teaspoons minced **fresh rosemary**

3 cups **chicken stock**

3 cups **whole milk**

2 tablespoons **dry sherry**

Kosher salt and **freshly ground black pepper**

1 cup **heavy cream**

2 **scallions**, white and green parts, thinly sliced, for garnish

1. In a Dutch oven or other heavy-bottomed pot over medium-low heat, cook the bacon until browned but not too crisp, 5 to 6 minutes. Using a slotted spoon, transfer the bacon to drain on a paper towel–lined plate, leaving the rendered fat in the pot.

2. Add the potatoes, leek, and rosemary to the pot, increase the heat to medium, and cook for 4 minutes. Reduce the heat to medium-low and stir in the stock and milk. Cover and cook at a gentle simmer for 1 hour. Remove from the heat and let the mixture cool for 15 minutes.

CORN CHOWDER
with Bacon

Man, I love this chowder. This is how it's supposed to be made (and the way I've done it since college): thick and full of corn, bacon, butter, cream—no skimping, no "healthier" substitutions. Enjoy this on a cold night in front of the fire (it's equally enjoyable on a summer evening when soup sounds like all you'd want). Our Cornbread with Sorghum Butter (page 67), flour tortillas, a stack of Ritz crackers, or a crusty loaf of Italian bread would be the perfect accompaniment to this.

SERVES 8 TO 10

---

8 slices **smoked bacon**, cut into small dice

3 tablespoons **unsalted butter**

1 large **yellow onion**, cut into ½-inch dice

½ **poblano pepper**, seeded and cut into ½-inch dice

2 **garlic cloves**, minced

½ cup **masa harina** (corn masa flour mix), such as Maseca brand (see Note on page 96)

5 cups **chicken stock**

1¼ pounds **Yukon Gold potatoes**, scrubbed well and cut into ½-inch chunks

Kernels from 10 ears of **yellow sweet corn** (about 8 cups), or 8 cups frozen corn kernels

½ teaspoon **smoked paprika**

Kosher salt and **freshly ground black pepper**

1 cup **heavy cream**

4 **fresh basil leaves**, rolled and cut into thin ribbons, or ½ teaspoon dried

1. In a Dutch oven or other heavy-bottomed pot over medium heat, cook the bacon until browned but not too crisp, about 6 minutes. Use a slotted spoon to transfer the bacon to a paper towel–lined plate, leaving the rendered fat in the pot.

2. Add the butter to the pot. Once it has melted, stir in the onion to coat and cook over medium heat for 5 minutes. Add the poblano and the garlic and cook, stirring, for 1 minute. Slowly whisk in the masa harina and gradually add 1 cup of the chicken stock, ¼ cup at a time. Whisk and continue to cook for 2 minutes, letting the mixture thicken into a roux that turns golden brown. Stir in the remaining 4 cups chicken stock until well combined.

2. Add the potatoes and cook for 2 minutes, stirring frequently. Reduce the heat to medium-low, add the corn kernels and smoked paprika, and season lightly with salt and black pepper. Stir, cover, and cook for 15 minutes more, or until the potatoes have softened slightly. Remove from the heat to cool slightly.

3. Transfer 3 cups of the mixture to a food processor or blender and purée until smooth. Return the purée to the pot, along with the cooked bacon, stirring until blended. Increase the heat to medium and cook for 5 minutes more, stirring as needed. Remove from the heat.

4. Stir in the cream and basil until well combined. Taste and season with more salt and pepper as needed. Serve warm. The soup can be covered and refrigerated for up to 3 days or frozen in an airtight container for up to 1 month.

SHRIMP STEW
with Okra & Tomatoes

Every time that I make this, I pine for a return trip to Martha's Vineyard. After our pals Alan Zuschlag and Keith Miller were the high bidders for a house rental there, they invited us along for a week. The least we could do was make seafood stew one night (though I also had packed a freshly baked blueberry pie) with ingredients found up the road at the farmers' market in West Tisbury. Inspired by a stew I enjoyed at the sorely missed Elizabeth on 37th restaurant in Savannah, Georgia, I went looking for fresh okra, corn, and tomatoes. The shrimp came from a seafood truck parked nearby. Use what's available and in season here—zucchini or summer squash works well, as do a variety of peppers. Serve with crusty white bread.

SERVES 8 TO 10

4 thick slices **smoky bacon**, cut into ½-inch dice

5 small **red potatoes**, rinsed and cut into ½-inch dice

8 tablespoons (1 stick) **unsalted butter**

2 pounds large **raw shrimp**, peeled and deveined, tails removed

Kernels from 4 ears of **fresh corn** (about 3 cups)

2 **poblano peppers**, seeded and cut lengthwise into very thin slices

1 medium **yellow onion**, halved crosswise and thinly sliced

5 garden-fresh **tomatoes**, cored and coarsely chopped

20 whole small **fresh okra**, tops trimmed slightly

2 teaspoons **adobo sauce** from canned chipotles

2 tablespoons **ketchup**

1 teaspoon **smoked paprika**

1 teaspoon **kosher salt**

1. In a Dutch oven or other heavy-bottomed pot over medium-low heat, cook the bacon until browned but not crisp, 5 to 6 minutes. Use a slotted spoon to transfer the bacon to drain on a paper towel–lined plate and reserve the rendered bacon fat for another use, if desired. Wipe out the pot.

2. Add 1 cup water and the potatoes to the pot and bring to a boil over high heat. Reduce the heat to medium and cook for 15 minutes, or until the potatoes are fork-tender and the water has almost evaporated. Stir in the butter until melted and cook for 4 minutes.

3. Add the reserved bacon, the shrimp, corn, poblanos, onion, tomatoes, okra, adobo sauce, ketchup, smoked paprika, and salt, stirring well to combine. Cover the pot and increase the heat to high. Cook until the shrimp are pink throughout, about 5 minutes, stirring occasionally and scraping the bottom of the pan. Serve hot. Leftovers can be refrigerated for up to 1 day.

OUR COMMUNITY OF ARTISANS

Joe Sink Pottery, page 213

SUMMER GAZPACHO

During my first of two tenures at *The Washington Post*, food critic Tom Sietsema, then an assistant on the Food desk, was writing a piece about local restaurant secrets and asked if I had a favorite dish for which I'd love to have the recipe. I thought immediately of the gazpacho, full of finely diced vegetables, at a dive on Pennsylvania Avenue near the entrance to Georgetown. It was so good that I waited each summer for it to appear on the menu, and more than once I bugged the chef about how he made it. He didn't share his recipe but rattled off a list of ingredients. Tom, ever dogged, cajoled the secret out of him and included it in that story, and I've made it every summer since.

Years later, Dwight and I had a gazpacho in seaside Barcelona that tasted exactly like this recipe, but it had been puréed into a creamy blend, while large chopped servings of vegetables were brought out in little bowls to add as desired. I liked the idea of the larger chunks and revisited my gazpacho project recently, making sure the veggies added bigger texture without becoming a choking hazard. The best success will come at the height of summer, when these fresh ingredients are abundant in a garden or a farmers' market. Please try it first just as I've written before making any substitutions, and cut all the vegetables into a same-size hefty dice; my suggestion is to keep the pieces less petite and more on the chunky side.

SERVES 8

2 medium **cucumbers**, coarsely diced

2 medium **red onions**, coarsely diced

2 medium **carrots**, trimmed, scrubbed well, and coarsely diced

1 medium **green bell pepper**, seeded and coarsely diced

2 **celery stalks**, including any leaves, coarsely diced

4 **red radishes**, trimmed and diced

1 firm but ripe **avocado**, peeled, pitted, and diced

1 tablespoon chopped **fresh parsley**

¼ cup chopped **fresh cilantro**

1 teaspoon **Worcestershire sauce**

¼ cup **extra-virgin olive oil**

¼ cup **red wine vinegar**

46 ounces canned **tomato juice**, well shaken

2 teaspoons **hot sauce**, preferably Tabasco

1¼ pounds ripe **tomatoes**, cored and diced

2 **garlic cloves**, minced

Kosher salt

Freshly ground black pepper

1. In a large nonmetallic bowl, combine all but ½ cup of the cucumbers, all but ½ cup of the red onions, all of the carrots, the green bell pepper, celery, radishes, half of the avocado, the parsley, half of the cilantro, the Worcestershire sauce, oil, vinegar, tomato juice, hot sauce, diced tomatoes, and garlic, stirring until well blended. Taste and season with salt and ½ teaspoon black pepper. Cover and refrigerate for at least 1 hour and up to 3 hours before serving.

2. Taste the gazpacho again and adjust the seasoning as needed. Ladle it into bowls and garnish them with the reserved cucumber, red onion, avocado, and cilantro or serve the gazpacho in a large serving bowl with the garnishes in side dishes, Barcelona-style. Serve immediately. Leftovers can be refrigerated in an airtight container for up to 1 day; any longer and the crisp veggies get mushy.

COOKIES
& BARS

109
CHEWY
GRANOLA BARS

110
BILLY REID'S
TOFFEE BARS

113
BLUEBERRY &
APRICOT BARS

115
RED TRUCK BROWNIES

116
ORANGE POPPY
SEED COOKIES

118
CASTAWAY COOKIES
with Lime & Coconut

119
MORAVIAN GINGER
COOKIES

121
HOMEMADE
GRAHAM CRACKERS

122
ICED ANIMAL COOKIES

123
ICEBOX FRUITCAKE

OUR
COMMUNITY
OF ARTISANS
Woodie Long Gallery,
page 213

CHEWY GRANOLA BARS

Our chunky granola is just about our biggest seller (food traveler Andrew Zimmern says it's the best in North America), and we know not to mess with a good thing. I think of our granola bar as a more portable version—the same great taste folks have come to love, with a little soft chew added in. These bars are a popular item for our customers to take along for hiking in the Blue Ridge Mountains or in Shenandoah National Park, and for cycling to our area's local vineyards and rivers; you'll enjoy these on any journey. We're giving you creative license with the mix-ins; feel free to substitute other dried fruit or nuts, but keep to the measurements given in the recipe so the total amounts of fruit and nuts stay the same.

MAKES 24 SMALL BARS

---

2 cups **quick-cooking oats**

¾ cup (packed) **light brown sugar**

½ teaspoon **kosher salt**

¼ teaspoon **ground cinnamon**

½ cup **sweetened shredded coconut**

½ cup sliced **almonds**

½ cup chopped **walnuts**

½ cup hulled **sunflower seeds**

½ cup **dried cranberries**

½ cup **dark or golden raisins**, or a combination, or dried blueberries

1 teaspoon **pure vanilla extract**

2 tablespoons **light corn syrup**

6 tablespoons **canola oil**

2 tablespoons **honey**

2 tablespoons **maple syrup**

1. Preheat the oven to 350°F. Grease a 13 × 9-inch rimmed baking sheet or pan with vegetable oil spray.

2. Measure out 1⅔ cups of the oats into a large mixing bowl. Pour the remaining ⅓ cup oats into a food processor or blender and pulse until finely ground. Add the ground oats to the bowl of quick-cooking oats.

3. Add the brown sugar, salt, and cinnamon to the bowl, stirring together until well combined. Add the coconut, almonds, walnuts, sunflower seeds, dried cranberries, and raisins and stir to combine.

4. In a separate bowl, whisk together the vanilla, corn syrup, oil, honey, maple syrup, and 1 tablespoon water. Add to the oat mixture and toss until well coated.

5. Spread the granola evenly into the prepared pan, all the way to the edges. Use a rubber spatula to press the granola gently into the corners, and then press down on the rest to achieve an even thickness.

6. Bake for 25 to 30 minutes, until the edges are golden brown and the mixture looks set. Use a knife to loosen the slab around the edges. Let cool in the pan for 10 minutes.

7. Use a knife or a bench scraper to cut the slab cleanly into bars of equal size. Portion to your preference: 6 bars long by 4 bars wide will give you 24, but slice larger, if desired. After cutting, let them cool completely in the pan for 20 minutes before removing. (It may be easier to cut the baked slab into halves, turn those out onto parchment paper on the counter, and finish cutting bars individually.) To store, wrap the individual bars in plastic wrap, then store in a zip-top bag or airtight container. The bars will keep at room temperature for up to 1 week or frozen for up to 2 months.

TOFFEE BARS

We made these bars at the request of fashion designer Billy Reid, who sent tins of them to fashion writers and editors to accompany the pandemic-altered virtual unveiling of his spring 2021 collection. I tinkered with his wife's grandmother's toffee bar recipe and shipped a batch to him overnight. I'll let Billy tell the story: "My first encounter with the English toffee bar was during a fortieth anniversary gathering for my wife's parents many years ago. There have been countless batches of this recipe served at nearly every family event I can remember. Our dear friends at the Red Truck Bakery have taken that recipe—chocolate, sweet and salty, almost-soft, cookie-cakelike delight—and advanced it in their own delicious way. Just don't tell my in-laws I said that." Mum's the word.

MAKES 50 BARS

NOTE: You can easily halve this recipe and bake it instead on a 13 × 9-inch baking sheet. Also, if you want to add a little decorative flair to the bars, you can do as we did when we made these for the fashion writers and editors referenced above: at the end of step 8, just after pressing the toffee brittle and walnuts into the melted chocolate, we piped on thin diagonal stripes of more melted chocolate to mimic the design of Billy Reid's signature heirloom ribbon.

FOR THE TOFFEE BRITTLE:

8 tablespoons (1 stick) **unsalted butter**

¼ teaspoon **kosher salt**

¾ cup **granulated sugar**

2 teaspoons **light corn syrup**

½ teaspoon **baking soda**

FOR THE SHORTBREAD BASE:

2 cups **walnut pieces**

1 pound (4 sticks) **unsalted butter**, at room temperature

2 cups (packed) **light brown sugar**

2 large **egg yolks**

2 teaspoons **pure vanilla extract**

3 cups **unbleached all-purpose flour**, sifted

½ teaspoon **kosher salt**

4 cups **semisweet chocolate chips** (24 ounces)

1. **Make the toffee brittle:** Lightly grease an 18 × 13-inch rimmed baking sheet with vegetable oil spray. Line it with parchment paper and grease the parchment as well.

2. In a deep saucepan over low heat, melt the butter. Increase the heat to medium and stir in the salt, granulated sugar, corn syrup, and 1 tablespoon plus 1½ teaspoons water. Cook, without stirring, until the temperature of the mixture registers 290°F on an instant-read or candy thermometer, 8 to 10 minutes. (Don't walk away; the bubbling mixture will quickly go from light to dark.)

3. Remove the saucepan from the heat. With a wooden spoon or rubber spatula, stir in the baking soda until well combined, scraping the bottom of the pan. The mixture should lighten and thicken. Pour it onto the parchment-lined baking sheet, spreading it evenly with an offset spatula. Let cool completely, 30 to 40 minutes, then break the toffee into small shards.

4. **Make the shortbread base:** Preheat the oven to 350°F. Spread the walnut pieces on a separate 18 × 13-inch rimmed baking sheet and toast for 5 minutes, until fragrant and lightly browned. Transfer to a bowl to cool.

recipe continues

OUR
COMMUNITY
OF ARTISANS

Billy Reid,
page 212

5. Lightly grease the same rimmed baking sheet with vegetable oil spray. Line it with parchment paper, then grease the parchment as well.

6. In the bowl of a stand mixer fitted with the paddle attachment, beat the butter and brown sugar on medium speed until lightened and creamy, about 2 minutes. Scrape down the sides of the bowl. Add the egg yolks one at a time, beating on medium speed until just combined after each addition. Scrape down the sides of the bowl, then add the vanilla and beat on medium speed until well blended. Scrape down the bowl again, then add the flour in two additions along with the salt, beating on medium speed until combined. The dough will be quite firm. Scrape it onto the parchment-lined baking sheet and press it into an even layer, all the way to the edges. Bake for 16 to 20 minutes, rotating from front to back halfway through, until the top is light golden brown and slightly puffed. Let the shortbread cool completely in the pan.

7. Place the chocolate chips in a heatproof bowl set over a saucepan of simmering water on the stovetop. Once they have begun to soften, stir until the chocolate is completely melted and smooth. Remove the bowl from the heat.

8. **Assemble the toffee bars:** Slide the cooled shortbread (still on parchment) onto a cutting board. Spread the melted chocolate evenly over the shortbread. Quickly scatter the toffee brittle shards evenly over the melted chocolate, followed by the toasted walnut pieces. Lightly press both those toppings into the chocolate to adhere. Let cool completely.

9. With a large, sharp knife, trim the four sides of the shortbread, creating a clean edge all the way around (trimmings make crumbly snacks for the cook, or a delicious topping for ice cream). Cut into 50 bars and serve. Store in an airtight container at room temperature for up to 4 days or stack the bars between layers of parchment in a freezer-safe container and freeze for up to 3 months.

BLUEBERRY & APRICOT BARS

Who knew how popular these bars would be at the bakery? They were an afterthought for us, born out of an overload of dried blueberries in our pantry, and now we're trying to keep up with the demand. Our cherry-and-white-chocolate version might be the most requested at the bakery, but the fruitiness and chewiness of this one, full of dried blueberries and dried apricots, is gaining momentum among customers. There's an unexpected little zing of lemon zest in the bars and in the icing, and that may well send these into first place.

MAKES 12 LARGE BARS

---

2 cups **unbleached all-purpose flour**, sifted

¾ teaspoon **baking powder**

½ teaspoon **baking soda**

¾ teaspoon **kosher salt**

¼ teaspoon **ground ginger**

¼ teaspoon **freshly grated or ground nutmeg**

1 cup (2 sticks) **unsalted butter**, at room temperature

1 cup (packed) **light brown sugar**

½ cup **granulated sugar**

½ teaspoon plus 1 teaspoon **freshly grated lemon zest**

2 large **eggs**

½ teaspoon **pure vanilla extract**

¼ teaspoon **pure almond extract**

10 ounces chopped **dried apricots** (about 1¼ cups)

2½ ounces **dried blueberries** (about 2 cups)

1 cup **confectioners' sugar**, sifted

1. Preheat the oven to 325°F. Grease a 13 × 9-inch rimmed baking sheet with vegetable oil spray.

2. In a medium bowl, whisk together the flour, baking powder, baking soda, salt, ginger, and nutmeg.

3. In the bowl of a stand mixer fitted with the paddle attachment, beat the butter, brown sugar, granulated sugar, and ½ teaspoon of the lemon zest on medium speed for 3 minutes, until light and fluffy. Add the eggs one at a time, beating on medium speed until just combined after each addition. Scrape down the sides of the bowl, then gradually add the flour mixture and beat on medium speed until just incorporated. Scrape down the sides again, then add the vanilla and almond extracts and continue to beat on medium speed until combined. Stir in the apricots and blueberries with a large spoon or rubber spatula until just combined.

4. Spread the mixture in the prepared baking sheet all the way to the edges, smoothing it with a spatula. Bake for 25 to 28 minutes, rotating the pan from front to back halfway through, until the top is light golden brown and puffed.

5. Meanwhile, in a medium bowl, mix the confectioners' sugar and the remaining 1 teaspoon lemon zest with 1 to 2 tablespoons water, as needed, until the icing is smooth, opaque, and barely pourable.

6. Let the bars cool completely in the pan, then use a spoon to drizzle the icing on top in zigzags. Cut 12 bars of equal size (roughly square). Store in an airtight container at room temperature for up to 2 days or refrigerate for up to 4 days.

RED TRUCK BROWNIES

At the bakery, brownies are the first thing we suggest whenever someone is looking for sweet finger-food bites for a large event—it's not much of a surprise that they are complete crowd-pleasers. We don't add nuts, and no one seems to miss them—the chocolate chips are unexpected inside and serve as good firm texture in the middle of a moist and rich brownie. I like to make these fairly large, but feel free to cut them smaller (or even larger!). We also sometimes cut the brownies into quarters and package them as brownie bites. And that's what my ninety-seven-year-old Aunt Molly has been asking for lately, because she can keep them in the freezer and grab a little nugget when the yearning for chocolate hits her. At Christmas, we break peppermint sticks or candy canes into small bits and press them into the top of the batter before baking.

MAKES 20 LARGE BROWNIES

1¼ cups **unsweetened cocoa powder**

9 large **eggs**

½ cup **canola oil**

1 cup (2 sticks) **unsalted butter**, at room temperature

3½ cups **sugar**

2 teaspoons **pure vanilla extract**

1½ cups **unbleached all-purpose flour**, sifted

1 teaspoon **kosher salt**

2 teaspoons **espresso powder** or very finely ground coffee

¾ teaspoon **freshly grated orange zest** (from 1 orange)

12 ounces (2 cups) **semisweet chocolate chips**

1. Preheat the oven to 350°F and position a rack in the upper third.

2. Grease a 17 × 12 × 1-inch jelly-roll pan or a baking pan with interior dimensions of roughly 15.6 × 10 inches with vegetable oil spray. Line the pan with parchment paper.

3. In the bowl of a stand mixer fitted with the paddle attachment, beat the cocoa powder, eggs, and oil on low speed until well combined. Add the butter and increase the speed to medium-low, beating just until smooth and creamy, about 1 minute. Scrape down the sides of the bowl.

4. Add the sugar and vanilla, beating on medium-low speed until well blended. Scrape down the sides of the bowl.

5. Whisk together the flour, salt, and espresso powder in a separate bowl or sift them onto a sheet of parchment paper. Add the flour mixture to the mixing bowl along with the orange zest and beat on low speed for 30 seconds, or until no trace of flour remains. Scrape down the sides of the bowl once more and add the chocolate chips. Beat on low speed for 1 minute, then increase the speed to medium and beat for 3 minutes more. The batter will be thick. Scrape the batter into the pan, smoothing the top and spreading it evenly to the edges.

6. Bake on the upper rack of the oven for 20 to 25 minutes, rotating the pan from front to back halfway through, or until a toothpick inserted into the center comes out clean or with just a few moist crumbs clinging to it. The brownies should be just set on the edges and still slightly soft on top.

7. Transfer the pan to a wire rack to cool completely. Use a knife to loosen the slab around the edges, then slide it out (on its parchment) onto a cutting board. Trim the edges, if desired, and cut it into 20 equal portions. Serve immediately or cool completely and wrap the brownies individually in plastic wrap and store in a zip-top bag or airtight container. The brownies will keep at room temperature for up to 2 days or in the freezer for up to 2 months.

ORANGE POPPY SEED COOKIES

The first baker I ever hired brought these cookies to his job interview at the bakery fifteen years ago, and the taste convinced me that the two of us were in sync. The fragrant cookies appear delicate but have some heft to them—enough to make them dunkable into a cup of hot tea or coffee. Swap out the orange zest with an equal amount of lemon zest to create lemon poppy seed cookies, another favorite at the bakery.

MAKES 24 LARGE COOKIES

---

1 tablespoon plus
  1 teaspoon **freshly
  grated orange zest**

¾ cup **sugar**

1½ cups **unbleached
  all-purpose flour**

½ teaspoon **baking powder**

Pinch of **kosher salt**

8 tablespoons (1 stick)
  unsalted butter, at room
  temperature

1 large **egg**, at room
  temperature

1 teaspoon **pure vanilla
  extract**

1 tablespoon **poppy seeds**

1. In a medium bowl, use a fork to stir the orange zest into the sugar until well blended.

2. Sift together the flour, baking powder, and salt onto a sheet of parchment paper or into a separate bowl.

3. In the bowl of a stand mixer fitted with the paddle attachment, beat the butter with the orange zest–sugar on medium speed for 2 to 3 minutes, until light and fluffy. Scrape down the sides of the bowl. Add the egg and vanilla and beat until incorporated. Add the flour mixture and the poppy seeds, beating until well combined and the poppy seeds are evenly distributed. The dough will be firm. Cover with plastic wrap, pressing it directly onto the surface of the dough. Refrigerate for at least 1 hour and up to 3 hours.

4. Preheat the oven to 350°F. Have ready two ungreased baking sheets.

5. Divide the chilled dough into 24 equal portions, rolling them into balls. Place 12 on each baking sheet, spacing the balls at least 2 inches apart. Use your palm to flatten each ball into a disk about 3 inches across.

6. Bake one sheet at a time for 7 to 9 minutes, rotating from front to back after 5 minutes, just until the cookies are very lightly browned on the edges yet still a bit soft at the center. Let the cookies sit on the baking sheet for a few minutes, then transfer them to a wire rack to cool completely. Store in an airtight container at room temperature for up to 3 days or freeze for up to 3 months.

CASTAWAY COOKIES

with Lime & Coconut

This is a treat that tastes like summer. Luckily, that's when we're making Key lime pies, so we use the juice of that fruit in these cookies, although we also use regular (Persian) lime juice. Either works great, and lime with coconut (cue Harry Nilsson's song) and white chocolate is a tropical trifecta. I named them Castaways as soon as I tasted them the first time, almost fifteen years ago.

MAKES 24 LARGE COOKIES

---

2 teaspoons **freshly grated lime zest** (from 1 large lime)

¾ cup **granulated sugar**

2 cups **unbleached all-purpose flour**, sifted

½ teaspoon **baking powder**

¾ teaspoon **kosher salt**

12 tablespoons (1½ sticks) **unsalted butter**, at room temperature

¾ cup (packed) **light brown sugar**

1 large **egg**

1½ teaspoons **pure vanilla extract**

¼ cup **fresh lime juice** (from 2 or 3 limes)

1 cup **sweetened shredded coconut** (4 ounces)

1 cup **white chocolate chips** (5 ounces)

1. In a medium bowl, use a fork to stir the lime zest into the granulated sugar. In a separate bowl, whisk together the flour, baking powder, and salt.

2. In the bowl of a stand mixer fitted with the paddle attachment, beat the butter, lime zest–sugar, and brown sugar on medium speed for 2 to 3 minutes, until light and fluffy. Scrape down the sides and bottom of the bowl. Add the egg, beating until incorporated, then the vanilla and the lime juice, mixing until combined. The mixture will look curdled; this is okay. Scrape down the sides of the bowl again.

3. Add the flour mixture and beat on low speed until well mixed. Add the coconut and white chocolate chips, mixing just until combined. Press plastic wrap directly onto the surface of the dough in the mixer bowl and refrigerate for at least 1 hour and up to overnight.

4. Preheat the oven to 350°F. Have ready two ungreased baking sheets.

5. Divide the chilled dough into 24 equal portions, rolling them into balls. Place 12 on each baking sheet, spacing the balls at least 2 inches apart. Use your palm to flatten each ball into a disk about 3 inches across.

6. Bake one sheet at a time for 12 to 14 minutes, rotating from front to back halfway through, or until the cookies are lightly browned on the edges yet still a bit soft at the center. Let the cookies sit on the baking sheet for a few minutes, then transfer them to a wire rack to cool completely. Store in an airtight container for up to 3 days or freeze for up to 3 months.

MORAVIAN
GINGER COOKIES

I send moms and dads to my grandmother's recipe for ginger cookies when they want a kid-friendly baking project for gift-giving or simply for enjoying at home. Plan ahead; traditionally, the dough is chilled several days before using, a wait time that might be difficult for kids to endure, but it also divides the project into manageable sessions. My grandmother kept the dough in the refrigerator for at least a week before rolling and baking; the longer you store it like this, the easier it is to handle and the more the flavor will develop. These paper-thin cookies are the traditional treat of Old Salem, North Carolina, founded in 1766 by members of the Moravian Church after leaving what is now part of the Czech Republic. This recipe might just rival those still available in the Old Salem bakery.

You'll need a 2-inch cookie cutter—a scalloped-edge one is traditional. If baking all of this dough in one day is too much to handle, you can freeze half the dough, well wrapped, for up to 2 months. What a nice surprise to come back to later.

MAKES 60 TO 66 COOKIES

¼ cup **vegetable shortening**

½ cup **molasses**

¼ cup (packed) **light brown sugar**

¼ teaspoon **ground ginger**

¼ teaspoon **ground cloves**

¼ teaspoon **ground cinnamon**

⅛ teaspoon **freshly grated or ground nutmeg**

⅛ teaspoon **ground allspice**

⅛ teaspoon **kosher salt**

¼ teaspoon **baking soda**

1¾ cups **unbleached all-purpose flour**, sifted, plus more for rolling

1. In a large saucepan over medium heat, whisk together the shortening, molasses, brown sugar, ginger, cloves, cinnamon, nutmeg, allspice, salt, and baking soda. Whisk until smooth and shiny, about 5 minutes. Remove from the heat.

2. Stir in the flour until well combined, forming an evenly dark brown dough that is quite firm. Divide the dough into two pieces and transfer to a lidded container to cool, then seal tightly and refrigerate for at least 2 days; however, the cookies turn out best when the dough has been refrigerated for a week.

3. Preheat the oven to 375°F. Lightly grease two baking sheets with vegetable oil spray or line them with parchment paper. Lightly flour a work surface and a rolling pin, using as little flour as possible.

4. Roll out each piece of dough until it is as thin as possible (you may find it's easier to roll it in portions between two sheets of lightly floured parchment). The finished cookies should be very thin and crisp, so don't be afraid to roll the dough even thinner than you think (even ⅛ inch thick is a little on the thick side). Use the cookie cutter to cut the dough into 2-inch rounds, transferring them to the baking sheets with a thin metal spatula and spacing them ½ inch apart. Re-roll scraps and re-chill the dough as needed. The rounds should look shiny.

5. Bake one sheet at a time for 4 to 5 minutes, rotating from front to back halfway through, or until the cookies are lightly browned and fragrant (they will crisp up more as they cool). Brush off any excess flour before letting them cool for a few minutes on the baking sheet. Use the metal spatula to transfer them to a wire rack to cool completely. Repeat with the rest of the cookie dough. Store the cookies in an airtight container at room temperature for up to 4 days or freeze for up to 6 months.

HOMEMADE GRAHAM CRACKERS

When I was digging through a box of old recipes that I've kicked under the bed of every house I've lived in, I found the beginnings of this jewel. The recipe card was stained with spilled ingredients, and when I found my Uncle Stan's handwritten comments at the bottom, I remembered that we once had made graham crackers for a Key lime piecrust at his Safety Harbor, Florida, home in the early 1980s. My staff rolled their eyes at taking on this project, and because we make nearly one thousand Key lime pies each year, I relented. But you're not off the hook at home: graham crackers made from scratch are great and easy to make. Crumbled into a crust, these crackers are used in our Chocolate Chess Pie (page 174), but they're addictive treats on their own just like their store-bought counterparts—and I'm kind of crazy about dipping them in melted milk chocolate. A 2½-inch-square cookie cutter or a rolling ravioli cutter will come in handy here.

MAKES 42 TO 46 SQUARE CRACKERS

---

4 tablespoons (½ stick) **unsalted butter**, at room temperature

½ cup (packed) **light brown sugar**

¼ cup **honey**

1 large **egg**

1½ cups **whole-wheat graham flour** (such as Bob's Red Mill), sifted, plus more as needed

¾ cup **unbleached all-purpose flour**, sifted

¾ teaspoon **kosher salt**

½ teaspoon **baking soda**

2 tablespoons **whole milk**, plus more as needed

Granulated sugar, for sprinkling (optional)

Milk chocolate chips, melted (optional)

1. Preheat the oven to 350°F. Lightly grease two rimmed baking sheets with vegetable oil spray.

2. In the bowl of a stand mixer fitted with the paddle attachment, beat the butter, brown sugar, and honey on medium speed until well blended. Add the egg and mix well. Scrape down the sides of the bowl with a flexible spatula.

3. In a separate bowl, whisk together the whole-wheat graham flour, all-purpose flour, salt, and baking soda.

4. Reduce the mixer speed to low and add half of the flour mixture to the bowl. Add the milk and the remaining half of the flour mixture, beating on low speed until the dough just comes together. If it's crumbly, add a little more milk. If it's too wet, add a little more of the graham flour. The dough should be firm, evenly caramel in color, and not sticky. Divide it in half.

5. Sprinkle some graham flour across a large sheet of parchment paper or plastic wrap on a work surface. Working with half of the dough at a time, place it on the floured surface and sprinkle the top with a little more graham flour. Cover it with a second piece of parchment or plastic wrap and roll out the dough into an evenly thin rectangle less than ¼ inch thick.

6. Uncover the dough and use a 2½-inch square cookie cutter, rolling ravioli cutter, or sharp knife to cut as many 2½-inch squares as you can, placing them on the baking sheets spaced ½ inch apart. Reroll scraps as needed.

7. Use a fork to prick the top of each square several times. Sprinkle the squares with granulated sugar, if desired. Bake one sheet at a time for 9 to 11 minutes, rotating from front to back halfway through, or until the crackers are slightly firm to the touch and the edges are turning light brown. Cool completely on the baking sheets on a wire rack, where they will crisp up.

8. Enjoy as is, or dip into melted milk chocolate to coat, if desired, and let set on a wire rack. Store graham crackers in an airtight container at room temperature for up to 5 days or freeze for up to 3 months.

ICED ANIMAL COOKIES

You don't see these around much anymore, but happening upon little pink- and white-frosted animal cookies, with tiny multicolored round sprinkles, takes me back to my childhood. Animal cookie cutters are easy to find online and in stores, and they are well worth the minimal investment for the fun of using the shapes; try to get cutters that are about 3 inches long. At the bakery, we ice and sprinkle just one side of the cookie, but to authentically re-create this throwback treat, double the amount of icing and coat and sprinkle one side, let it fully dry, and then repeat with the other side.

MAKES 24 TO 36 (3-INCH) COOKIES

FOR THE COOKIES:

12 tablespoons (1½ sticks) **unsalted butter**, at room temperature

1 cup **granulated sugar**

1 large **egg** plus 1 large **egg yolk**

2 teaspoons **pure vanilla extract**

2½ cups **unbleached all-purpose flour**, plus more for rolling

½ teaspoon **baking powder**

½ teaspoon **kosher salt**

FOR THE ICING:

2 cups **confectioners' sugar**, sifted

2 tablespoons **whole milk**

1 tablespoon **light corn syrup**

½ teaspoon **pure vanilla extract**

Red food coloring

Multicolored round sprinkles (rainbow nonpareils)

1. **Make the cookies:** In the bowl of a stand mixer fitted with the paddle attachment, beat the butter and granulated sugar on medium speed for 2 minutes, until light and fluffy. Scrape down the sides of the bowl with a flexible spatula. Add the egg and egg yolk one at a time, beating well after each addition. Reduce the speed to low and add the vanilla, mixing until well combined. Scrape down the bowl again.

2. Sift together the flour, baking powder, and salt onto parchment paper or into a large bowl. On low speed, gradually add the flour mixture to the butter mixture, mixing until just combined; do not overmix. The dough may be clumpy but should still hold together. Gather the dough into a mass and divide it in half, flattening a bit and wrapping each portion in plastic wrap. Refrigerate for at least 3 hours and up to overnight.

3. Preheat the oven to 325°F. Line two baking sheets with parchment paper.

4. Lightly flour your rolling pin and work surface. Unwrap one chilled dough half and roll it out to a thickness of about ¼ inch. Cut out cookie shapes using 3-inch animal cookie cutters, transferring the shapes to a baking sheet as you work and spacing the cookies at least 1 inch apart. (You may also want to flour the cutters between uses to prevent sticking.) Reroll scraps as needed. Repeat with the remaining chilled dough.

5. Bake one sheet at a time for 8 to 10 minutes, rotating it from front to back halfway through, or until the cookies are just lightly golden in the center and barely browned on the edges. Let them sit on the baking sheet for a few minutes, then transfer the cookies to a wire rack to cool completely.

6. **Make the icing:** In a medium bowl, use a fork to whisk together the confectioners' sugar, milk, corn syrup, and vanilla. Gradually whisk in 2 tablespoons water until the icing consistency is smooth and spreadable but not too runny (add a little bit more water if too thick, or more confectioners' sugar if too runny). You should have a generous 1 cup. Transfer half of the icing to a separate bowl and cover with plastic wrap; this will be your white icing. To the first bowl, stir in just a tiny drop of red food coloring, mixing until the color is a little pinker than cotton candy (you want it light pink, definitely not red).

7. Place a wire rack over newspaper (or that piece of parchment you used in step 2). Working in batches, arrange the cookies on the rack, coating the surface of half of them with the pink icing and immediately applying sprinkles. Let dry completely. Repeat with the remaining cookies using the white icing and sprinkles. Let dry completely for up to 4 hours. Store in an airtight container for up to 3 days.

ICEBOX FRUITCAKE

Who knew this funny little gem would be our most requested Christmas recipe? Dwight's mom, Dot, used to prepare this retro treat each December for her family. The source of the recipe was always a bit of a mystery, and we first thought she made it up. It requires no baking and needs just a simple mixing of ingredients that are then pressed into a loaf pan and refrigerated until set. And like most fruitcakes, the name of this recipe might call to mind less-than-exciting desserts, but don't be fooled into thinking that's the case here—with the sweetness of candied cherries, dates, coconut, and even marshmallows, this cake is really delicious and incredibly addictive. Eventually, Dot's secret was exposed when we discovered that the recipe had originally been printed on the side of a box of graham crackers back in the 1950s (and the cake was even made inside the waxed box). It wouldn't have remained a secret for too long, anyway—I later found the identical cake in my grandmother's recipe box. I introduced it at the bakery as sort of a joke the first Christmas we were open, and it's been a big hit each year since then.

MAKES ONE 9 × 5-INCH LOAF

1 (14- to 15-ounce) box **graham crackers** (3 sleeves)

1 cup chopped **pecans**

1 cup chopped **pitted dates**

1½ cups (packed) **candied cherries** (12 ounces), or 1 (10-ounce) jar maraschino cherries, drained and syrup reserved

1 cup (packed) **sweetened shredded coconut**

1½ cups **mini marshmallows**

1 (14-ounce) can **sweetened condensed milk**

1. Lightly grease a 9 × 5-inch loaf pan with vegetable oil spray. Crumble or crush the graham crackers into chunks no larger than ½ inch (but not crumbs).

2. Lightly grease a large bowl with vegetable oil spray. Add the crushed graham crackers, pecans, dates, cherries, coconut, and marshmallows. Gradually pour in the sweetened condensed milk and mix well, scraping the bowl repeatedly with a flexible spatula. Add 2 tablespoons water (or the reserved cherry syrup, if using), mixing well just until the mixture comes together (you can add up to 2 more tablespoons water, if the mixture seems dry).

3. Spoon the mixture into the prepared loaf pan, pressing down the mixture evenly, including the corners, with your hands. Cover with plastic wrap, pressing the plastic against the mixture, and refrigerate for at least 6 hours and up to overnight, until the cake is firm and set. To serve, slice the cake inside the pan into ¼-inch-thick slices and keep it chilled. The loaf can be refrigerated for up to 2 months or frozen in an airtight container for up to 4 months.

DINNER

127
CARROT, PARSNIP & LEEK POTPIES

129
PORK TENDERLOIN
with Rosemary & Blueberries

130
MID-JULY TOMATO PIE

133
CORN CRAB CAKES
with Jalapeño Mayonnaise

134
PEANUT GINGER CHICKEN
with Cucumber Salsa

136
BAKED CHICKEN
with Oaxacan Mole Sauce

139
ROAST CHICKEN
with Guava & Pineapple

140
MUSHROOM-RICOTTA LASAGNE
with Port Sauce

143
CHUNKY MEATLOAF
with Plenty of Bacon

145
SWEET POTATO & POBLANO ENCHILADAS
with Oaxacan Mole Sauce

Carrot, Parsnip & Leek
POTPIES

Potpies are comfort food, so it's no surprise that they're among the top sellers year-round at the bakery. I've been working on a vegetarian version, and I knew it had to include my favorite root vegetables: carrots and especially parsnips in a creamy leek sauce. These potpies are quite easy to replicate at home, and I like to bake them in 6-inch-round, 2-inch-tall pie plates and serve them as individual, or at least more manageable, portions. However, you can also bake the filling and crust in a single 9-inch pie plate for a hearty, traditionally larger potpie if you prefer. (Ovenproof bowls or disposable aluminum foil pans will work as well.) One critical step to remember is piercing the top crust with a knife or punching out a shape in the center in order to vent the pie. If the filling isn't bubbling out of the very center, the potpies haven't fully baked.

MAKES FOUR 6-INCH POTPIES, OR ONE 9-INCH PIE

FOR THE FILLING:

8 tablespoons (1 stick) **unsalted butter**

¾ cup diced **yellow onion**

1 medium **leek**, white and light green parts, cut into thin rounds and rinsed well

2 teaspoons **kosher salt**

Freshly ground black pepper

2 **garlic cloves**, minced

2 medium **carrots**, trimmed, scrubbed well, and cut into ¾-inch dice

4 medium **parsnips**, peeled and cut into ¾-inch dice

2 small **sweet potatoes**, peeled and cut into ¾-inch dice

1 tablespoon **powdered vegetable base**, such as Knorr's Vegetable Recipe Mix or Better Than Bouillon Seasoned Vegetable Base

¼ cup **unbleached all-purpose flour**

1 cup **heavy cream**

¼ teaspoon **dried sage**

1 teaspoon minced **fresh rosemary**

½ teaspoon **fresh thyme leaves**, or ¼ teaspoon dried

Pinch of **freshly grated or ground nutmeg**

¾ teaspoon **curry powder**

FOR THE CRUSTS:

Unbleached all-purpose flour, for dusting

1½ recipes (3 disks) **Savory Pie & Quiche Crust** (page 128), or 4 store-bought crusts (see Note)

1 large **egg**

Flaky sea salt and **coarsely ground black pepper**, for sprinkling

NOTE: Store-bought crust is always thinner than homemade crust, so if you're using store-bought, you'll need 4 disks to get the right coverage for these pies.

1. **Make the filling:** In a large pot, melt the butter over low heat. Stir in the onion, leek, kosher salt, and pepper to taste and cook for 15 minutes, stirring occasionally, until the onion is translucent. Stir in the garlic and cook for 2 minutes, until golden brown. Pour in 1 cup water.

2. Increase the heat to medium and stir in the carrots, parsnips, and sweet potatoes. Cook for 1 minute. Stir in the vegetable base and cook for 1 minute more.

3. Add the flour, stirring until the vegetables are evenly coated. Reduce the heat to low and cook for 5 to 7 minutes, until nicely thickened, stirring often. The flour coating (roux) will brown a little bit, but don't let it burn.

4. Whisk in the heavy cream, sage, rosemary, thyme, nutmeg, and curry powder and simmer for 1 minute more. Remove from the heat and let the filling cool completely (otherwise you'll melt the dough when you assemble the potpies). The cooled filling can be stored in an airtight container for up to 2 days.

5. **Make the crusts:** Dust a work surface with flour and roll out the 3 disks of dough. Cut the disks into four 9-inch rounds and four 7½-inch rounds (use inverted bowls as templates), rerolling the scraps as needed. Without stretching the dough, gently drape each larger dough round into a 6-inch pie pan, letting the dough drape over the

recipe continues

sides. Gently press the dough into the bottom and up the sides without stretching it.

6. Divide the cooled filling evenly among the four pie shells.

7. In a small bowl, use a fork to stir together the egg and 1 tablespoon water. Brush the rim of each filled pie shell with the egg wash, then set a smaller round of dough atop each and press the edges of the bottom and top crusts together with your fingers. Trim the dough around the outside edge of the pans to about ½ inch. Roll the outside edges of dough just inside the rim and crimp.

8. Brush the top crusts with more egg wash, cut a couple of slits in the center of each potpie, and sprinkle with the flaky sea salt and coarse black pepper. At this point you can proceed with baking or freeze and bake the pies later. (For freezing, wrap each pie tightly in plastic wrap, seal in freezer storage bags, and freeze for up to 3 months.)

9. **Bake the pies:** Preheat the oven to 400°F. Place the potpies on a rimmed baking sheet and bake for 45 to 65 minutes (if baking from frozen, add another 15 minutes), rotating the baking sheet from front to back after 30 minutes, until the mixture is bubbling out of the center slits and the crusts are deep golden. (If the edges of the potpies are browning too quickly, after 30 minutes cover the potpies loosely with foil.)

10. Let the pies cool slightly before serving. You can serve them straight from the pie plates or transfer the potpies to a serving plate. Here's the way we do it at our house: Place a small plate upside down on the pie. Holding on to both the pie pan and the plate, carefully invert them. Remove the pie pan. Place a dinner plate upside down on what is the bottom of the pie and, carefully holding the pie and both plates, flip it right side up and serve.

SAVORY PIE & QUICHE CRUST

This crust is almost identical to our Classic Piecrust (page 169), which is featured in many of our sweet pies. However, this version swaps the sugar and citrus zests for fresh rosemary or thyme, which complements the fillings in our quiches and savory pies, and we also add some cheese. If you're making a single-crust pie or quiche, freeze one disk of this dough for another use.

MAKES 2 DISKS, ENOUGH FOR TWO 10-INCH CRUSTS

3½ cups **unbleached all-purpose flour**, sifted, plus more as needed

1 teaspoon **kosher salt**

12 tablespoons (1½ sticks) **unsalted butter**, chilled and cut into cubes

¼ cup **vegetable shortening**, chilled

1 large **egg yolk**

2 ounces **Parmigiano-Reggiano** or **cheddar cheese**, freshly grated (½ cup)

1 teaspoon chopped **fresh rosemary** or **thyme** (or a mixture of both)

½ cup **cold water**, plus more as needed

1. In a large bowl, whisk together the flour and salt. Add the butter and shortening and, using your fingers, two knives, or a pastry blender, work them into the flour mixture until they are reduced to pea-size pieces. Add the egg yolk, cheese, and rosemary, mixing until combined. Gradually add the cold water and mix just until a dough comes together. If it is crumbly, add a bit more water, 1 teaspoon at a time. If it seems sticky, add a bit more flour.

2. Divide the dough in half and form each one into a disk. Wrap them separately in plastic wrap or put each disk in a freezer storage bag, seal, and refrigerate for 30 minutes before using, or freeze the dough for up to 1 month, thawing it in the refrigerator for 2 hours before using.

PORK TENDERLOIN
with Rosemary & Blueberries

We became the new owners of our farmhouse on the Friday before a Memorial Day weekend. On that Saturday morning, I walked around behind the chicken coop and picked a large bowlful of ripe blueberries from several heirloom bushes that could be at least eighty years old. A trip to the local grocery store to start stocking our kitchen yielded pork tenderloin on sale, and here's the first meal we made out in the country. It was good enough to make again for a dinner at the first group event held at our new Marshall bakery location just before we opened. Fresh rosemary and a bit of Grand Champion Peach Jam tie the pork and blueberries together. Corn Ice Cream (page 198) and Salted Caramel Apple Pie (page 168) might be the way to finish it off.

SERVES 4

1 (1½-pound) **pork tenderloin**, trimmed of excess fat

Kosher salt and **freshly ground black pepper**

2 tablespoons **extra-virgin olive oil**

2 tablespoons **unsalted butter**

1 medium **yellow onion**, finely chopped

1 teaspoon **freshly grated ginger**

½ cup **apple cider**

1 teaspoon **apple cider vinegar**

1 pint (2 cups) **fresh blueberries**, stemmed and rinsed

2 tablespoons finely chopped **fresh rosemary**

3 tablespoons **Grand Champion Peach Jam** (page 206) or store-bought peach jam

1. Lightly season the pork on all sides with salt and pepper. In a large cast-iron skillet over high heat, heat the oil just until shimmering. Add the pork to the skillet, turning to brown it on all sides, about 5 minutes per side. Reduce the heat to medium and cook for 20 minutes, turning it occasionally, or until the center of the pork registers 145°F on an instant-read thermometer. Transfer the pork to a cutting board and cover loosely with foil.

2. Reduce the heat to low and add the butter to the skillet. Once it has melted, stir in the onion and ginger. Cook for 15 minutes, until the onion is golden brown. Stir in the apple cider and vinegar, using a wooden spoon to dislodge any browned bits from the bottom of the pan. Continue to cook over low heat for about 5 minutes, until the mixture has thickened. Stir in the blueberries, rosemary, and the peach jam. Taste and season with salt and pepper. Let the sauce simmer for 3 minutes more, until the mixture is heated through. Let cool slightly.

3. Uncover the pork and slice it into ½-inch-thick pieces on the cutting board before transferring the meat to plates or a large platter. Serve with the blueberry sauce.

TOMATO PIE

I included our recipe for the end-of-season Green Tomato Pie in my previous cookbook, and, although it is a delicious dish, folks wanted to know whether they could use ripe red heirloom tomatoes in a pie. Sure! Here I've done exactly that, with some changes, and it is even more scrumptious. This pie is a stunner—best suited for the tastiest, beefiest tomatoes available—so I've always got an eye out for Cherokee Purples, Brandywines, and Mr. Stripeys. The open-faced recipe calls for a single piecrust; our Savory Pie & Quiche Crust recipe (page 128) makes two, so make the full recipe and freeze half, well wrapped, for another use. Like, well, another tomato pie.

MAKES ONE 10-INCH PIE

½ recipe (1 disk) **Savory Pie & Quiche Crust** (page 128), or 1 store-bought crust

Unbleached all-purpose flour, for dusting

2 tablespoons **cornmeal**

7 medium **tomatoes**, preferably in a variety of colors, sliced into ⅓-inch-thick rounds and drained (see Note)

7 **cooked bacon slices**, drained and cut into 1-inch pieces

16 large **fresh basil leaves**

¾ cup **mayonnaise**

2 large **eggs**

6 ounces **cheddar cheese**, grated (1½ cups)

4 ounces **Parmigiano-Reggiano** cheese, freshly grated (1 cup), plus more (optional) for garnish

2 tablespoons **unbleached all-purpose flour**

Pinch of **ground cayenne pepper**

½ teaspoon **smoked paprika**

3 **scallions**, white and green parts, chopped, plus more (optional) for garnish

1. Preheat the oven to 350°F. Place a wire rack inside a rimmed baking sheet.

2. Dust a work surface with flour and roll out the pie dough into a 13-inch round. Fold it gently (don't stretch it) into a 10-inch pie plate. Trim and crimp the edges. Transfer the pie plate to the refrigerator for 20 minutes to ensure the crust is well chilled before baking.

3. Remove the pie plate from the refrigerator and sprinkle the cornmeal evenly over the bottom of the crust. Layer a third of the sliced tomatoes over the cornmeal. Scatter half the bacon pieces over the tomatoes. Repeat with one more layer of each: half of the remaining sliced tomatoes and all of the basil leaves, evenly scattered on top, followed by the remaining bacon.

4. In a medium bowl, whisk together the mayo, eggs, cheddar, Parmesan, flour, cayenne, smoked paprika, and scallions. Spread the mixture evenly over the bacon layer, all the way to the crimped piecrust edges.

5. Arrange the remaining sliced tomatoes in an attractive pattern on top of the mayo mixture.

6. Place the pie on top of the rack set in the baking sheet. Bake for 45 to 60 minutes, rotating the sheet from front to back after 30 minutes, until the pie is bubbling hot, the edges of the crust are deep golden brown, and the mayo layer has taken on some color.

7. Let cool for 15 minutes on a wire rack before serving. If desired, garnish with more chopped scallions and Parmesan.

NOTE: You'll want to get the tomatoes as dry as possible before baking them. To drain them of excess moisture, lay out the tomato slices on a platter or baking sheet covered with paper towels. Let sit for 5 minutes before patting them dry with additional paper towels.

CORN CRAB CAKES

with Jalapeño Mayonnaise

Because we live in the Chesapeake Bay watershed, I truly know that the less filler used in a crab cake, the purer the results. I love a crab cake with nothing more than a bit of egg to hold it together, but I'm here to sell you on thinking a bit differently about crab cakes—this version is my favorite way to prepare them. Cornbread crumbs bind the lump crab with peppers and corn, making this a standout dish. Topping the crab cakes with a jalapeño-cilantro mayonnaise sends it skyward. Brenda Day, the wife of one of Dwight's former business partners, first introduced us to her version of these. I've made entrée-size servings to great acclaim, and for cocktail events I've knocked the size down to something small that can be handled in one bite. I always get asked for the recipe, so now I can hand them this book. The jalapeño-cilantro mayo goes inside the crab cakes as well, and the robust roasted corn partners nicely with the surprise of red onion. Even better, our crab cakes are broiled, not fried. Starring in pairs on the plate (you'll want two crab cakes per person), these are the best dressed-up crab cakes you'll ever enjoy.

MAKES 8 CRAB CAKES

FOR THE JALAPEÑO MAYONNAISE:

1½ cups **mayonnaise**

2 tablespoons chopped **red onion**

1 tablespoon chopped **fresh cilantro**

½ teaspoon **dry mustard**

1 tablespoon seeded and finely chopped **jalapeño pepper**

FOR THE CRAB CAKES:

½ cup **Jalapeño Mayonnaise**, plus more for serving

1 large **egg**, beaten

1 teaspoon **dry mustard**

¼ teaspoon crushed **red pepper flakes**

½ teaspoon **kosher salt**

½ teaspoon **freshly ground black pepper**

½ cup **yellow corn kernels**, fresh or frozen (thawed and drained if frozen)

½ cup diced **red or green bell pepper**

2 tablespoons diced **red onion**

1 tablespoon chopped **fresh parsley**

¾ cup crumbled **cornbread**, homemade (page 67) or store-bought, slightly stale or dry

1 pound **lump crabmeat**, picked over

Cilantro sprigs, for garnish

1. **Make the Jalapeño Mayonnaise:** Combine the mayo, red onion, cilantro, dry mustard, and jalapeño in a food processor or blender and purée until smooth. Transfer to a small bowl, cover, and refrigerate.

2. **Make the crab cakes:** Position a rack 4 to 6 inches from your oven's broiler element and preheat the broiler.

3. In a large bowl, stir together ½ cup of the Jalapeño Mayonnaise with the beaten egg. Add the dry mustard, red pepper flakes, salt, black pepper, corn, bell pepper, red onion, parsley, and crumbled cornbread, stirring until thoroughly combined. Fold in the crabmeat and then shape the mixture into 8 equal-size crab cakes.

4. Grease a baking sheet with vegetable oil spray in areas just large enough to be covered by the crab cakes and arrange them on it at least 1 inch apart. Broil for a total of 8 to 10 minutes, flipping them over halfway through, until browned on both sides. If the crab cakes are browning too quickly, move the oven rack down.

5. Let cool slightly, then place 2 crab cakes on each plate. Add a dollop of the jalapeño mayonnaise atop each crab cake, then garnish each with a cilantro sprig.

PEANUT GINGER CHICKEN
with Cucumber Salsa

Dwight loves fresh-from-the-garden cucumbers sliced and tossed with a bit of vinegar and sugar, so we planted them (and enjoyed them) every year until the groundhogs and raccoons caught on. Before that, we ended up with more than we could use, so I'd make a salsa with the cucumbers, sugar, and vinegar, adding a little bit of jalapeño spicy heat, that paired nicely with an Asian-peanut baked chicken, which is a bit like a chicken satay in a big baking dish. If a peanut allergy exists in your household, consider using almond butter (I sometimes substitute Big Spoon Roasters' Fiji Ginger almond butter).

SERVES 4 TO 6

FOR THE CHICKEN:

½ cup **creamy peanut butter**

¾ cup **unsweetened apple cider**, warmed slightly in the microwave

2 tablespoons **peanut oil**

3 tablespoons **soy sauce**

2 tablespoons **apple cider vinegar**

½ cup **chili sauce** (not hot sauce), such as Heinz brand

1 tablespoon plus 1 teaspoon minced **garlic**

2 tablespoons **freshly grated ginger**

12 **boneless, skinless chicken thighs**

FOR THE CUCUMBER SALSA:

¼ cup **apple cider vinegar**

2 tablespoons **peanut oil**

1 tablespoon **sugar**

1 cup peeled, seeded, and diced **cucumber** (1 medium)

2 **scallions**, white and green parts, trimmed and finely chopped

2 tablespoons chopped **fresh cilantro**

1 small **jalapeño pepper**, seeded and minced

1. **Make the chicken:** In a medium bowl, stir together the peanut butter and the warmed apple cider until smooth. Add the oil, soy sauce, vinegar, and chili sauce, stirring until well combined. Stir in the garlic and ginger.

2. Preheat the oven to 375°F. Lightly grease a 13 × 9-inch baking dish or pan with vegetable oil spray.

3. Spread a thin layer of the peanut sauce on the bottom of the baking dish. Add the chicken thighs, tucking each one into a bundle so they don't overlap, and cover with the remaining peanut sauce. Bake, uncovered, for 35 to 40 minutes, or until tender, cooked through, and the internal temperature registers 165°F on an instant-read thermometer.

4. **Meanwhile, make the cucumber salsa:** In a medium bowl, thoroughly whisk together the vinegar, oil, and sugar. Stir in the cucumber, scallions, cilantro, and jalapeño. Let sit at room temperature while the chicken cooks.

5. Serve 2 or 3 chicken thighs on each plate, spooning any sauce and pan juices over the top, with a heap of the cucumber salsa alongside.

BAKED CHICKEN
with Oaxacan Mole Sauce

Gather round: here is what I consider the best single dish in my repertoire. Of all my cooking experiences, nothing tops the week I spent in a former convent in Oaxaca, Mexico, as chef Rick Bayless taught our small group to cook the local cuisine (food writer and Southern Foodways Alliance director John T. Edge was in my class, and we remain friends fifteen years later). Rick calls mole (pronounced MOL-ay) "the soul of the Mexican kitchen," and it is the sauce you've always heard about: a complex purée made with chiles, fruit, nuts, and chocolate. Rick's recipe was the initial inspiration for this version, just as my friends Rolando Juarez and Karen Barroso opened their restaurant Guajillo in Rosslyn, Virginia, and invited me into their kitchen to learn to cook mole their way. So here's the best of both.

I'm always astounded at how perfect this resulting recipe tastes, and I love to make it. What a superior mole adds to other dishes is beyond comprehension, and this sauce will make you a convert—and quite proud—when using it, as here, for chicken breasts or thighs; chili (page 97); enchiladas (page 145); and even dabbed next to roasted carrots (page 154). The chicken itself goes particularly well with rice or roasted vegetables served alongside.

SERVES 4

4 large **boneless, skinless chicken breasts**, or 8 boneless, skinless chicken thighs

Kosher salt and **freshly ground black pepper**

4 cups **Oaxacan Mole Sauce** (recipe follows)

White sesame seeds

1 medium **white onion**, thinly sliced

1. Preheat the oven to 400°F.

2. Pat the chicken dry with paper towels. Season it all over with salt and pepper and place the chicken in a shallow 13 × 9-inch baking dish. Pour the mole sauce over the chicken, turning to coat and cover it evenly. Sprinkle with the sesame seeds and scatter the sliced onion evenly over the top. Roast for 40 to 50 minutes, until the chicken is cooked through and its internal temperature registers 165°F on an instant-read thermometer. Let rest for 5 minutes before serving.

OUR COMMUNITY OF ARTISANS

Woodie Long Gallery, *page 213*

OAXACAN MOLE SAUCE

The mole sauce, made with red chiles, is not difficult, but it is *involved*, with many ingredients and procedures. But please know that you can't mess this up (as long as you don't forget to stir the sauce on the stovetop). What's more, you can make it two days ahead, or even longer if you make a big batch and keep it in your freezer. Consider substituting fresh peaches for the pineapple, as I do when they're ripe and juicy. Search out pasilla de Oaxaca smoked chiles, an amazing product full of gorgeous, robust flavor. They are available, along with dried ancho chiles, Mexican oregano, and Mexican canela at worldspice.com. Trust me.
MAKES 10 CUPS

FOR THE BASE:

10 medium **dried ancho chiles**, stemmed, seeded, and opened flat (if you can find smoked pasilla de Oaxaca chiles, substitute just 2 or 3)

10 unpeeled **garlic cloves**

1 tablespoon **cumin seeds**, toasted in a skillet and freshly ground

1 teaspoon **freshly ground black pepper**

2 teaspoons **dried oregano**, preferably Mexican

¼ teaspoon **ground cloves**

1½ cups **chicken broth**, plus more as needed

FOR THE MOLE:

5 to 6 tablespoons **peanut or vegetable oil**, plus more as needed

1 **plantain**, peeled and sliced ¼ inch thick

3 **plum tomatoes**, halved lengthwise

½ cup (2 ounces) **walnut halves or pieces**

½ cup (2 ounces) whole **raw or blanched almonds**

½ cup (2 ounces) **salted or unsalted roasted peanuts** (optional)

1 medium **white onion**, thinly sliced

½ cup **raisins**

1 cup **crushed pineapple** (fresh or canned)

½ teaspoon **ground cinnamon** or Mexican canela

3 ounces **Mexican chocolate**, chopped (about ½ cup), such as 1½ disks of the Ibarra brand

3 slices **firm white bread**, toasted, 3 flour tortillas, or 4 corn tortillas

5½ cups **chicken broth**

1½ tablespoons **light brown sugar**

2 to 3 teaspoons **kosher salt**

1. **Make the base:** Heat a large skillet or griddle over medium heat and add the opened chiles a few at a time (make sure your exhaust fan is on). Press down on the chiles with a heatproof spatula for 5 seconds, or until they make a crackling sound, then flip them over and repeat. Add the toasted chiles to a bowl of hot water to soak for 30 minutes, making sure they remain submerged. Drain the chiles and set aside, discarding the liquid.

2. Meanwhile, in the same skillet, toast the garlic over medium heat for 15 minutes, turning once, until the cloves have softened and slightly blackened. Let cool, then trim off any hard ends and peel them.

3. In a blender, combine the chiles, garlic, ground cumin, black pepper, oregano, and cloves. Add 1½ cups of the chicken broth and purée until smooth, adding more broth if needed and stopping to scrape down the sides of the blender occasionally. Transfer the mixture to a bowl.

4. **Make the mole:** In the same skillet, heat 1 tablespoon of the oil over medium heat. When the oil is shimmering, add the plantain and cook, flipping as needed, until browned on both sides. Use a slotted spoon to transfer the plantains to a plate. Add the tomatoes cut-side down to the skillet and cook for 4 minutes, then flip and cook for about 7 minutes more, until the skins start to blacken and blister. Transfer the tomatoes and the plantains to the emptied blender.

5. In a large Dutch oven or other heavy-bottomed pot, heat 2 tablespoons of the oil over medium-low heat. Add the walnuts, almonds, and peanuts (if using), stirring often until toasted and fragrant, about 4 minutes. Use a slotted spoon to transfer the nuts to the blender. If the pot seems dry, add 1 tablespoon of the oil. Stir in the onion, cooking until lightly browned, about 9 minutes. Stir the raisins into the onions and cook until plump, about 1 minute more; remove the pot from the heat.

6. Transfer the contents of the pot to the blender along with the pineapple, cinnamon, chocolate, and toasted bread, tearing the latter into pieces as you work. (You may need to do this in batches.) Add 1½ cups of the broth and purée the ingredients until smooth, stopping to scrape down the sides of the blender as needed.

7. Add 2 tablespoons of the oil to the emptied pot to coat the bottom and heat it to medium-high. Add the reserved chile base and cook, stirring continuously, until the base has thickened and become darker, about 8 minutes. Add the puréed mixture from the blender and continue to cook, stirring frequently, for 8 minutes more, or until very thick.

8. Reduce the heat to medium-low and add the remaining 4 cups broth. Partially cover the pot and simmer for 1 hour, stirring often, until the mole is thick and fragrant. Stir in the brown sugar and add salt to taste. Remove the pot from the heat and let the mole cool. Transfer the mole to a freezer-safe storage bowl. The mole can be refrigerated for up to 2 days or frozen for up to 6 months.

OUR
COMMUNITY
OF ARTISANS

Shawn Ireland (Our
North Carolina
Pottery Pals),
page 212

ROAST CHICKEN
with Guava & Pineapple

The meal I enjoy cooking most for early fall dinners with friends, when I don't mind turning on the oven and heating up the kitchen but still want a reminder of summer, is this roast chicken, glazed with guava and scented with freshly toasted and ground cumin—the fruit packs a punch of tropical flavor, and the whole thing is a crowd-pleaser. Guava jelly and guava juice, the stars of this recipe, are readily available in the international aisle of many grocery stores and at Latin markets (the guava products are more important than the pineapple—I have a friend who is allergic to it, and it's fine to leave out the pineapple). This chicken is a stunner on its own, but I love serving it with Cornbread with Sorghum Butter (page 67), Roasted Heirloom Carrots with Rosemary & Harissa (page 154), and even Aunt Darla's Green Pea Salad (page 150).

SERVES 4 TO 6

FOR THE CHICKEN:

1 tablespoon **cumin seeds**, toasted in a skillet and freshly ground

Kosher salt and **freshly ground black pepper**

3 **garlic cloves**, minced

2 tablespoons **extra-virgin olive oil**

3 tablespoons **fresh lime juice** (from 1 or 2 limes)

1 (5-pound) **roasting chicken**, patted dry, giblets removed

FOR THE GLAZE:

12 ounces **guava jelly** (1 generous cup)

1½ cups **guava juice or nectar**

5 tablespoons **hot pepper jelly**

1 tablespoon **soy sauce**

2 tablespoons **ketchup**

½ cup **fresh lime juice** (from 3 or 4 limes)

1 tablespoon **cumin seeds**, toasted in a skillet and freshly ground

2 teaspoons **smoked paprika**

1 teaspoon **ground allspice**

1 teaspoon **kosher salt**

1 tablespoon **cold water**

1 (8-ounce) can **crushed pineapple in heavy syrup**

1. **Prepare the chicken:** In a large zip-top food storage bag, combine the freshly ground cumin, a generous pinch each of salt and pepper, the garlic, oil, and lime juice. Add the chicken and seal the bag, pressing out any excess air. Massage the marinade into the chicken with the bag closed. Refrigerate for at least 3 hours and up to overnight.

2. Preheat the oven to 400°F. Line a roasting pan or baking dish (preferably one that's not much larger than the chicken) with aluminum foil.

3. Remove the chicken from the marinade (discard the marinade) and set the chicken in the pan, breast-side up. Cover the chicken loosely with foil and roast for 45 minutes.

4. **Meanwhile, make the glaze:** In a medium saucepan, combine the guava jelly, guava juice, hot pepper jelly, soy sauce, ketchup, lime juice, freshly ground cumin, smoked paprika, allspice, and salt. Add the cold water, bring to a boil over medium-high heat, and cook, stirring occasionally, about 2 minutes. Reduce the heat to medium and continue to cook for 15 to 20 minutes, stirring often, until the glaze is glossy and has thickened and reduced by nearly half. Remove from the heat but leave it in the pan. You should have about 2 cups of the glaze. At this point, the glaze can be covered and stored in the refrigerator for up to 2 days. Before using, heat the glaze in a saucepan just long enough to make it spreadable again.

5. After 45 minutes of roasting the chicken, remove the roasting pan from the oven and brush the bird all over with one-third of the guava glaze. Return the chicken, uncovered, to the oven and continue to roast for 30 to 45 minutes more, using half of the remaining glaze to brush the chicken, until the juices run clear when a fork is inserted in the thigh or a meat thermometer inserted in the thigh (not touching the bone) registers 165°F.

6. Transfer the chicken to a serving platter. Bring the remaining glaze to a simmer in the same saucepan over medium heat. Stir in the pineapple and any pineapple syrup and cook just until heated through. Serve the pineapple-guava glaze alongside the chicken.

MUSHROOM-RICOTTA LASAGNE
with Port Sauce

While in my early twenties, I was in San Francisco alone for an afternoon Giants baseball game at Candlestick Park. I had dinner at Greens, perched on a pier overlooking the bay and the Golden Gate Bridge. Redwood burl tables filled the room, and chef Deborah Madison headed the kitchen. I ordered the vegetarian lasagne, and I haven't forgotten the impression it made on me as Greens called me back for many more meals over the years.

Two decades later, I was at a dinner in Florida celebrating the twentieth anniversary of the planned community of Seaside and seated next to a woman who introduced herself as . . . Deborah Madison. I'm sure my jaw dropped and I was a fawning idiot the rest of the night. Deborah, who had left Greens to focus on cookbook writing, told me about a newer lasagne recipe that Greens executive chef Annie Somerville had created. I tracked down Annie, who had just retired after her thirty-eighth year at Greens, and she shared the recipe with me. It is involved and time-consuming to undertake—you'll be making a mushroom sauce, a ricotta custard, an herb béchamel sauce, maybe even a terrific mushroom stock, and then assembling it all—so I spread the prep over a couple of days and stick it all in the fridge, ready to put together.

MAKES ONE 13 × 9-INCH LASAGNE

FOR THE MUSHROOM SAUCE:

½ ounce **dried porcini mushrooms**

1 tablespoon **extra-virgin olive oil**

1 medium **yellow onion**, cut into ¼-inch dice (about 1 cup)

½ teaspoon **kosher salt**, plus more as needed

Freshly ground black pepper

5 **garlic cloves**, minced

½ cup **good-quality port**, such as Ficklin Vineyards

3 tablespoons **unsalted butter**

¼ cup **unbleached all-purpose flour**

3 cups **Rich Mushroom Stock** (page 211) or a good-quality store-bought mushroom broth

FOR THE MUSHROOMS AND LEEKS:

2 tablespoons **extra-virgin olive oil**

2 large **leeks**, white parts only, halved lengthwise, thinly sliced, and rinsed well

¾ teaspoon **kosher salt**

Freshly ground black pepper

½ teaspoon **ground thyme**

5 **garlic cloves**, minced

1 pound **white button mushrooms**, stemmed, rinsed well, and cut into thick slices (about 5 cups)

¼ cup **good-quality port**, such as Ficklin Vineyards

¼ cup chopped **fresh mixed herbs**, such as thyme, marjoram, and parsley

FOR THE RICOTTA CUSTARD:

About 2 cups **Black Pepper Ricotta** (page 209), or 1 pound store-bought whole-milk ricotta

2 large **eggs**, beaten

1 ounce **Parmigiano-Reggiano** cheese, grated (about ⅓ cup)

3 pinches of **freshly grated or ground nutmeg**

½ teaspoon **kosher salt**

¼ teaspoon **freshly ground black pepper**

FOR THE HERB BÉCHAMEL SAUCE:

2½ cups **whole milk**

Several **fresh herb sprigs** tied together, such as parsley, sage, thyme, and marjoram

2 tablespoons **unsalted butter**

3 tablespoons **unbleached all-purpose flour**

¼ teaspoon **kosher salt**

¼ teaspoon **freshly ground black pepper**

FOR THE LASAGNE:

3 ounces **Parmigiano-Reggiano** cheese, grated (about 1 cup)

4 ounces **Gruyère cheese**, grated (about 1½ cups)

1 pound **fresh pasta sheets**, or as needed

1. **Make the mushroom sauce:** Place the dried porcini mushrooms in a medium bowl and cover with warm water. Soak for 10 minutes, then strain them through a fine-mesh strainer into a separate bowl, reserving the soaking liquid and discarding any grit. Finely chop the mushrooms, discarding any pieces that are hard or tough.

recipe continues

OUR
COMMUNITY
OF ARTISANS

Jugtown Pottery,
page 213

2. In a medium saucepan, heat the oil over medium heat until shimmering. Stir in the onion, salt, and a few pinches of pepper. Cook until the onion begins to release its moisture, 5 to 7 minutes. Add the garlic and the chopped mushrooms. Cook for 2 to 3 minutes, then add the port and the strained mushroom soaking liquid. Continue to cook at a simmer over medium heat for about 8 minutes, until the pan is nearly dry. Transfer the mixture to a bowl.

3. In the same saucepan, melt the butter over low heat. Whisk in the flour to form a roux. Cook for 2 to 3 minutes, stirring constantly. Whisk ½ cup of the mushroom stock into the roux to make a paste, then whisk in another ½ cup of the stock to thin it. Gradually add the remaining 2 cups stock and, once it has been incorporated, add the onion-porcini mixture, making sure to include any accumulated juices in the bowl. Increase the heat to medium and cook the sauce for 8 to 10 minutes, until it has thickened nicely. Taste and season with additional salt if needed. If not using immediately, cool and refrigerate the sauce in an airtight container for up to 2 days.

4. **Make the mushrooms and leeks:** In a large skillet, heat 1 tablespoon of the oil over medium heat. Stir in the leeks, ¼ teaspoon salt, a few pinches of pepper, and the thyme and cook for 2 minutes. Add half of the garlic, cover, and steam until the leeks are tender and slightly golden, 7 to 8 minutes. Transfer to a bowl.

5. Wipe out the skillet and place it over high heat with 1½ teaspoons of the oil. When the oil is shimmering, add half of the mushrooms and season with ¼ teaspoon salt and a few pinches of pepper. Cook the mushrooms, without stirring—at this point they'll begin to stick to the pan, but you want to let them get a good sear on the bottom—until they're golden, then stir once and continue to sear for 1 to 2 minutes. Add half of the remaining garlic, stir again, then add half of the port to deglaze the pan, stirring with a wooden spoon to dislodge any browned bits from the bottom. Transfer the mushroom mixture to the bowl with leeks. Add the remaining 1½ teaspoons oil to the pan and cook the remaining mushrooms as directed. Transfer the cooked mushrooms to the bowl. Add 3 tablespoons of the chopped herbs, reserving the remaining 1 tablespoon for serving. If not using immediately, cool, cover, and refrigerate for up to 2 days.

6. **Make the ricotta custard:** Stir together the ricotta and eggs in a bowl until well blended. Add the Parmesan, nutmeg, salt, and pepper, mixing thoroughly. If not using immediately, cover and refrigerate for up to 2 days.

7. **Make the herb béchamel sauce:** In a large saucepan, heat the milk with the herb bundle over medium-low heat, until warmed through and fragrant, about 5 minutes. In a separate saucepan, melt the butter over low heat. Add the flour and cook, whisking continuously, to form a roux. Discard the herb bundle. Add ½ cup of the warm milk to the roux, whisking constantly to form a paste, then gradually pour in the remaining 2 cups warm milk, whisking until smooth. Add the salt and pepper. Increase the heat to medium and cook for 7 to 10 minutes, whisking frequently, until the béchamel has slightly thickened and is smooth.

8. **Assemble the lasagne:** Reserve ⅓ cup of the Parmesan (to sprinkle on top) and toss the remaining Parmesan and the Gruyère together in a medium bowl. Spread a third of the mushroom sauce on the bottom of a deep 13 × 9-inch baking dish and cover it with one layer of the pasta sheets. Pour half of the remaining sauce over the pasta, followed by all of the mushroom-leek mixture. Add another layer of pasta and spread the ricotta custard evenly over it. Add another layer of pasta and scatter half the Parmesan-Gruyère mixture on top. Add the remaining sauce, the remaining Parmesan-Gruyère mixture, and the final layer of pasta, in that order. (You may have some pasta sheets left over.) Pour all the béchamel sauce over the lasagne, spreading it evenly to cover the edges. (At this point you could cover and refrigerate the lasagne and bake it the next day; bring to room temperature while the oven preheats.)

9. Preheat the oven to 350°F. Grease the underside of a sheet of aluminum foil with vegetable oil spray and use it to loosely cover the lasagne. Bake for 20 minutes, then uncover and scatter the reserved ⅓ cup Parmesan on top. Return the lasagne to the oven, uncovered, and bake until the béchamel sauce has set, the Parmesan has melted, and the lasagne is golden brown on top, 20 to 30 minutes. The pasta should be tender. Scatter the reserved tablespoon of chopped herbs on top as soon as the lasagne comes out of the oven. Let it rest for 10 minutes or so before serving (any sooner and it will be too loose to cut).

CHUNKY MEATLOAF
with Plenty of Bacon

I grew up with this meatloaf—it's my mom's recipe. I've added more bacon to it over the years, and I bet my siblings wouldn't find anything wrong with that. At home, I like to heat up leftover slices of the meatloaf in a stovetop grill pan, creating nice charred diagonal lines on the surface. The Roasted Heirloom Carrots with Rosemary & Harissa (page 154) are perfect companions.

SERVES 8

FOR THE MEATLOAF:

1 tablespoon **unsalted butter**

1 tablespoon **canola oil**

1 medium **yellow onion**, coarsely chopped

2 teaspoons **minced garlic**

2 **celery stalks**, including any leaves, finely chopped

1 **red bell pepper**, seeded and coarsely chopped

2 teaspoons **ground thyme**

1 tablespoon **kosher salt**

1 teaspoon **freshly ground black pepper**

1 large **egg**

2 teaspoons **Worcestershire sauce**

½ cup **chili sauce** (not hot sauce), such as Heinz brand, or ketchup

1 cup **bread crumbs** (use focaccia, panko, crackers, or cornbread) or oats

2 tablespoons finely chopped **fresh parsley**

3 pounds **ground beef** (90 percent lean) or store-bought meatloaf mix (beef, lamb, or veal)

10 slices **thick-sliced smoked bacon**

FOR THE GLAZE:

¼ cup **chili sauce**, such as Heinz brand, or ketchup

2 teaspoons **maple syrup**

1 tablespoon **Dijon** (either coarse or smooth) or yellow mustard

2 teaspoons **Worcestershire sauce**

1 teaspoon **hot pepper sauce**, such as Tabasco

Ketchup, for drizzling

1. **Make the meatloaf:** In a Dutch oven or other large heavy-bottomed pot over medium-low heat, combine the butter and oil. Once the butter has melted, add the onion, garlic, celery, and bell pepper, stirring to coat. Cook for 6 minutes, stirring a few times, until the vegetables have softened. Stir in the thyme, salt, and black pepper and cook for 1 minute more. Remove the pot from the heat and let the mixture cool slightly.

2. In a liquid measuring cup, use a fork to stir together the egg, Worcestershire sauce, and chili sauce, then pour the mixture into the pot with the vegetables. Add the bread crumbs and parsley, stirring with a wooden spoon until thoroughly combined. Add the ground beef and mix well with the spoon or your clean hands so the vegetables are evenly distributed. Cover and refrigerate for 20 minutes.

3. Preheat the oven to 400°F. Grease a 13 × 9-inch glass baking dish with vegetable oil spray and place it on a baking sheet.

4. **Make the glaze:** In the same liquid measuring cup, use a fork to stir together the chili sauce, maple syrup, mustard, Worcestershire sauce, and hot pepper sauce.

5. Add the chilled meatloaf mixture to the prepared baking dish. With clean hands, form it into a rounded loaf centered in the pan, about 10 inches long and 4 inches tall. Spoon the glaze across the loaf and down the sides. Arrange the bacon slices diagonally across the top of the loaf, tucking the ends underneath, and encircle the loaf with any bacon that's left over. Drizzle stripes of ketchup diagonally (in the opposite direction of the diagonal bacon) and evenly across the top.

6. Bake the meatloaf for 1 hour, rotating it from front to back halfway through, or until the center of the loaf feels firm and the bacon on top is nicely browned. If the meatloaf is browning too quickly, reduce the oven temperature to 375°F and cover the baking dish with aluminum foil. Continue to cook until the center is no longer pink and the internal temperature is 155°F to 160°F.

7. Transfer the baking dish to a cooling rack and let the meatloaf rest, uncovered, for 15 minutes, which will allow some of its juices to reabsorb. Drain any remaining juices before serving.

SWEET POTATO & POBLANO ENCHILADAS
with Oaxacan Mole Sauce

I love the way sweet potatoes work with a honey-sweetened goat cheese and our Oaxacan Mole Sauce. Make the sauce ahead of time, store it in your freezer, and bring it to room temperature for dishes such as this. With the mole prep out of the way, this is a quick dish to pull together. Be spontaneous: the last time I made this, I switched out the sweet potatoes and squash for cooked and peeled shrimp, which is extraordinary with the mole and goat cheese. Either way, Nita's Corn Salad with Tomatoes & Basil (page 153) is a great match for these.

SERVES 6

1 large **sweet potato**, peeled and cut into ½-inch cubes

2 tablespoons **extra-virgin olive oil**

Kosher salt and **freshly ground black pepper**

1 medium **poblano pepper**, halved lengthwise, seeded, and cut into thin 1-inch-long strips

1 medium **yellow summer squash**, trimmed and cut into ½-inch cubes

½ large **red onion**, cut into ¼-inch dice

1 (15-ounce) can **black beans**, rinsed and drained

8 ounces **plain goat cheese**, crumbled

2 teaspoons **honey**

3¼ cups **Oaxacan Mole Sauce** (page 137) or store-bought enchilada sauce

12 (6-inch) **corn tortillas**

1½ cups **Pickled Red Onions** (page 209)

2 cups (8 ounces) shredded **Monterey Jack cheese**

¼ cup (packed) **fresh cilantro leaves**, for garnish

1. Preheat the oven to 400°F.

2. In a large bowl, toss the sweet potato with 1 tablespoon of the olive oil on a rimmed baking sheet. Season with salt and pepper and roast for 10 minutes, stirring halfway through, until tender and golden brown. Meanwhile, toss the poblano and squash with the remaining 1 tablespoon olive oil and season with salt and pepper. Remove the sweet potatoes from the oven, sliding them with a wooden spoon to the bowl of poblano and squash and stirring gently to combine. Spread the veggies evenly on the baking sheet. Return the pan to the oven and roast for an additional 10 minutes, until the sweet potatoes are browned all over and the squash is golden. Remove from the oven and reduce the temperature to 350°F.

3. Transfer the roasted sweet potatoes, poblano, and squash back to the large bowl. Add the red onion, black beans, goat cheese, honey, and ¼ cup of the mole sauce, stirring gently to combine and evenly coat everything. (If your mole was frozen and thawed, thin it with a little water.)

4. Spread a thin layer of the remaining mole sauce on the bottom of a 3-quart rectangular baking dish. Fill each tortilla with ⅓ cup of the veggie filling, rolling and placing the tortillas seam-side down in the baking dish. Spread or pour the remaining mole sauce evenly over the rolled tortillas. Scatter the pickled red onions over the sauce and sprinkle the Jack cheese evenly across the top.

5. Bake for 20 to 25 minutes, or until the cheese is bubbling and the edges are browned. Serve 2 enchiladas per plate, garnished with the cilantro.

SIDES

148
BAKED BEANS
with Molasses, Honey & Bacon

150
AUNT DARLA'S
GREEN PEA SALAD

151
EILEEN'S COLESLAW

151
PARSNIP PURÉE

153
NITA'S CORN SALAD
with Tomatoes & Basil

154
ROASTED
HEIRLOOM CARROTS
with Rosemary & Harissa

157
WATERMELON SALAD
with Grilled Halloumi

158
SQUASH CASSEROLE
with Corn & Crunchy Bread Crumbs

BAKED BEANS

with Molasses, Honey & Bacon

When the fireplace is ablaze, these navy beans are usually in our oven. James Beard gets most of the credit here, but I can't leave well enough alone and felt a need to add some layers of flavor over the years. I make these with Allan Benton's smoked bacon (intense smokiness is important), molasses, honey, maple syrup, a decent amount of cumin, and a pinch of curry. The recipe takes very little work, with most of the time devoted to baking—the key is a very low-temperature oven that bakes the beans slowly for 6 to 8 hours, leaving you free to go about other things in your day as you please. Nestling the onion in the center of the pot infuses everything with its flavor—and the treat is to slice it up to mix back into the pot or enjoy on the side. The beans work very well with a slab of Cornbread with Sorghum Butter (page 67) or with a simple grilled chicken breast served on top, or accompanying Chunky Meatloaf with Plenty of Bacon (page 143). Our favorite part of this dish: enjoying these leftovers after a day in the fridge, when the flavors have become even richer.

SERVES 4 TO 8

2 cups **dried navy beans**, picked over

1 teaspoon **kosher salt**, plus more as needed

½ cup (packed) **light brown sugar**

½ cup **molasses, honey, or sorghum syrup**, or a combination

1 tablespoon **maple syrup**

½ teaspoon **Worcestershire sauce**

1 tablespoon **dry mustard**

1 tablespoon plus 1½ teaspoons **whole cumin seeds**, toasted in a skillet and freshly ground, or 2 teaspoons ground cumin

1 teaspoon **curry powder**

1 teaspoon **freshly ground black pepper**

1 medium **yellow onion**

1 pound **smoky bacon**, coarsely chopped

1. Rinse the beans well and soak them in 2 quarts water overnight. Drain the beans and place them in a large pot. Add 1 teaspoon salt and cover the beans with 2 inches water. Bring to a boil, then reduce the heat and gently simmer, stirring occasionally with a wooden spoon, for about 30 minutes, until the beans are barely tender. Drain the beans and place them in a large bowl, discarding the cooking liquid.

2. In a small bowl, use a fork to whisk together the brown sugar, molasses, maple syrup, Worcestershire sauce, dry mustard, ground cumin, curry powder, and pepper. Add the mixture to the beans and stir to coat.

3. Preheat the oven to 250°F. Boil a kettle of water.

4. Peel the onion, leaving it whole. Place it in the center of a large ovenproof saucepan with a tight-fitting lid or a Dutch oven, and scatter the chopped raw bacon around it.

5. Pour the beans over the bacon in the pot. Add enough of the boiled water to just barely cover the beans. Cover tightly and bake 4 to 5 hours, until the beans have softened further but are not broken apart.

6. Remove from the oven, uncover, and give the beans a stir. Taste and add salt as needed. Return the pot to the oven, uncovered, and bake for an additional 2 to 3 hours, until the sauce is thicker, the beans are darker, and the surface is a bit crusty.

7. Remove the onion and coarsely chop it, serving it atop, mixed in, or alongside the beans.

OUR
COMMUNITY
OF ARTISANS

Mark Hewitt Pottery,
page 213

GREEN PEA SALAD

My Aunt Darla, from "BristolTennessee" (her family says it as one word to differentiate from those on the other side of State Street in Bristol, Virginia), is famous around our parts for her smoky pimento cheese recipe we use at the bakery. I was privy to another one of her Bristol delicacies: a chilled green pea salad that she brought out on special occasions. The crunch of cold chopped water chestnuts against the crisp peas in a creamy mayo dressing is worth the wait at a holiday meal, but I've taken to mixing up this cool dish in the summer to pair with crunchy foods like fried chicken and soft-shell crabs. My pal Travis Milton, a Virginia chef who hails from Darla's neck of the woods—albeit on the far *north* side of State Street—makes a version with bacon fat, cheese, and fresh herbs. That's a bit involved for Darla's kin, but I'm offering up some optional ingredients here to keep peace in the hills. If you can find May peas, English peas, or sugar snap peas at the farmers' market, as Travis does, grab those, although Darla and I both prefer to use frozen green peas, which really are just as good as fresh—but don't use off-color, mushy, canned peas. Darla doesn't include shredded cheese, as others do, because the salad is best after a day in the fridge, and she thinks the cheesy texture becomes too soggy. In one last text to Darla about her recipe, I asked if she didn't add just a *bit* of sugar. "Honey, I add sugar to *everything,* even gravy. When are you coming down to give me some sugar?"

SERVES 8 TO 10

3 thick slices **smoky bacon** (optional)

1 teaspoon **apple cider vinegar**

1½ cups **mayonnaise**

2 teaspoons **sugar**

Kosher salt and **freshly ground black pepper**

1 small head **iceberg lettuce**, cored and coarsely chopped

1 small **red onion**, finely chopped

1 (8-ounce) can **water chestnuts**, drained and chopped

2 pounds **green peas**, frozen and thawed, or fresh, drained (see Note)

1. In a medium skillet over medium heat, cook the bacon, if using, until crisped, 5 to 6 minutes. Use a slotted spoon to transfer the bacon to a paper towel–lined plate to drain, then coarsely chop it. Reserve 2 teaspoons of the rendered bacon fat, discarding the rest or saving it for another use.

2. Transfer the reserved bacon fat (if using) to a medium bowl. Use a fork to whisk the vinegar into the bacon fat, then whisk in the mayonnaise and sugar until well blended. If not using bacon, just whisk together the vinegar, mayonnaise, and sugar until well blended. Season with the salt and pepper to taste. Cover and refrigerate until ready to use.

3. In a large bowl, combine the lettuce, red onion, water chestnuts, and the chopped bacon (if using). Add the peas and stir gently (don't smash the peas) until evenly distributed.

4. Fold in the mayonnaise dressing until the ingredients are evenly coated. Cover and refrigerate for at least 2 hours before serving.

NOTE: If using fresh peas, quickly blanch them in boiling water for 1 minute or less, then shock them in a bowl of ice water before draining and using.

EILEEN'S COLESLAW

Eileen Hill was a neighbor of ours in her eighties who lived directly across the street from us in Arlington, Virginia. We bought the house in which she grew up, built by her father in 1919. During our renovation, she brought over food for us, including what she called "Eileen's famous coleslaw." The slaw is finely chopped, almost minced. I thought I preferred coarsely chopped coleslaw, but this indeed turns out great (and a food processor is a great help with all the chopping). Her thoughts on our renovation? "You made my old house well again."

SERVES 6 TO 8

1 large head **cabbage**, cored and coarsely chopped (about 9 cups)

1 medium **onion**, coarsely chopped

2 **green bell peppers**, seeded and cut into chunks

2 **carrots**, trimmed, peeled, and cut into chunks

2 **celery stalks**, trimmed and cut into chunks

2 tablespoons **apple cider vinegar**

¼ cup **sugar**

1 tablespoon **kosher salt**

1 tablespoon **freshly ground black pepper**

½ cup **mayonnaise**, plus more as needed

1 tablespoon **celery seed**

1. Working in batches as needed, pulse the cabbage in a food processor just until finely chopped. Transfer the cabbage to a large mixing bowl. Repeat with the onion, pulsing it until finely chopped, and add it to the cabbage. Continue to pulse (separately) the bell peppers, the carrots, and finally the celery. Mix all the finely chopped items together until well combined.

2. Add the vinegar to the bowl and stir. Add the sugar, salt, black pepper, mayonnaise, and celery seed, mixing until evenly distributed. If the slaw does not seem well coated, add a little more mayonnaise. Cover and refrigerate for 1 hour, restirring before serving. The slaw can be refrigerated for up to 2 days.

PARSNIP PURÉE

It's rare to see parsnips listed on a restaurant menu, although I never stop looking for them—especially in the fall and winter, peak seasons for this root vegetable. I love its sweet, unique flavor, slightly spicy and vaguely nutty, and I often serve it as a side dish just as I would mashed potatoes. Try to find parsnips that are roughly the same thickness and not too fat, as the larger ones can have woody cores.

SERVES 6 TO 8

2 tablespoons **unsalted butter**

1 small **yellow onion**, thinly sliced

1 **garlic clove**, thinly sliced

1 (3-inch-long) **celery stalk** with some leaves, thinly sliced

1 pound **parsnips**, trimmed, peeled, and thinly sliced

½ cup **heavy cream**

½ cup **whole milk**

⅛ teaspoon **curry powder**

Kosher salt

1. In a large saucepan over medium-low heat, melt the butter. Stir in the onion and gently sauté until barely golden, stirring occasionally, about 10 minutes. Stir in the garlic and celery and continue to cook for about 4 minutes more, until fragrant and tender.

2. Add the parsnips, cream, and milk to the saucepan and stir everything to coat. Increase the heat to medium-high, just until the mixture comes to a boil, then reduce the heat to medium-low, cover, and simmer until the parsnips are soft, 10 to 12 minutes.

3. Uncover and continue to cook until the liquid has reduced by half, about 6 minutes. Stir in the curry powder and season with salt to taste. Let cool slightly.

4. Transfer the mixture to a blender or food processor and purée until smooth. Serve warm.

NITA'S CORN SALAD
with Tomatoes & Basil

We know and love April McGreger from her days spent cooking up the sumptuous jams and preserves we kept on our bakery's retail shelves, until she surprised us all in a short email saying that she's hanging up her Farmer's Daughter company apron for good. She has since shared an adapted recipe for her mom's corn salad with *Garden & Gun* magazine, and every time I made it for our catering events and posted the results on Instagram, I got swooning comments from friends who had then made it themselves. I chatted with April about her mom Nita's original and true version, and she laughed when telling me that Nita never measured ingredients, didn't write down a vital ingredient (such as the roasted red pepper juice from a jar), and avoided herbs in her dish until influenced by her daughter. "She makes this all year long," April says, "definitely using frozen sweet corn or even (gasp!) canned shoepeg corn. It's a working woman's recipe, so shortcuts are the norm!" This is one of my favorite summer dishes in the book.

SERVES 6 TO 8

NOTE: While April and her mom have given their blessing to use frozen corn if you need to, I sure would urge you to make this with fresh corn in the height of summer.

6 ears of **corn**, shucked, or 4½ cups frozen corn, thawed and drained (see Note)

1 cup **multicolored cherry or grape tomatoes**, halved

¼ cup diced **red onion**

1 medium **cucumber**, peeled, seeded, and coarsely chopped

¼ cup chopped **roasted red bell peppers** from a jar, plus 3 tablespoons liquid

½ teaspoon **kosher salt**, plus more as needed

½ teaspoon **freshly ground black pepper**, plus more as needed

2 tablespoons **extra-virgin olive oil**

3 tablespoons **mayonnaise**

¼ cup **fresh basil leaves**, rolled up and thinly sliced

1. If using fresh corn, bring a large pot of water to a boil. Have a large bowl of ice water ready.

2. If you're using fresh corn, add the ears to the pot and boil for 2 minutes, then immediately transfer the corn to the ice-water bath to cool for 30 seconds. Drain on a cooling rack over newspaper or paper towels until cool enough to handle. (If you're using thawed and drained frozen corn, skip this step and simply add the corn to the large bowl in step 3.)

3. Scrape the kernels from the corn cobs into a large bowl. Add the tomatoes, red onion, cucumber, roasted red peppers and their liquid, salt, and pepper and mix well.

4. Pour in the oil and toss until everything is evenly coated. Spoon in the mayonnaise, mixing to evenly coat. Cover and refrigerate for at least 1 hour. Taste and season with more salt and pepper, as needed. Stir in the basil just before serving.

ROASTED HEIRLOOM CARROTS
with Rosemary & Harissa

My friends know I love carrots in all forms—puréed to make a side dish, freshly juiced, or even in cakes and muffins. One pal of mine, Patrick Hurley from Raleigh, is a potter, and he created a rectangular ceramic pot for me in which to roast my favorite vegetable, the preparation I love the best. As soon as rainbow-colored heirloom carrots start appearing at the farmers' market in late spring and through the fall, I buy a bunch for their extra sweetness and visual appeal. Orange carrots work perfectly, of course—though it is worth getting a fresh bunch from the market rather than loose ones at the grocery store. Finely chopped fresh rosemary, good olive oil, and sea salt elevate this simple dish. Having spent some time in Tunisia, I became fascinated by the country's harissa, a hot chile pepper paste, and I use it to brighten up these carrots without turning them fiery. These carrots are a multi-season crowd-pleaser alongside Roast Chicken with Guava & Pineapple (page 139), Mid-July Tomato Pie (page 130), or Pork Tenderloin with Rosemary & Blueberries (page 129).

SERVES 6

1. Preheat the oven to 400°F and line a rimmed baking sheet with parchment paper or a silicone liner.

2. Cut the carrots on the diagonal into large chunks of equal size (and cut any noticeably thicker carrots in half lengthwise), placing them in a large bowl as you work. Toss with the oil, rosemary, and harissa until evenly coated. Season generously with the flaky salt and pepper.

3. Spread the carrots on the prepared baking sheet in a single layer and roast for 25 to 35 minutes, shaking the pan to toss the carrots halfway through, until the carrots are tender, sizzling, and browned on the edges.

24 **fresh carrots**, trimmed and peeled, preferably multicolored and of equal size

2 tablespoons **extra-virgin olive oil**

1 tablespoon finely chopped **fresh rosemary**

2 teaspoons **harissa**

Flaky sea salt

Freshly ground black pepper

WATERMELON SALAD
with Grilled Halloumi

The dog days of summer call for a cooling watermelon-and-tomato salad. Many recipes include feta, which adds a creamy bite to the sweetness of the fruit, but I think that cheese crumbles too easily and doesn't much vary the texture of the salad. Dixie Grimes, chef at Alexe van Beuren's beloved BTC Old-Fashioned Grocery in Water Valley, Mississippi—the unofficial headquarters of the town's annual Watermelon Carnival— introduced me to grilling halloumi cheese and cutting it into small cubes, which is the way she prepares it at her Dixie Belle Café and is what inspired this recipe. The cheese has a high melting temperature with a pleasant texture that doesn't fall apart. It plays well with fresh herbs (and I include three here), fresh fruit and veggies, and a sassy little dressing.

SERVES 8 TO 10

NOTE: Halloumi is easy to find in the specialty cheese section of most grocery stores, but if you can't find it, you can use a 12-ounce block of feta in its place.

FOR THE DRESSING:

¼ cup **extra-virgin olive oil**

¼ cup **fresh lime juice** (from 2 or 3 limes)

1 teaspoon **minced garlic**

3 tablespoons **honey**

1 tablespoon chopped **fresh cilantro**

1 tablespoon chopped **fresh mint**

1 teaspoon **kosher salt**

2 teaspoons **freshly ground black pepper**

FOR THE WATERMELON SALAD:

Extra-virgin olive oil

2 (8-ounce) packages **halloumi cheese**, cut in ½-inch slices (see Note)

6 cups seeded or seedless diced **red watermelon**

2 pints **heirloom cherry tomatoes** in assorted colors, halved

2 medium **cucumbers**, seeded and cut into thin half-moons

1 medium **red onion**, thinly sliced crosswise

1 **red or green bell pepper**, seeded and cut into thin strips

1 large **jalapeño pepper**, seeded and cut into very thin strips

6 **fresh basil leaves**, stacked, rolled, and cut into very thin ribbons

1. **Make the dressing:** Combine the olive oil, lime juice, garlic, honey, cilantro, mint, salt, and black pepper in a small mason jar. Seal and shake for 1 minute, until emulsified and smooth. Refrigerate for up to 1 week.

2. **Make the salad:** Heat a cast-iron skillet over medium heat until hot but not smoking. Add just enough olive oil to coat the bottom of the pan. Add the slices of halloumi and sear both sides, flipping with tongs or a spatula, to a medium golden brown, about 5 minutes total. Transfer them to a cutting board. (If you're using feta cheese, skip this step and simply add chunks to the salad.)

3. In a large serving bowl, toss together the watermelon, tomatoes, cucumbers, red onion, bell pepper, jalapeño, and basil until just incorporated. Cut the slices of grilled halloumi into small cubes and add them to the bowl. Toss with enough dressing to lightly coat and serve immediately.

SQUASH CASSEROLE
with Corn & Crunchy Bread Crumbs

Lunch at a tiny café off the beaten path in Savannah, Georgia, led to the best squash casserole I'd ever eaten, and I was crushed when the owner wouldn't budge on sharing its secrets. "That's our most popular dish, and I'm not giving that recipe to anyone," she snapped at me. I got the feeling that I had been the guy who asked the question she'd heard one too many times. This recipe is the result of spending too many summers trying to duplicate that dish's subtle sweetness, creaminess, and crunch. Feel free to make it your own: If you have an abundance of zucchini, then substitute some for the summer squash. Cherry tomatoes would be great in it as well—just cut a handful in half and scatter them in along with the corn. And if you want it a bit meatier, nothing goes better with this dish than ½ cup or so of coarsely chopped cooked bacon, which you can add to the dish at the same time as the corn.

SERVES 6 TO 8

4 pounds **yellow squash**, trimmed and sliced into ⅓-inch-thick rounds

8 ounces **cream cheese**, at room temperature

½ cup **half-and-half**

1 large **egg**

1½ cups **plain panko bread crumbs**

6 ounces **Gruyère or Asiago cheese**, shredded (1½ cups)

4 ounces grated **Parmigiano-Reggiano cheese**, freshly grated (1 cup)

½ cup chopped **fresh parsley**

1 tablespoon chopped **fresh basil**, or 2 teaspoons dried

1 tablespoon **unsalted butter**, plus 2 tablespoons melted

2 medium **yellow onions**, thinly sliced crosswise

2 **garlic cloves**, minced

2 cups **fresh or frozen corn kernels** (thawed and patted dry if frozen)

Kosher salt and **freshly ground black pepper**

1. Preheat the oven to 350°F and position a rack in the center. Grease a 13 × 9-inch baking dish with vegetable oil spray.

2. Bring a large pot of water to a boil over medium-high heat. Add the squash and cook for 5 minutes, or until barely tender. Drain into a colander in the sink.

3. In a large bowl, whisk together the cream cheese, half-and-half, egg, 1 cup of the panko, the Gruyère, ½ cup of the Parmesan, the parsley, and basil.

4. Melt 1 tablespoon butter in a large sauté pan or deep skillet over medium heat. Stir in the onions and cook, stirring occasionally, until lightly browned and tender, about 6 minutes. Stir in the garlic and cook for 1 minute more, until fragrant. Remove from the heat.

5. Add the parcooked squash to the pan along with the cream cheese mixture. Stir in the corn and season with salt and pepper to taste. Pour the mixture into the prepared baking dish and spread it out evenly. Cover tightly with foil and bake on the center rack for 20 minutes.

6. Meanwhile, in a medium bowl, combine the 2 tablespoons melted butter, the remaining ½ cup panko, and the remaining ½ cup Parmesan, tossing to coat evenly.

7. Remove the casserole from the oven and uncover. Sprinkle the panko-Parmesan mixture evenly across the top. Move the rack to the upper third of the oven and return the casserole to the rack. Continue to bake, uncovered, for 10 minutes more, or until the Parmesan in the topping has melted and the casserole is heated through. Turn on the broiler and, very briefly, broil to create a golden crust, watching closely so it does not burn. Let the casserole sit for a few minutes before serving.

DESSERTS

162
BLUE RIBBON BLUEBERRY PIE
with Ginger

165
SOUR CHERRY PIE
with a Hint of Almond

166
LEMON CHESS TART

168
SALTED CARAMEL APPLE PIE

170
VIRGINIA PEANUT PIE

172
BILL SMITH'S ATLANTIC BEACH PIE

174
CHOCOLATE CHESS PIE
with Graham Cracker Crust

175
BANANA PUDDING
with Homemade Vanilla Wafers

177
APPLE CRISP

178
OLD-FASHIONED STRAWBERRY SHORTCAKES

180
DOT'S PEACH COBBLER
with Crystallized Ginger

181
CARROT CAKE
with Chantilly Cream

183
LEXINGTON BOURBON CAKE

184
FLOURLESS CHOCOLATE TRUFFLE CAKE

187
MARTHA WASHINGTON'S GREAT CAKE

189
TRIPLE-CHOCOLATE CAKE

191
CARAMEL CAKE
with Pecans

193
ORANGE CAKE

195
NOYES BIRTHDAY CAKE

197
PEACH POUND CAKE

198
CORN ICE CREAM

BLUE RIBBON BLUEBERRY PIE
with Ginger

Behold the purest taste of summer. At the bakery, I'm always asked which is my favorite pie, and my honest answer is, "Whatever we're making right now," because we're a seasonal bakery and (aside from Libby's 100 percent pumpkin purée, which becomes particularly handy in November) we don't use anything canned or frozen in our pies. When a certain local fruit is no longer available, I'm then excited to move on to the next harvest available from our area farmers.

But I must say I especially look forward to blueberry season at the bakery and at the farmhouse. We have several huge and ancient blueberry bushes at our farm, and we race to get to them before the birds do, using the blueberries on cereal, in pancakes and waffles, and in my homemade pies and other desserts. This is a straight-up fresh blueberry pie made just the way we do at the bakery, with a bit of lemon zest and ginger to bring out the best of the berries, which back in the day made it worthy of my blue ribbon at the Arlington County Fair. Try it with Corn Ice Cream (page 198)—a glorious combination that tastes like long, lazy July days.

MAKES ONE 10-INCH DOUBLE-CRUST PIE

1. Preheat the oven to 375°F. Place a wire rack inside a rimmed baking sheet.

2. In a large bowl, mix together the sugar, cornstarch, crystallized ginger, salt, and lemon zest. Add the blueberries and toss to coat. Let sit for a few minutes to allow the berries to release their juices.

3. Lightly flour a work surface and a rolling pin. Roll out one disk of pie dough into a 13-inch round. Drape it into a 10-inch pie pan, leaving some overhang around the edges. Pour the blueberry mixture into the bottom crust and dot the top of the fruit with the cubes of butter.

4. Roll out the second disk of dough and set it over the filling. Trim and crimp the edges, sealing in the filling. Cut a few slits in the center.

5. Use a fork to whisk together the egg and 1 tablespoon water in a small bowl. Brush the top with the egg wash.

6. Carefully place the pie on the rack set in the baking sheet. Bake for 70 to 90 minutes, rotating the sheet from front to back after the first 30 minutes, or until the exact center of the filling is bubbling right up out of the slits. (If it isn't, the filling hasn't yet thickened and set—don't rush it.) Let cool on a separate wire rack before serving. The pie can be kept at room temperature for 2 days, then wrapped and refrigerated for up to 3 additional days.

¾ cup **sugar**

¼ cup plus 2 tablespoons **cornstarch**

1 tablespoon finely chopped **crystallized ginger**

Pinch of **kosher salt**

½ teaspoon **freshly grated lemon zest**

5 cups **fresh blueberries** (about 1¾ pounds), stemmed and rinsed

Unbleached all-purpose flour, for rolling

1 recipe (2 disks) **Classic Piecrust** (page 169), or 2 store-bought crusts

2 tablespoons chilled **unsalted butter**, cut into cubes

1 large **egg**

SOUR CHERRY PIE
with a Hint of Almond

I always slightly wince at the term "sour cherry." The cherries themselves are not really sour but rather are not overly sweet (which is fine by me), which makes them the best cherry for pies. The variety is properly called Montmorency cherries, and you'll find them for a fleeting week or two at the farmers' market under that name, or referred to as "sour cherries" or "tart cherries" or even "pie cherries." Just make sure they're not Bing cherries and that they have a nice bright red color. You know, like a cherry pie.

My farmhouse is home to four Montmorency cherry trees, given to us as a housewarming present by our pals Mark White and Linda Kosovych. When we have a good crop and can harvest before the critters get to the trees, their fruit makes its way into pies and cherry jam that I make at home and at the bakery. Don't underestimate the role the small amount of almond extract plays in this recipe: rather than really imparting an almond flavor, it boosts the intensity of the cherries immensely. The lattice top, an easy undertaking, makes this a beauty, as does some vanilla ice cream alongside.

MAKES ONE 10-INCH LATTICE-TOP PIE

---

5 cups (about 2 pounds) fresh or frozen **pitted sour cherries** (thawed and drained if frozen)

¾ cup **granulated sugar**

¼ cup plus 2 tablespoons **cornstarch**

¼ teaspoon **kosher salt**

½ teaspoon **pure almond extract**

Unbleached all-purpose flour, for dusting

1 recipe (2 disks) **Classic Piecrust** (page 169), or 2 store-bought crusts

2 tablespoons chilled **unsalted butter**, cut into cubes

1 large **egg**

Turbinado sugar, for sprinkling

Vanilla ice cream, for serving (optional)

1. Preheat the oven to 425°F. Set a wire rack inside a rimmed baking sheet.

2. Place the cherries in a large mixing bowl. In a small bowl, stir together the granulated sugar, cornstarch, salt, and almond extract. Pour the sugar mixture over the cherries and toss to coat evenly.

3. Dust a work surface and a rolling pin with flour and roll out one disk of pie dough into a 13-inch round, press it into a 10-inch pie pan or plate, and trim the edges about an inch wider than the pie pan. Roll out the second disk of dough into a 13 × 8-inch rectangle. Cut the dough from one of the shorter 8-inch sides into 6 wide, equal-size strips.

4. Use a flexible spatula to stir the cherries again and scrape down the sides of the bowl. Fill the pie shell with the cherry mixture, scraping any remaining liquid and filling into the pie. Scatter the cubed butter over the filling.

5. Create a lattice crust by laying 3 of the fat strips of dough across the pie horizontally, then laying the remaining 3 strips across them perpendicularly. Weave the top strips of dough over and under those on the bottom. Trim the ends of the latticed strips about 1 inch from the pie rim and roll and crimp the edges, blending the lattice with the bottom crust on the pie plate rim.

6. In a small bowl, use a fork to whisk together the egg and 1 tablespoon water. Brush the egg wash over the lattice top and on the edges of the pie. Sprinkle generously with turbinado sugar.

7. Carefully place the pie on the rack set in the baking sheet. Bake for 25 minutes, then reduce the oven temperature to 375°F. Rotate the baking sheet from front to back and continue to bake for 35 to 45 minutes more, until the pie filling is bubbling through the lattice (if the center isn't bubbling, the filling hasn't yet thickened and you'll have a liquid-y pie).

8. Let cool on a separate wire rack for 30 minutes. Serve with vanilla ice cream, if desired. The pie can be kept at room temperature for 2 days, then wrapped and refrigerated for up to 3 additional days.

LEMON CHESS TART

In the mid-1980s, I was invited to judge the design and photography of garden books in a competition sponsored by *Southern Living* magazine. Part of the event's attraction, for me, was spending a weekend in Birmingham, Alabama. I feel only a teensy bit sorry that I didn't join my hosts for dinner, as Dwight and I had our sights set on a reservation at the best restaurant in town: Frank Stitt's newish Highlands Bar & Grill. The lemon chess tart we had for dessert that night inspired the version we make at the bakery, and it was ten years later— after Frank and Pardis Stitt had become friends of ours—that I confessed I had lifted the recipe from his 2004 cookbook as a bakery offering, giving him full credit. They laughed and offered up any recipe I wanted, as long as they received our granola for life. Done.

A note about full-fat buttermilk: Our lemon chess tarts inexplicably failed us once when they didn't set up properly and were too liquid-y. We retraced our steps, knowing we had done everything correctly. We finally found that our dairy supplier had substituted nonfat buttermilk for our usual standing order of full-fat buttermilk, and it ruined the batch. This tart needs all that fat. And a note about Meyer lemons: We like to use Meyer lemons whenever possible. They have a more rounded flavor than regular lemons, with added nuances of orange and a sweeter, not-so-bitter taste.

MAKES ONE 9-INCH TART

---

1 **Pâte Sucrée Tart Shell** (page 169)

FOR THE FILLING:

2 tablespoons **freshly grated lemon zest** (from 2 lemons)

1 cup plus 2 tablespoons **sugar**

1½ teaspoons **cornstarch**

½ teaspoon **pure vanilla extract**

Pinch of **freshly grated or ground nutmeg**

Pinch of **kosher salt**

1½ cups **full-fat buttermilk** (do not use low-fat or nonfat)

3 large **eggs**

4 tablespoons (½ stick) **unsalted butter**, melted and cooled

2 tablespoons **fresh lemon juice** (from 1 lemon)

Whipped cream (see page 175), for serving (optional)

1. Prepare the tart shell and set it aside.

2. **Make the filling:** In a medium bowl, use a fork to stir the lemon zest into the sugar and let it infuse for a few minutes. Stir in the cornstarch, then mix in the vanilla, nutmeg, and salt until evenly distributed.

3. In the bowl of a stand mixer fitted with the whisk attachment, beat the buttermilk on medium-low speed until frothy. Replace the whisk with the paddle attachment. Beat in the eggs, butter, and lemon juice. Scrape down the sides of the bowl with a flexible spatula, then add the sugar-cornstarch mixture and beat on low speed just to combine. The mixture should look slightly thickened. Cover the bowl with plastic wrap and refrigerate for 2 hours.

4. Preheat the oven to 350°F. Place the tart shell (in its pan) on a baking sheet.

5. Remove the bowl with the lemon filling from the fridge. Whisk the filling just until smooth (in case it separated a bit while chilling) and pour it into the tart shell. Gently pop any big air bubbles. Bake for 40 to 50 minutes (start checking after 40 minutes), carefully rotating the baking sheet from front to back halfway through, until the filling looks just set but still a bit jiggly in the center. Cool the tart on a wire rack.

6. Carefully run a knife around the rim to loosen the crust. Set the tart pan on a small bowl or glass, reach under, and evenly push up the removable bottom, along with the tart, through the pan. Leave the tart on its bottom plate, or carefully transfer the tart to a flat serving platter. Refrigerate until well chilled, at least 2 hours and up to 3 days. Serve with whipped cream, if desired.

SALTED CARAMEL APPLE PIE

My bakery is on the edge of the Shenandoah Valley—at the core (ha ha) of apple country—so I'm always playing with apple recipes. Just over the Blue Ridge Mountains are our friends at J.Q. Dickinson Salt-Works, and their salt is the perfect finish to the combination of apple and caramel. I like using Honeycrisp and Granny Smith apples (the sweet and slightly tart varieties pair nicely with the sweet caramel). And when it comes to savoring a slice, I recall my dad's line: "Apple pie without some cheese is like a kiss without a squeeze." He always had a good-size hunk of cheddar waiting on his plate.

MAKES ONE 10-INCH PIE

NOTE: The process for making the caramel calls for close attention, so don't wander off!

FOR THE CARAMEL SAUCE:

1 cup **sugar**

½ cup **heavy cream**, at room temperature

8 tablespoons (1 stick) **unsalted butter**, at room temperature

1 teaspoon **pure vanilla extract**

1½ teaspoons **fine sea salt**

FOR THE PIE:

6 to 8 **Honeycrisp and Granny Smith apples**, peeled, cored, and sliced medium thick (8 cups)

1¼ cups **sugar**

½ cup **cornstarch**

¼ teaspoon **ground cinnamon**

¼ teaspoon **freshly grated or ground nutmeg**

1 recipe (2 disks) **Classic Piecrust** (recipe follows), or 2 store-bought crusts

2 tablespoons chilled **unsalted butter**, cut into small cubes

1 large **egg**

Flaky sea salt, for sprinkling

Cheddar cheese, for serving (optional)

1. **Make the caramel:** In a deep saucepan, stir together the sugar and ¼ cup water. Bring to a boil over high heat, brushing down the sides with a wet pastry brush to prevent sugar crystals from forming. Continue cooking on medium-high to high heat for 10 to 15 minutes without stirring (but keep an eye on it consistently to prevent it from scorching), until the mixture has thickened and turned a deep golden brown but is not too dark. Remove from the heat.

2. Use a wooden spoon to gradually and carefully stir the cream into the caramel, then add the butter, vanilla, and fine sea salt, stirring until thoroughly combined and smooth. Partially cover the saucepan to keep the caramel warm to easily spoon over the apples later.

3. **Make the pie:** Preheat the oven to 375°F. Place a wire rack inside a rimmed baking sheet.

4. Place the apples in a large bowl. In a medium bowl, use a fork to stir together the sugar, cornstarch, cinnamon, and nutmeg. Pour the sugar mixture over the apples and toss to coat evenly.

5. Roll out one disk of pie dough into a 13-inch round, press it into a 10-inch pie pan, and trim the edges. Fill the pie shell with the apple mixture, packing the slices so there are no large gaps. Pour or spoon the warm caramel sauce over the apples, letting it run between the slices. Scatter the cubes of butter over the apples.

6. Roll out the second disk of dough into an 11-inch round and set it over the filling. Trim and crimp the edges to seal all the way around. Cut a few slits in the center of the top crust.

7. In a small bowl, use a fork to whisk together the egg and 1 tablespoon water. Brush the egg wash over the top of the pie and along the edges. Generously sprinkle the flaky sea salt on top.

8. Place the pie on the rack set in the baking sheet and bake for 60 to 75 minutes, rotating the baking sheet from front to back halfway through, until the pie filling is bubbling through the center slits (if the center isn't bubbling, the filling hasn't yet thickened and you'll have a liquid-y pie). Cover the pie loosely with foil if the edges are browning too quickly.

9. Transfer the pie to a separate wire rack to cool for 30 minutes. Serve each portion with a slice of cheddar cheese, if desired. The pie can be kept at room temperature for 2 days, then wrapped and refrigerated for up to 4 days.

CLASSIC PIECRUST

This buttery crust is infused with citrus zest and remains a customer favorite at the bakery. It's also featured in our first cookbook, but as the base for plenty more recipes in this collection, it deserves its own place here as well. You can make the crusts in advance, too—with frozen disks of dough on hand, you'll be a step ahead in making not only the Salted Caramel Apple Pie (previous page) but also Sour Cherry Pie with a Hint of Almond (page 165), Virginia Peanut Pie (page 170), Blue Ribbon Blueberry Pie with Ginger (page 162), and Peach Hand Pies (page 49). And if you're making a pie that only needs one crust, freeze the other one for later.

MAKES 2 DISKS, ENOUGH FOR TWO 10-INCH CRUSTS

3½ cups **unbleached all-purpose flour**, sifted

1 teaspoon **kosher salt**

2 tablespoons plus 1 teaspoon **sugar**

12 tablespoons (1½ sticks) chilled **unsalted butter**, cut into cubes

¼ cup chilled **vegetable shortening**

1 large **egg yolk**

1½ teaspoons **freshly grated orange zest**

1½ teaspoons **freshly grated lemon zest**

½ cup **cold water**, plus more as needed

1. In a large bowl, whisk together the flour, salt, and sugar. Using your fingers, two knives, or a pastry blender, cut in the chilled butter and shortening until they are reduced to pea-size pieces. (Alternatively, combine the flour, salt, and sugar in a food processor, add the butter and shortening, and pulse until reduced to pea-size pieces, then transfer to a large bowl.)

2. Add the egg yolk and citrus zests, stirring with a spatula until well blended. Gradually add the cold water, stirring just until the dough comes together. If it's crumbly, add more water, 1 teaspoon at a time.

3. Divide the dough in half, forming each one into a disk. Wrap the disks individually in plastic wrap and refrigerate for at least 30 minutes and up to 1 day before using. The dough can also be sealed in freezer storage bags and frozen for up to 1 month; thaw for 2 hours in the refrigerator before using.

PÂTE SUCRÉE TART SHELL

8 tablespoons (1 stick) **unsalted butter**, at room temperature

¼ cup **granulated sugar**

½ teaspoon **freshly grated lemon zest**

1 large **egg yolk**

½ teaspoon **pure vanilla extract**

1¼ cups **unbleached all-purpose flour**, plus more for dusting

½ teaspoon **kosher salt**

1. In the bowl of a stand mixer fitted with the paddle attachment, cream the butter, sugar, and lemon zest on medium speed until fluffy and pale yellow, 5 to 7 minutes. Scrape down the sides of the bowl with a flexible spatula. Add the egg yolk and vanilla, beating on medium speed until combined. Turn off the mixer and add the flour and salt all at once. Beat on the lowest speed, just until clumps of dough begin to gather and the sides of the bowl are mostly clean.

2. Turn out the contents of the mixer bowl onto a lightly floured work surface. Use your hands to smudge the dough mixture repeatedly on the counter until well incorporated and holds together. Shape the dough into a brick shape and wrap it in plastic wrap. Refrigerate for at least 1 hour and up to a day before using.

3. Lightly flour a rolling pin. Unwrap the chilled dough and place it on a floured work surface. Roll from the center of the dough out toward the edges, rotating to form a round of dough about 11 inches in diameter. Roll the circle onto a rolling pin, for ease of transferring, and drape the dough into a shallow 9-inch tart pan with a removable bottom. (Do not stretch the dough; if it tears, carefully smudge it back into one piece in the pan.) Push and pinch the dough into the sides of the pan, allowing it to hang over the rim just slightly. Use the rolling pin to trim the dough edge by rolling it across the rim of the pan. Set aside until ready to use.

VIRGINIA PEANUT PIE

Food & Wine released its list of "The Best Pie in Every State" just before Thanksgiving 2021, and when I saw our new pie representing the Commonwealth of Virginia, I knew better than to quickly post the accolades on social media. My exhausted team would have walked out as they anticipated a new crush of pie orders. I'll let *Food & Wine* describe the pie I had introduced just a few months earlier:

"Dating back to colonial times and still a staple in the small towns throughout the Old Dominion, the peanut pie is about as uniquely local as you can get around here, dessert-wise. Too bad, then, that many people find the classic recipe to be a stodgy affair—one possible reason you don't see it on every dessert menu in the region, something that for a long time bugged baker Brian Noyes, whose cult favorite Red Truck Bakery is widely regarded as one of the best in the state. Starting out with the best Virginia peanuts, the Red Truck version gives the old girl a beautiful upgrade, incorporating crumbles of chocolate cake, coconut, and a bit of hot honey, which balances nicely with locally produced hickory syrup. You've never had a pie quite like this."

We use big fat Virginia peanuts from the Marks family of Southampton County, the heart of Virginia peanut country. The hot honey adds a bit of zing to the filling, and I like how the hickory syrup plays with the peanuts. Top with whipped cream (or the Chantilly cream on page 181) or vanilla ice cream.

MAKES ONE 10-INCH PIE

Unbleached all-purpose **flour**, for dusting

½ recipe (1 disk) **Classic Piecrust** (page 169), or 1 store-bought crust

¾ cup (packed) **crumbled chocolate cake**, homemade (such as leftover Triple-Chocolate Cake on page 189) or store-bought

3 large **eggs**

4 tablespoons (½ stick) **unsalted butter**, melted and cooled

¾ cup (packed) **light brown sugar**

1 teaspoon **freshly grated orange zest**

¼ teaspoon **kosher salt**

¼ cup **sorghum syrup** or **dark corn syrup**

¼ cup **light corn syrup**

¼ cup **hickory syrup**, preferably Falling Bark Farm Hickory Syrup, or **maple syrup**

2 tablespoons **hot honey**

2 tablespoons **apple cider** or **apple juice**

½ teaspoon **pure vanilla extract**

¼ cup **sweetened shredded coconut**

1 cup **roasted unsalted peanuts**, chopped, plus ½ cup whole peanuts

Vanilla ice cream, whipped cream (see page 175), or Chantilly cream (page 181), for serving (optional)

1. Dust a work surface and a rolling pin with flour and roll out the piecrust dough into a 13-inch round. Fold the dough over your rolling pin and gently transfer it to a 10-inch pie plate; don't stretch the dough when fitting it in. Trim and crimp the edges.

2. Preheat the oven to 375°F.

3. Spread the cake crumbs evenly over the bottom of the pie dough.

4. In a large bowl, whisk the eggs. Add the melted butter, brown sugar, orange zest, salt, sorghum syrup, light corn syrup, hickory syrup, hot honey, cider, and vanilla, whisking until smooth and thickened. Stir in the coconut and the chopped peanuts, then pour the mixture evenly over the cake crumbs. (A few crumbs may float up; that's okay.) Scatter the whole peanuts evenly across the top of the pie.

5. Place the pie on a baking sheet and bake for 40 to 50 minutes, rotating the baking sheet from front to back halfway through, until the crust is golden brown and the filling has puffed and set.

6. Let cool completely on a wire rack before serving or storing. If desired, serve with vanilla ice cream or whipped cream. The pie can be kept at room temperature for 5 days or wrapped and frozen for up to 2 months.

**OUR
COMMUNITY
OF ARTISANS**

Belmont Peanuts,
page 212

Bill Smith's
ATLANTIC BEACH PIE

Bill Smith, former chef of the legendary and dearly missed Crook's Corner in Chapel Hill, grew up in New Bern, North Carolina, in the '50s, enjoying various interpretations of this chilled summer treat on nearby Atlantic Beach.

Relying on the boardwalk memories of his youth, Bill concocted a version of what he called Atlantic Beach Pie for a Carolina-themed meal at a Southern Foodways Alliance conference, and after a couple hundred guests enjoyed it there, he added it to his restaurant's lineup. It quickly became a favorite on the dessert menu, and the supply was exhausted every night, as were Bill and his staff. Soon NPR was broadcasting a story about the pie, and Bill was asked to make several hundred servings for the Atlanta Food & Wine Festival. He now sees the life of this dessert as never-ending but his own existence jeopardized by the pie's notoriety ("This pie," he says, "will be the death of me"), which might shed some light on why he retired after thirty years in the kitchen. The lack of that pie at his farewell dinner at UNC did not go unnoticed by me, and I queried him about whether he's done with it. "I still make the pie occasionally. Since I've retired, I'm rarely asked to make it by the truckload anymore, thank heavens."

With Bill's approval and guidance, we've been baking Atlantic Beach Pie at the bakery on summer weekends, and it creates a fear of missing out (yes, that was a group of customers waiting outside our doors for that pie 30 minutes before we opened). The allure here is not just the juice and zest of lemon and lime, but the unusual and very mandatory saltine cracker crust, calling to mind the salt air and water of its roots—so no substitutions in the recipe are allowed.

MAKES ONE 9-INCH PIE

FOR THE CRUST:

60 **saltine crackers** (not reduced-sodium; about 1⅔ sleeves)

3 tablespoons **sugar**

9 tablespoons (1 stick plus 1 tablespoon) **unsalted butter**, at room temperature

FOR THE FILLING:

1 (14-ounce) can **sweetened condensed milk**

4 large **egg yolks**

¼ cup **fresh lemon juice** (from 2 lemons)

¼ cup **fresh lime juice** (from 2 to 3 limes)

Whipped cream (see page 175), for topping

Freshly grated zest of ½ lemon

Freshly grated zest of ½ lime

Flaky sea salt, for sprinkling

1. Preheat the oven to 350°F.

2. **Make the crust:** In a medium bowl, crumble the crackers finely with your hands; don't crush until they're dust but just very small pieces (a few larger pieces are okay). Sprinkle in the sugar, then knead in the butter with your hands until the crumbs hold together like dough. Press the mixture into a 9-inch pie plate. Chill for at least 15 minutes, then bake for 18 minutes, or until the crust is a light golden color. Transfer to a wire rack to cool completely.

3. **Make the filling:** While the crust is cooling, pour the condensed milk into a medium bowl. Use a whisk (or an electric mixer, if desired) to beat in the egg yolks, then whisk in the lemon and lime juice until thoroughly combined. At that point, stop whisking and let the mixture thicken for a couple of minutes. With a rubber spatula, spread the filling into the cooled piecrust, smooth the top, and bake for 16 minutes, until the filling has set. Let cool for 5 minutes.

4. Refrigerate the pie uncovered for at least 1 hour or overnight (like a Key lime pie, it must be cold and firm to be sliced). Just before serving, cover the top of the chilled pie with a good amount of whipped cream and top with the lemon and lime zests. Sprinkle with flaky salt, slice the pie, and serve. Cover and refrigerate any leftovers for up to 3 days.

CHOCOLATE CHESS PIE
with Graham Cracker Crust

While seasonal fruit is the basis of my favorite pies, the winter proves a little problematic in that regard, so chocolate chess pie fits right into the season. At the bakery, we originally baked chocolate chess pie in a regular piecrust, but when we had a supply of graham cracker crumbs left over after we finished the summer's Key lime pies, I thought about s'mores and knew this was a winning combination.

MAKES ONE 9-INCH PIE

FOR THE CRUST:

1¾ cups finely ground **graham cracker crumbs**, homemade (page 121) or store-bought (about 9 full-size crackers)

¾ cup **sugar**

7 tablespoons **unsalted butter**, melted

¼ teaspoon **ground cinnamon**

FOR THE FILLING:

2 large **eggs**

1 (5-ounce) can **evaporated milk**

4 tablespoons (½ stick) **unsalted butter**, melted and cooled

1 teaspoon **pure vanilla extract**

5 tablespoons **unsweetened cocoa powder**

1¾ cups **sugar**

¼ cup **cornstarch**

1 teaspoon **freshly grated orange zest**

Whipped cream (see page 175) or Chantilly Cream (page 181), for serving (optional)

1. Preheat the oven to 375°F.

2. **Make the crust:** In a medium bowl, stir together the graham cracker crumbs, sugar, melted butter, and cinnamon until well blended. Press the mixture into a 9- or 9.5-inch pie plate. Bake for 8 minutes, until fragrant and lightly browned; let cool.

3. Reduce the oven temperature to 325°F. Place the pie plate and baked crust on a baking sheet. Set aside.

4. **Make the filling:** In a large bowl, whisk together the eggs, evaporated milk, melted butter, and vanilla until well blended. Add the cocoa and whisk thoroughly, scraping down the sides of the bowl with a flexible spatula. Add the sugar and cornstarch, whisking until smooth. Stir in the orange zest and scrape down the sides once more.

5. Pour the filling into the prebaked piecrust; do not overfill. Gently pop any big air bubbles on the surface. Bake for 50 to 55 minutes, carefully rotating the baking sheet from front to back halfway through, until a thin crust has formed on the surface (the center of the pie will still have a little wiggle). Transfer the pie to a wire rack to cool completely.

6. Serve with whipped cream or Chantilly cream, if desired. The pie can be kept at room temperature for 2 days or wrapped and refrigerated for up to an additional 3 days.

BANANA PUDDING
with Homemade Vanilla Wafers

I'm a North Carolina barbecue fan, and I can't walk away from that meal without ending it with a big scoop or two of banana pudding with plenty of vanilla wafers. It took ten years to get this favorite dessert into our lineup at Red Truck, and because we're a bakery, I insisted from Day One that we make the cookies ourselves. They're not difficult to undertake, and the taste is worth the effort. Use the full yield of the vanilla wafers.

SERVES 8 TO 10

FOR THE VANILLA WAFERS:

1¾ cups **unbleached all-purpose flour**, sifted

½ teaspoon **kosher salt**

1 teaspoon **baking powder**

8 tablespoons (1 stick) **unsalted butter**, at room temperature

½ cup **sugar**

1 large **egg**

1 tablespoon plus 2 teaspoons **pure vanilla extract**

1 tablespoon **whole milk**

FOR THE PUDDING:

¾ cup **sugar**

3 tablespoons **cornstarch**

¼ teaspoon **kosher salt**

2 large **eggs** plus 1 large **egg yolk**, lightly beaten

2 cups **whole milk**

3 tablespoons chilled **unsalted butter**, cut into 6 equal pieces

1 teaspoon **pure vanilla extract**

3 firm **bananas**, sliced into rounds ¼ inch thick

FOR THE WHIPPED CREAM:

1 cup chilled **heavy cream**

2 tablespoons **sugar**

1. **Make the vanilla wafers:** In a medium bowl, sift together the flour, salt, and baking powder. In the bowl of a stand mixer fitted with the paddle attachment, beat the butter and sugar on medium speed for 2 minutes, just until fluffy, scraping down the sides of the bowl with a spatula after 1 minute. Add the egg, beat for 30 seconds more, and scrape down the sides again. Add the vanilla and milk and mix on low speed for 15 seconds. Add the flour mixture and beat on low speed until just combined. Cover the bowl with plastic wrap and refrigerate for at least 20 minutes and up to 2 hours.

2. Preheat the oven to 350°F. Line two baking sheets with parchment paper. Scoop the batter into teaspoon-size balls and arrange them 1 inch apart on the prepared baking sheets. Press each ball with the heel of your hand to flatten it slightly. Bake one sheet at a time, rotating it from front to back halfway through, for 12 to 15 minutes, until the wafers are golden brown. Transfer to a wire rack to cool completely.

3. **Make the pudding:** Combine the sugar, cornstarch, and salt in a large saucepan. Over low heat, add the eggs and yolk and whisk to combine. Add the milk, whisking for 1 minute, until blended. Raise the heat to medium-low and continue to cook, stirring constantly, until the mixture reaches 175°F to 180°F, 6 to 10 minutes, or until the mixture thickens and bubbles around the edges and looks smooth. Remove the saucepan from the heat and whisk in the butter, one piece at a time, making sure each one is fully incorporated before adding the next. Whisk in the vanilla. Transfer the mixture to a bowl and press a round of parchment paper directly on the surface of the pudding. Refrigerate for 2 hours or until set.

4. Spread a small amount of the pudding into a large glass bowl or an 8 × 8-inch baking dish (aim for a 1- to 2-inch layer of pudding). Cover the pudding with a layer of vanilla wafers, followed by a layer of banana slices. Spoon a third of the remaining pudding on top of the bananas. Repeat the layering process, using all the bananas and most of the wafers (save enough to top the pudding later), and ending with a layer of the remaining pudding.

5. **Make the whipped cream:** In the bowl of a stand mixer fitted with the whisk attachment, beat the cream and sugar on medium speed until stiff peaks form. Spoon the whipped cream over the top layer of the pudding, spreading it to cover the pudding completely. Top with the remaining vanilla wafers. Refrigerate the pudding for at least 30 minutes before serving. Cover and refrigerate any leftovers for up to 3 days.

Apple Crisp.

4 c. peeled + sliced apples
1 T lemon juice
1/3 c. sifted Flour.
1 c. oats - uncooked
1/2 c. firmly packed Br. sugar
1/2 t salt
1 t cinnamon
1/2 c. butter - melted.

Place apples in Bak. dish. Sprinkle wit lemon juice. Combine dry ingred. + melted butter, Mix till crumbly.

(over

APPLE CRISP

My grandparents settled in western North Carolina, home to the state's apple country nestled among the Blue Ridge Mountains, where some 150 orchards are located. It was an amusing sight, I'm sure, as the locals watched my grandmother maneuver her large black Cadillac through the groves to a parking area, where I would jump out and grab a wooden basket for picking. She clued me in about mixing apple varieties to improve the taste and texture of baked goods, and we picked Granny Smiths, Romes, Fujis, Mutsus, and Crispins to use in pies and cobblers. My favorite project at her house was the simplest: an oat-based crumble atop a baking dish of apple slices. When softened vanilla ice cream was scooped alongside, our smiles were even wider.

SERVES 4

1. Preheat the oven to 375°F. Lightly grease a 9 × 9-inch baking dish with vegetable oil spray.

2. Add the apple slices to the baking dish, making sure they completely cover the bottom of the dish. Sprinkle the apples with the lemon juice. In a small bowl, mix together the granulated sugar and ½ teaspoon of the cinnamon, then sprinkle this evenly over the fruit.

3. In a medium bowl, stir together the flour, oats, brown sugar, salt, and the remaining 1 teaspoon cinnamon. Pour in the melted butter and mix just until the ingredients are crumbly. Spoon the oat mixture evenly over the apples.

4. Bake for 30 minutes, or until the apples are tender and the topping is golden brown. Serve warm, with whipped cream or ice cream, if desired.

4 cups peeled, cored, and medium-sliced **apples**, such as Granny Smith or Honeycrisp (about 3 large apples)

1 tablespoon **fresh lemon juice**

1 tablespoon **granulated sugar**

½ teaspoon plus 1 teaspoon **ground cinnamon**

½ cup **unbleached all-purpose flour**

1 cup **old-fashioned rolled oats**

¾ cup (packed) **light brown sugar**

½ teaspoon **kosher salt**

12 tablespoons (1½ sticks) **unsalted butter**, melted

Whipped cream (see page 175) or vanilla ice cream, for serving (optional)

STRAWBERRY SHORTCAKES
Old-Fashioned

We were always excited about strawberry season in California, which meant picking our own berries for my mom's homemade strawberry shortcake that we enjoyed nearly every Saturday from April through July. She would make a heavy biscuit dough, with extra sugar and cream, as the base to soak up the juice of the berries. Inspired to make that dessert at the farmhouse, I played with my biscuit recipe, sweetening it up and replacing some of the buttermilk with cream just like my mom did. It stayed a little lighter than hers, but the juices soaking into the shortcake took me right back to her kitchen.

SERVES 8

FOR THE SHORTCAKES:

2¾ cups **unbleached all-purpose flour**, sifted, plus more as needed

2¼ teaspoons **baking powder**

¾ teaspoon **baking soda**

2 teaspoons **kosher salt**

2 tablespoons **granulated sugar**

8 tablespoons (1 stick) chilled **unsalted butter**, cut into cubes, plus 4 tablespoons (½ stick), melted

¾ cup **heavy cream**

1 cup **full-fat buttermilk**

Turbinado sugar, for sprinkling

FOR THE FRUIT:

2 quarts hulled **strawberries**

¾ cup **granulated sugar**

2 cups **whipped cream** (see page 175), for serving

1. **Make the shortcakes:** In a large bowl, use a fork to whisk together the flour, baking powder, baking soda, salt, and granulated sugar. Add the butter to the flour mixture and use your fingers or a pastry cutter (do not use a mixer) to incorporate it, until the butter is broken down into pea-size pieces.

2. Whisk together the heavy cream and the buttermilk in a liquid measuring cup. Add the mixture to the dry ingredients all at once, and use a spatula or a plastic scraper to fold in the liquid mixture as quickly and as gently as possible. Flour your hands and reach into the bowl and under the dough, flipping it around to combine. The dough will be wet but manageable.

3. Turn out the dough onto a lightly floured surface, and, working lightly, use your hands to pat it into a rectangle about 1 inch tall. Lightly sprinkle flour across the top of the dough and pat it with your hands until the flour has been absorbed.

4. Flour the bottom of the dough and your work surface. With the scraper, fold the dough in half lengthwise and repeat flouring it and patting it out with your hands. Repeat the process a total of four times. Pat the dough into a rectangle about 1 inch tall.

5. Preheat the oven to 400°F. Line a baking sheet with parchment paper.

6. Dip a 3-inch biscuit cutter into flour and cut as many shortcakes as you can from the dough, pressing straight down with the cutter without twisting. Place the shortcakes on the baking sheet so they are nearly touching one another. Reshape the scraps as needed to form a total of 8 shortcakes. Bake for 14 to 16 minutes, rotating the baking sheet from front to back halfway through, until the tops are golden brown. Transfer the finished shortcakes to a wire rack, brush the tops with the melted butter, and sprinkle with turbinado sugar. Let cool.

7. **Meanwhile, prepare the fruit:** Place 1 cup of the strawberries in a medium bowl and mash them with a fork or the back of a spoon. Cut the remaining berries in half (or quarters if they're large) and add them to the bowl along with the granulated sugar, mixing to coat them evenly. Let sit for 30 minutes to macerate and allow the syrupy juices to develop.

8. To assemble the shortcakes, use a fork to deeply poke around the equator of each shortcake, creating a top-and-bottom line of separation, and carefully pull them apart. Set one or two bottoms on each serving plate. Spoon the macerated strawberries and their juices evenly over all of the bottoms and replace the tops. Add a dollop of whipped cream to each plate and serve.

DOT'S PEACH COBBLER
with Crystallized Ginger

I recently found a handwritten note from Dwight's mom, Dorothy McNeill, thanking me for getting her peach cobbler recipe into *The Washington Post* when I worked there years ago. Dot, as her friends knew her, made this dessert in a funny little style, with a thin butter-based cobbler batter rising up through the fruit while baking. I thought it worthy enough to include in a *Post* Food section roundup of the best dishes of summer. Dot had a way around the kitchen that left me mesmerized: her thin cornbread was poured, like a mini pancake, into a layer of hot oil shimmering in a skillet. She cooked up a mean fried okra that I still hanker after, and we make her unique Icebox Fruitcake (page 123)—very 1950s—at the bakery each December. Long before I opened a bakery, I daydreamed about having a little coffee and dessert joint somewhere, and even considered naming it after her: Dot's Cup & Saucer. Longtime friends still remind me of that, and that often leads me to ponder a new venture.

SERVES 8

8 tablespoons (1 stick) **unsalted butter**

4 large ripe **peaches**, peeled, pitted, and cut into medium slices (about 3 cups)

1¼ cups **sugar**

1 tablespoon plus 1½ teaspoons finely chopped **crystallized ginger**

1 cup **unbleached all-purpose flour**

2 teaspoons **baking powder**

½ teaspoon **kosher salt**

1 cup **whole milk**

1 teaspoon **pure vanilla extract**

Vanilla ice cream, for serving (optional)

1. Preheat the oven to 350°F. Place the butter in a 13 × 9-inch baking dish.

2. In a large bowl, combine the peaches, ¾ cup of the sugar, and the crystallized ginger, tossing to distribute everything evenly.

3. In a separate large bowl, whisk together the flour, the remaining ½ cup sugar, the baking powder, and salt.

4. Place the baking dish in the oven for 3 to 5 minutes, just until the butter has melted. (Don't let it burn.) Meanwhile, whisk the milk and vanilla into the flour mixture until well blended. The batter will be thin.

5. Transfer the hot baking dish to the stovetop and tilt it just enough so the melted butter coats the entire bottom. Pour the batter evenly over the melted butter, without stirring. Spoon the peach mixture over the batter, again without stirring. Pour any fruit juices from the bowl evenly across the fruit.

6. Return the baking dish to the oven. Bake for 40 to 50 minutes, rotating the baking dish from front to back halfway through, until the batter has risen to the top around the peaches and is crisp and browned. The puffed-up batter will sink a bit after baking. Serve warm with ice cream, if desired.

CARROT CAKE
with Chantilly Cream

This cake was always waiting for me when I visited my grandmother in Hendersonville, North Carolina. It's rich and chunky with walnuts and pineapple, and she liked to tell me it was healthy because of the carrots. She topped the cake with cream cheese frosting, which I wasn't (and still am not) a fan of, so I tried to talk her into using dollops of whipped cream instead. I got one of "those looks" from her, and we compromised on Chantilly cream, a dressed-up version of whipped cream flavored with orange. She admitted later that I might be onto something.

MAKES ONE 13 × 9-INCH CAKE

FOR THE CAKE:

2 cups **unbleached all-purpose flour**

1½ cups **sugar**

2 teaspoons **baking soda**

1 teaspoon **kosher salt**

1 teaspoon **ground cinnamon**

¾ teaspoon **freshly grated or ground nutmeg**

½ teaspoon **ground cloves**

1 (14- to 16-ounce) can **crushed pineapple in juice**, drained, with ½ cup juice reserved (see Note)

½ cup **canola oil**

3 large **eggs**

1 teaspoon **pure vanilla extract**

2 cups shredded **carrots** (from 3 trimmed and well-scrubbed large carrots)

1 cup chopped **walnuts**

FOR THE CHANTILLY CREAM:

1 teaspoon **freshly grated orange zest**

¼ cup **sugar**

⅔ cup chilled **heavy cream**

1 teaspoon **pure vanilla extract**

2 teaspoons chilled **fresh orange juice**

2 tablespoons chilled **sour cream**

NOTE: If the amount of pineapple juice you get from the can does not total ½ cup, just add enough water to the juice to yield ½ cup total.

1. **Make the cake:** Preheat the oven to 350°F. Generously grease a 13 × 9-inch baking pan with vegetable oil spray. Line the bottom with parchment paper.

2. Sift together the flour, sugar, baking soda, salt, cinnamon, nutmeg, and cloves onto a sheet of parchment paper.

3. In the bowl of a stand mixer fitted with the paddle attachment, combine the flour mixture, reserved pineapple juice, and oil, beating on low speed until combined. Add the eggs one at a time, incorporating each one before adding the next, and add the vanilla. Beat on medium speed for 2 minutes, scraping down the sides of the bowl with a flexible spatula as needed. Remove the bowl from the mixer. Use the spatula to fold in the drained pineapple, carrots, and walnuts until evenly distributed.

4. Scrape the batter into the prepared pan. Bang the pan on the counter a few times to get rid of any air bubbles. Bake for 30 to 40 minutes, rotating the pan from front to back halfway through, until the cake starts to pull away from the sides of the pan and a toothpick inserted into the center comes out clean. Transfer the pan to a wire rack to cool the cake completely (keep the cake in the pan).

5. **Make the Chantilly cream:** In a small bowl, use a fork to stir the orange zest into the sugar, letting the mixture sit for a couple of minutes to infuse.

6. In the clean bowl of a stand mixer fitted with the whisk attachment, combine the heavy cream, vanilla, and orange juice and beat on medium speed for 1 minute, or until well combined. Add the sugar-zest mixture and the sour cream, beating on medium speed just until soft peaks form, about 3 minutes. (Do not overbeat.) You should have about 2 cups.

7. Serve each portion of carrot cake with a dollop of the Chantilly cream on top. Cover and refrigerate any leftover Chantilly cream for up to 2 days.

OUR COMMUNITY OF ARTISANS

Meg Nottingham Walsh, artist, *page 212*

LEXINGTON BOURBON CAKE

A trip to Lexington, Kentucky, for a Southern Foodways Alliance–VisitLex cocktail event inspired this bourbon-fueled cake. The featured cocktail included a robust ginger ale, fresh ginger, and a generous pour of good bourbon. This cake packs in a quadruple threat of ginger—fresh, crystallized, ground, and even ale. Echoing the bite of the ginger, the glaze gets its kick from ghost peppers thanks to a bourbon-honey liqueur made by Wild Turkey Distillery. Our friend Benny Hurwitz, Wild Turkey Distillery's brand ambassador, turned us onto the stuff; it's available in most areas and is what we use in the glaze. You want a hearty ginger ale with a bite, so try to find a craft brand such as Maine Root rather than the usual convenience store offering.

MAKES ONE 10-INCH BUNDT CAKE

FOR THE CAKE:

2 teaspoons **freshly grated lemon zest**

2 teaspoons **freshly grated orange zest**

2½ cups **sugar**

3 cups **unbleached all-purpose flour**

1 teaspoon **baking soda**

½ teaspoon **baking powder**

1 teaspoon **kosher salt**

½ cup **canola oil**

8 tablespoons (1 stick) **unsalted butter**, at room temperature

6 large **eggs**

½ teaspoon **pure vanilla extract**

1 cup **good-quality bourbon**, such as Maker's Mark or Wild Turkey

½ cup **ginger ale**, such as Maine Root Ginger Brew

1 cup **sour cream**

1 tablespoon plus 1½ teaspoons chopped **crystallized ginger**

1 teaspoon **ground ginger**

1 tablespoon plus 1 teaspoon grated **fresh ginger**

FOR THE GLAZE:

2 tablespoons **unsalted butter**

¼ cup **sugar**

¼ cup **good-quality bourbon**

¼ cup **Wild Turkey American Honey Sting** (bourbon honey liqueur) (or increase the bourbon to ½ cup)

¼ cup **honey**, preferably hot honey (see page 212)

½ teaspoon **ground ginger**

1. **Make the cake:** Preheat the oven to 350°F. Lightly grease the inside of a 10-inch Bundt-style pan with vegetable oil spray, then coat it again.

2. In a medium bowl, use your fingers to work the lemon and orange zests into the sugar until well combined. Let the mixture sit for a few minutes.

3. In a separate bowl or on a sheet of parchment paper, sift together the flour, baking soda, baking powder, and salt.

4. In the bowl of a stand mixer fitted with the paddle attachment, beat the oil, butter, and the citrus zest–sugar mixture on medium speed for 3 minutes, or until light and fluffy. Scrape down the sides of the bowl with a flexible spatula. Add the eggs one at a time, beating well on medium speed after each addition. With the mixer off, add the vanilla, bourbon, and ginger ale, then continue to beat until combined. The mixture will look curdled; that's okay.

5. Reduce the mixer speed to low and add the flour mixture in three additions, alternating with the sour cream and beginning and ending with the flour. Mix after each addition until just blended. Remove the bowl from the mixer and use a rubber spatula or wooden spoon to stir in the crystallized ginger, ground ginger, and fresh ginger until well combined.

6. Transfer the batter to the prepared pan, smoothing the surface. Bake for 50 to 65 minutes, rotating the pan from front to back after 25 minutes, or until a toothpick inserted into the thickest part of the cake comes out clean. Let cool in the pan for 15 minutes, then invert onto a wire rack set over a rimmed baking sheet. Trim the bottom of the cake so it's evenly flat, as needed, then turn it trimmed-side down on the rack.

7. **Meanwhile, make the glaze:** In a small saucepan over low heat, melt the butter. Whisk in the sugar, bourbon, Wild Turkey American Honey Sting, honey, and ground ginger, stirring until the sugar and honey have dissolved and the glaze is smooth, about 4 minutes. While the cake is still warm, brush the glaze all over the cake repeatedly, letting it soak in before brushing on more. Allow the cake to cool completely.

FLOURLESS CHOCOLATE TRUFFLE CAKE

I knew that my training at King Arthur Baking Company's campus in Norwich, Vermont, was worth the cost after I learned to make this cake there. It's deeply fudgy and rich, gluten-free, and just plain spectacular. I've tweaked the recipe over the years and played with the topping to come up with a feathery design that's easy to replicate at home. My team at the bakery ships these all over the country, and the only quibble we've received is that the top turns goopy if the UPS box is left outside on a hot summer's day. That complaint was quickly withdrawn in a second cheery email from the cake's recipient after he'd dragged his finger through the melted chocolate on the plastic wrap, eating it clean.

MAKES ONE 8-INCH CAKE

FOR THE CAKE:

8 tablespoons (1 stick) **unsalted butter**, plus more for the pan

1¼ cups **semisweet chocolate chips**

¾ cup **granulated sugar**

½ teaspoon **freshly grated orange zest**, or ¼ teaspoon pure orange extract

¼ teaspoon **kosher salt**

2 teaspoons **ground espresso**

1 teaspoon **pure vanilla extract**

½ cup **unsweetened cocoa powder**

3 large **eggs**

FOR THE GANACHE & GLAZE:

1 cup **semisweet chocolate chips**

½ cup **heavy cream**

½ cup **confectioners' sugar**, plus more as needed

1. **Make the cake:** Preheat the oven to 375°F. Grease a metal 8-inch round cake pan with butter (a cake or tart pan with a removable bottom works best here) and place an 8-inch parchment round in the bottom.

2. Melt the butter in a medium saucepan over medium-low heat. Add the chocolate chips, stirring until melted and well combined.

3. In the bowl of a stand mixer fitted with the paddle attachment, combine the sugar and the orange zest and beat on low speed until well blended, about 30 seconds. Keeping the speed on low throughout, add the salt, espresso, vanilla, and cocoa powder, beating for another 30 seconds. Add the eggs one at a time, beating just until smooth. Stop to scrape down the sides and bottom of the bowl with a rubber spatula and beat again for another 30 seconds. Add the melted chocolate-butter mixture, and beat just until combined. Continue to scrape the bowl and the paddle (where the zest may collect) with the spatula as needed.

4. Pour the batter into the prepared pan, smoothing the surface with a spatula and eliminating any air bubbles. Bake for 25 minutes, or until a skin has formed on the top and the center appears set and not shiny. Let it cool for 5 minutes, then run a paring knife around the edges of the cake (which may be crumbly) and invert it onto a serving plate. Let the cake cool completely.

5. **Meanwhile, make the ganache and glaze:** In a small saucepan, melt the chocolate chips over low heat and then whisk in the heavy cream. Remove from the heat to cool and thicken. In a small bowl, use a fork to whisk together the confectioners' sugar and 1 to 2 teaspoons water to make a glaze, adding more confectioners' sugar or water, as needed, so that it's opaque and thick enough to pipe through a small tip inserted into a pastry bag (or clip off a bottom corner of a freezer bag just enough to create a small hole).

6. Use an offset spatula to spread the chocolate ganache on top of the cake, right to the edge (if it drips down the sides a bit, that's okay). Let it set for 1 minute, then pipe parallel lines of the white glaze across the ganache. Quickly run the tip of a thin knife perpendicularly across the lines, alternating directions from one side of the cake to the other to create a zigzag feather pattern. Let set completely before serving. Keep the cake well wrapped at room temperature for up to 3 days or freeze for up to 3 weeks—just don't refrigerate, as that tends to dry out the cake.

OUR
COMMUNITY
OF ARTISANS

George Washington's
Mount Vernon,
page 213

Martha Washington's
GREAT CAKE

Swirls of lore surround this cake, one of the few culinary remnants of the Washington-Custis families surviving from the late 1700s. I first heard about this concoction from the staff at Mount Vernon, gracious hosts of two of my book-signing events at George Washington's historic estate just over the river from D.C., about an hour east of the bakery. Martha and George served this moist, hefty cake—sort of a cross between a panettone and a fruitcake—to their family and guests at Mount Vernon on special occasions, such as a Christmas dinner or an Epiphany party, that the estate's enslaved kitchen staff would have baked for them. My friend David Ferriero, Archivist of the United States, located the original recipe for me at Tudor Place in Georgetown, written in the hand of Martha Washington's second granddaughter, Martha Parke Custis Peter. It was a large cake, built for a real party—it yielded nearly one hundred servings and called for forty eggs and five pounds of fruit.

With assistance from Marian Burros of *The New York Times* (who put my bakery on the map a dozen years ago) and with guidance from the Mount Vernon staff and an adaptation they showed me created by culinary historian Nancy Carter Crump for the book *Dining with the Washingtons*, I've whittled the recipe down to a more-manageable tube pan cake that serves 8 to 12. Made with Madeira and brandy (I like to use Virginia-made apple brandy from our neighbors at Catoctin Creek Distilling Company), it benefits from aging a few days and up to a couple of months (like fruitcake) and pairs nicely with afternoon tea or coffee. What's better, we top it off with an orange buttercream frosting and bring it out on George's birthday each February 22.

MAKES ONE 9-INCH TUBE PAN CAKE

FOR THE CAKE:

1½ cups (packed) **golden raisins** (about 5¼ ounces)

1 cup (packed) **dried currants** (5 ounces)

1 cup **fresh orange juice**

¾ cup (packed) chopped **candied orange peel** (about 4½ ounces)

½ cup (packed) chopped **candied lemon peel** (3 ounces)

¼ cup **Madeira, dry port,** or **Marsala**

1¼ cups **brandy**, plus more as needed

12 tablespoons (1½ sticks) **unsalted butter**, at room temperature

1½ cups **granulated sugar**

3 large **eggs**, separated

1 teaspoon **fresh lemon juice**

3 cups **unbleached all-purpose flour**, sifted

½ teaspoon **freshly grated or ground nutmeg**

½ teaspoon **ground mace**

2 teaspoons **freshly grated orange zest** (from 1 large orange)

1 medium **tart apple**, such as Granny Smith, cored and coarsely chopped

½ cup slivered **almonds**

Boiling water, for the pan

FOR THE FROSTING:

3 cups **confectioners' sugar**, sifted, plus more as needed

2 tablespoons **freshly grated orange zest** (from 1 large orange)

12 tablespoons (1½ sticks) **unsalted butter**, at room temperature

1½ teaspoons **pure vanilla extract**

3 tablespoons plus 1 teaspoon **whole milk**

1. **Make the cake:** In a medium bowl, combine the raisins, currants, and orange juice, making sure the dried fruit is submerged (add water if needed to cover). In a separate medium bowl, combine both of the candied citrus peels and pour in the Madeira, tossing to coat. Cover each bowl with plastic wrap and let them sit at room temperature for at least 5 hours and up to overnight. Strain the contents of the two bowls over separate liquid measuring cups (or other containers), reserving the rehydrated fruit and peels separate from their liquids. Combine the reserved orange juice and Madeira with ¾ cup of the brandy in a large liquid measuring cup.

recipe continues

2. Place a rectangular baking pan on the lower oven rack fill it halfway with just-boiled water (this will create a moist heat in the oven that is necessary for this cake). Preheat the oven to 350°F. Lightly grease a tube pan or 9-inch Bundt pan with vegetable oil spray, then grease it again to thoroughly coat.

3. In the bowl of a stand mixer fitted with the paddle attachment, beat the butter on medium speed until light and fluffy, about 2 minutes. Scrape down the sides of the bowl. Add the granulated sugar, ½ cup at a time, beating well on medium speed after each addition. In a separate bowl, use a fork to whisk the egg yolks until smooth. Add the lemon juice to the egg yolks, then pour the mixture into the butter-sugar mixture, beating on medium speed until fluffy, about 2 minutes. Scrape down the bowl.

4. In another bowl or on a sheet of parchment paper, stir together the flour, nutmeg, mace, and orange zest. Add the flour mixture to the mixing bowl in three additions, beginning and ending with the flour mixture and alternating with the brandy mixture, beating after each addition on medium-low speed until smooth. Remove the bowl from the mixer. Use a sturdy spatula to stir in the reserved golden raisins and currants, citrus peels, chopped apple, and slivered almonds until evenly distributed. The batter will be creamy and thick.

5. In a separate bowl, beat the egg whites with a whisk until soft peaks form. Use the same sturdy spatula to gently fold half into the cake batter, then fold in the remaining beaten egg whites just until no trace of white remains. (Do not overmix.) The batter should be noticeably lightened.

6. Spoon the batter into the prepared cake pan, smoothing the top, and place on the middle oven rack, above the rectangular pan filled with water. Bake for 20 minutes, then, with the cake still in the oven, reduce the temperature to 325°F and bake for an additional 60 to 70 minutes, until a toothpick inserted all the way to the bottom of the cake comes out clean. The surface should be slightly cracked and spring back when gently pressed. When the water in the rectangular pan has cooled, remove the pan from the oven and discard the water.

7. Transfer the cake pan to a wire rack to cool for 30 minutes, then dislodge the cake from the pan (invert it if you're using a Bundt pan).

8. Wrap the cake in a few layers of cheesecloth, then brush with the remaining ½ cup brandy, or more as needed, so that the cheesecloth is damp. Once the wrapped cake has completely cooled, place it in an airtight container or wrap it tightly in aluminum foil. Let it sit at room temperature for at least 3 days and up to a few months, checking to make sure the cheesecloth is not dry. If it is, brush on more brandy.

9. On the day you'll be serving the cake, **make the frosting:** In the bowl of a stand mixer fitted with the paddle attachment, beat the confectioners' sugar, orange zest, butter, vanilla, and milk on medium speed until the frosting is fluffy and thick enough to swirl and spread, about 3 minutes. (If it seems thin, add a bit more confectioners' sugar to thicken it.)

10. Unwrap the cake and frost it all over, swiping the frosting into swirls with an offset spatula. Store at room temperature, covered, for up to 2 days. This cake can be sliced, individually wrapped in plastic, and frozen for up to 2 weeks.

TRIPLE-CHOCOLATE CAKE

The kid favorite. The parent favorite. This is a moist and rich fudgy cake, with chunks of chocolate chips adding good texture, and a third hit of chocolate that is spread across the top and drips down the sides. Please don't skip any of the ingredients—the taste of the brewed coffee is imperceptible (to kids and any adults who don't care for it), but it significantly punches up the flavor of the cocoa, as does the hint of orange zest. This cake goes so well with ice cream that a family-owned dairy, Moo Thru, just south of us in Remington, Virginia, now mixes chunks of the cake into their mint, peppermint, chocolate, and vanilla ice creams. We carry all those flavors at both bakery locations, and they're popular choices to order alongside this cake—double triple-chocolate cake is not a bad thing.

MAKES ONE 9-INCH BUNDT CAKE

FOR THE CAKE:

1 teaspoon **freshly grated orange zest**

2 cups **granulated sugar**

½ teaspoon **baking soda**

¾ teaspoon **baking powder**

¾ teaspoon **kosher salt**

2¼ cups **unbleached all-purpose flour**, sifted

1 cup **hot and strong brewed coffee**

1 cup **unsweetened cocoa powder**

1 cup **canola oil**

2 teaspoons **pure vanilla extract**

2 large **eggs**

¾ cup **sour cream**

1 cup **semisweet chocolate chips**

FOR THE GLAZE:

¾ cup **semisweet chocolate chips**

¾ cup **heavy cream**

3 tablespoons **unsalted butter**, at room temperature

1 cup **confectioners' sugar**, sifted

1. **Make the cake:** Preheat the oven to 350°F. Grease a 9-inch Bundt pan with vegetable oil spray.

2. In the bowl of a stand mixer fitted with the paddle attachment, add the orange zest to the granulated sugar and beat on low speed. Let it sit for a minute, then add the baking soda, baking powder, salt, and flour, beating on low speed to combine.

3. In a small bowl, use a fork to whisk together the hot coffee and the cocoa until well blended. Add the oil and whisk until the mixture is smooth. Let cool.

4. With a flexible spatula, scrape the cooled coffee mixture into the mixer bowl. Beat on low speed until well combined, about 2 minutes, scraping the bowl and paddle (where the zest may collect) as needed.

5. Rinse out the small bowl and use it to whisk together the vanilla, eggs, and sour cream. Using the spatula, scrape the mixture into the chocolate batter. Beat on medium speed for 2 minutes, or until well blended and shiny. Remove the bowl from the mixer and fold in the chocolate chips with the spatula until evenly distributed.

6. Pour the batter into the prepared pan, scraping the bowl clean. Bake for 45 to 60 minutes, until a toothpick or knife inserted into the thickest part of the cake comes out clean.

7. Let the cake cool in the pan for 10 minutes (this will build up a little condensation, which helps release the cake) and then carefully invert the Bundt pan onto a wire rack. After 5 more minutes, lift the pan off the cake and let it cool completely. Trim the bottom of the cake so it's evenly flat, then place it flat-side down on the rack.

8. **Make the glaze:** Place the chocolate chips in a heatproof bowl.

9. In a small saucepan over medium heat, bring the cream to a simmer (but do not boil). Pour the cream over the chocolate and let stand for 2 minutes. Add the butter and whisk until smooth. Add the confectioners' sugar, whisking until smooth, shiny, and thick. Let cool about 10 minutes. Stir and then spoon it over the top of the cake, letting it run down the sides.

CARAMEL CAKE
with Pecans

This is the cake that crashed our website. Fashion designer Billy Reid told me that he pined for a family cake that his grandmother made: "It was sort of a caramel cake mixed with a cream cheese–like pound cake. It had a slightly crusty top and a little creamy thing mixing in as well, and it dripped with a caramel coating. There may have been pecans. Is that something you might be able to mess with?" I rolled up my sleeves to tackle the challenge. In the bakery's kitchen, I dipped into a bubbling pot of caramel sauce, rich with cream and butter, that was destined for our Salted Caramel Apple Pie (page 168). I added the caramel to my cake batter, along with a fistful of pecans. Knowing how well caramel and apples play together, I poured in some apple juice to add another layer of flavor. I baked it in a Bundt pan and later brushed even more warm caramel onto the cake so that it soaked into the crumb.

I shipped the finished cake to Billy, and he told me that I had nailed it. I wrote about the experience for *Garden & Gun* magazine and provided the recipe for a two-layer cake version, and now everyone wanted that fragile cake shipped to them (but since layer cakes don't travel well, we instead put this Bundt version on our website). And a good cake can get even better: if you're up for taking this to the next level, do as the distillers of Maker's Mark Kentucky Straight Bourbon Whisky requested for their large corporate order—add a good pour of bourbon to the batter and as a brush-on. (I was happy to oblige.) And when *New York Times* food writer Julia Moskin asked me for a recipe using apple liqueur, I replaced the apple juice with apple brandy from Catoctin Creek Distilling Company up the road from us in Purcellville, Virginia, which elevated the cake even further—especially when you brush the sides of the cake with apple brandy before

adding more caramel. Julia says it's one of the best Bundt cakes the *Times* has ever featured.

MAKES ONE 9-INCH BUNDT CAKE

FOR THE CARAMEL SAUCE:

1½ cups **sugar**

1 cup **heavy cream**, at room temperature

1 cup (2 sticks) **unsalted butter**, in pieces, at room temperature

1 tablespoon **pure vanilla extract**

½ teaspoon **kosher salt**

FOR THE CAKE:

2 cups **sugar**

8 tablespoons (1 stick) **unsalted butter**, at room temperature

4 tablespoons **cream cheese**, at room temperature

4 large **eggs**, at room temperature

1 teaspoon **pure vanilla extract**

2½ cups **unbleached all-purpose flour**

2 teaspoons **baking powder**

¼ teaspoon **kosher salt**

¾ cup **whole milk**

¼ cup **unsweetened apple juice**, bourbon, or apple brandy, plus more for brushing

1 cup coarsely chopped **pecans**

1. **Make the caramel sauce:** In a deep saucepan, stir the sugar and ½ cup water until mixed. Bring to a boil over high heat, brushing down the sides with a wet pastry brush to prevent sugar crystals from forming on the sides of the pan. Without stirring, continue to cook on high heat for 15 to 20 minutes, until the mixture is bubbling at a slower pace and has turned a deep golden brown but not too dark. (This calls for close attention, so don't wander off!) Remove the saucepan from the heat.

2. Use a wooden spoon to gradually and carefully stir the cream into the caramel, then add the butter, vanilla, and salt, stirring until thoroughly combined and smooth. You should have about 2½ cups; you'll use some of the caramel sauce

recipe continues

in the cake batter, and the rest for brushing on the cake.

3. **Make the cake:** Preheat the oven to 350°F. Lightly grease the inside of a 9-inch Bundt-style pan with vegetable oil spray, then grease it again to thoroughly coat it.

4. In the bowl of a stand mixer fitted with the paddle attachment, beat the sugar, butter, and cream cheese on medium speed until light and fluffy, about 2 minutes. Scrape down the sides of the bowl. Reduce the speed to medium-low, add ½ cup of the caramel sauce, and beat until combined. Add the eggs one at a time, beating well after each addition. Add the vanilla and beat until just combined.

5. In a medium bowl, sift together the flour, baking powder, and salt. In another bowl, combine the milk and the apple juice. Add the flour mixture to the mixer bowl in three additions on medium-low speed, beginning and ending with the flour and alternating with the milk and apple juice, beating after each addition until well combined. Remove the bowl from the mixer and fold in the pecans just until evenly distributed.

6. Pour the batter into the prepared pan. Bang the filled pan on the counter a couple of times to release any air bubbles. Bake for 45 to 60 minutes, until the cake starts to pull away from the sides of the pan and a toothpick inserted into the thickest part of the cake comes out clean.

7. Let the cake sit in the pan for 15 minutes; the condensation will help the cake eventually release. Set a wire rack on a rimmed baking sheet. Carefully turn the cake out onto the rack, nudging it with a knife if necessary. Trim the bottom of the cake so it's evenly flat, then place it trimmed-side down on the rack.

8. Brush the cake all over with apple juice, as desired. Slightly warm the remaining caramel sauce and brush a light coat over the cake. Let the first coat soak in, then repeat with additional coats of the caramel sauce until you've used it all. Cool the cake for 1 hour before serving; the caramel will become somewhat set and much less sticky.

OUR COMMUNITY OF ARTISANS

Catoctin Creek Distilling Company, *page 212*

ORANGE CAKE

I grew up in California back when the citrus groves outnumbered the cul-de-sacs, and orange trees were everywhere. On the banana seat of my Sting-Ray bike, I raced my brothers, sisters, and friends through the orchards, and we'd usually finish by throwing rotten fruit at one another until we were chased off by the farmhands. Our neighborhood really did have an intense aroma of oranges and lemons, and that memory led to the bakery's seasonal Meyer lemon cake. Customers missed the citrus cake in the fall and winter, so I worked on a year-round orange cake—which is delightful at Christmas and very close to the one that my mom brought out at her Tupperware home parties back in the '60s. To me, it's all about the orange zest in the frosting.

MAKES ONE 9-INCH BUNDT CAKE

FOR THE CAKE:

3 cups **unbleached all-purpose flour**, sifted, plus more for dusting

3 tablespoons **freshly grated orange zest** (from 2 large oranges)

2½ cups **granulated sugar**

1 teaspoon **baking soda**

½ teaspoon **baking powder**

1 teaspoon **kosher salt**

½ cup **canola oil**

8 tablespoons (1 stick) **unsalted butter**, at room temperature

6 large **eggs**

1 teaspoon **pure vanilla extract**

½ cup **fresh orange juice** (from 3 small oranges)

1 cup **sour cream**

FOR THE SYRUP:

¼ cup **fresh orange juice** (see Tip)

½ cup **granulated sugar**

FOR THE GLAZE:

2 cups **confectioners' sugar**, sifted, plus more as needed

2 tablespoons **freshly grated orange zest** (from 1 large orange)

2 tablespoons **fresh orange juice**

TIP: The orange juice for the syrup can be squeezed from the 2 large oranges you have zested for the cake.

1. **Make the cake:** Preheat the oven to 350°F. Lightly grease a 9-inch Bundt pan with vegetable oil spray and dust it evenly with flour, tapping out any excess.

2. In a medium bowl, use your clean fingers to work the orange zest into the granulated sugar so it's evenly distributed. Let sit for a few minutes to allow the orange to infuse the sugar. In a separate bowl, whisk together the flour, baking soda, baking powder, and salt.

3. In the bowl of a stand mixer fitted with the paddle attachment, beat the oil, butter, and the sugar-zest mixture on medium speed until light and fluffy, about 3 minutes. Scrape down the sides of the bowl and the paddle. Add the eggs one at a time, beating well after each addition. Beat in the vanilla and the orange juice.

4. With the mixer on low speed, add the flour mixture in three additions, beginning and ending with the flour mixture and alternating with the sour cream, beating after each addition until just blended. The batter should be creamy and smooth.

5. Scrape the batter into the prepared pan, smoothing the surface with a spatula. Bake for 50 to 60 minutes, rotating the pan from front to back after 25 minutes, until a toothpick inserted into the thickest part of the cake comes out clean and the cake has pulled away slightly from the sides of the pan. Let cool in the pan for 10 minutes, then carefully invert the cake onto a wire rack set over a baking sheet to cool further. Trim the bottom of the cake, as needed, so it's evenly flat.

6. **Meanwhile, make the syrup:** In a small saucepan, combine the orange juice, granulated sugar, and ¼ cup water over low heat, stirring until the sugar has dissolved. Brush the syrup all over the cake, waiting a few minutes between applications to let it soak in.

7. **Make the glaze:** In a medium bowl, whisk the confectioners' sugar, orange zest, orange juice, and 1 tablespoon water until smooth, opaque, and quite thick; add either more confectioners' sugar or another tablespoon of water if needed. Spoon the glaze over the top of the cake, letting it run down the sides. Let it set before serving.

NOYES BIRTHDAY CAKE

For generations, this white cake—with a Swiss meringue–type white frosting that has melted chocolate poured over the top—was trotted out for birthdays in the Noyes family. My dad introduced it to our immediate family, as did his father to his, and it goes back at least to my great-grandfather at the Noyes ancestral home, Edgewater Farm, near Waterloo, Nebraska (now owned by my cousins Mac and Laura Burford). This dessert is the jewel in our family's food legacy, and, no, it's not a vanity project—this has been the name of the cake through the ages. I was heartsick when I couldn't locate a copy of the long-surviving recipe for this cookbook, and at the last minute—after I finished writing it, and as I was moving cookbooks from my house to the farmhouse—my grandmother's small spiral-bound book entitled "Kitchen Secrets" fell out of the pile. In a bit of happenstance (this seems to occur frequently to me, and my recipe tester Bonnie Benwick refers to it in Yiddish as *beshert* or destiny), the cover slid off and the first loose page inside was the recipe for this cake, written in my grandmother's hand. It took some tweaking to bring it into the current day (with original instructions like "add butter the size of a walnut"), and my very understanding editor let me sneak it into the desserts lineup.

My cousin Carol Clark has since sent me her own copy of the same recipe, written by my great-grandmother, whose notes attest to the magic of the frosting: "This is really a plain cake, but it takes practice to get the frosting just right. The cake is better when it is several days old. It is very good, almost like candy." Herewith, the cherished single-layer version true to the historic family recipe, although I sometimes double the recipe to make a two-layer cake for larger events.

MAKES ONE 8-INCH SINGLE-LAYER CAKE (CAN BE DOUBLED FOR FAMILY GATHERINGS)

FOR THE CAKE:

1½ cups **unbleached all-purpose flour**, plus more for dusting

1 cup **sugar**

8 tablespoons (1 stick) **unsalted butter**, at room temperature

2 large **egg whites** (see Tip)

2 teaspoons **pure vanilla extract**

1¾ teaspoons **baking powder**

½ cup **whole milk**

FOR THE FROSTING:

4 large **egg whites** (see Tip)

1 cup **sugar**

Pinch of **kosher salt**

2 teaspoons **pure vanilla extract**

5 ounces **unsweetened chocolate**, chopped

TIP: You'll have 6 egg yolks left over—which is just the right amount for making our Corn Ice Cream (page 198).

1. **Make the cake:** Preheat the oven to 350°F. Lightly grease an 8-inch round pan (with 2-inch sides) with vegetable oil spray and dust the inside evenly with flour, tapping out any excess.

2. In the bowl of a stand mixer fitted with the paddle attachment, beat the sugar and the butter on medium speed until light and fluffy, about 3 minutes. Stop to scrape down the sides of the bowl and the paddle. Add half of the egg whites, beating well to incorporate, then the remaining half. Add the vanilla and beat to combine.

3. In a large bowl or on a sheet of parchment paper, sift together the flour and baking powder. Reduce the mixer speed to low and add the flour mixture in three additions, beginning and ending with the flour and alternating with the milk, beating after each addition until just blended (do not overmix). The batter should be creamy and smooth.

4. Scrape the batter evenly into the prepared pan, smoothing the surface with a spatula. Rap the pan on the counter a few times to release any air bubbles. Bake for 30 to 40 minutes, until a toothpick inserted into the thickest part of the cake comes out clean and the cake has pulled away slightly from the sides of the pan. Let cool in the pan for 10 minutes, then carefully invert

recipe continues

the cake onto a wire rack set over a baking sheet to cool completely. Trim the cake, as needed, so that it sits flat.

5. **Meanwhile, make the frosting:** In the clean bowl of a stand mixer fitted with the whisk attachment, combine the egg whites, sugar, and salt. Fill a medium saucepan with a few inches of water and bring it to a simmer. Place the mixing bowl over the simmering water, making sure the water doesn't touch the bottom of the bowl. Gently whisk the mixture until the egg whites are very warm to the touch and the sugar has dissolved, about 5 minutes. Be patient and continue to whisk until the mixture no longer feels grainy (rub the mixture between your fingers to test it). Keep the pan of simmering water on the stove; you'll be using it again. Add a little more water to it, if needed.

6. Rinse and dry the mixer's whisk attachment and return it to the mixer, along with the bowl of the warm egg white mixture. Beat on medium-low speed until foamy, about 3 minutes. Gradually increase the speed to medium-high and beat until shiny, stiff peaks form, about 4 minutes. Add the vanilla and beat just until combined. Frost the cake as soon as possible (for best consistency), smoothing the top with an offset spatula, while keeping the sides fluffy and wavy with swirls and peaks.

7. Place the chocolate in a separate bowl and set it over the pan of simmering water, again making sure the water does not touch the bowl. Stir the chocolate just until it's fully melted and smooth, then remove the bowl from the pan. Let cool for 1 minute, then stir once to mix. You'll want to pour the chocolate quickly before it thickens.

8. Use an offset spatula to spread the melted chocolate in a large circle evenly over the smooth top of the frosted cake just up to the edge of the cake. You can gently nudge some of the chocolate to start spilling over the side, if desired.

PEACH POUND CAKE

I love this simple, summery pound cake—a treat to embrace the peak of peach season that is best made with ripe, juicy peaches rather than frozen fruit. Even more peaches find their way into the glaze. For a peaches-and-cream-like finish (and your own happiness), add a dollop of whipped cream to each plated slice.

MAKES ONE 10-INCH TUBE PAN CAKE

FOR THE CAKE:

1 cup (2 sticks) **unsalted butter**, at room temperature

2½ cups **granulated sugar**

5 large **eggs** plus 1 large **egg yolk**, at room temperature

3 cups **unbleached all-purpose flour**, sifted

½ teaspoon **baking powder**

¼ teaspoon **ground ginger**

¼ teaspoon **kosher salt**

1 teaspoon **pure vanilla extract**

½ teaspoon **pure almond extract**

½ cup **sour cream**

1 to 2 large ripe **peaches**, peeled, pitted, and chopped (1½ cups)

FOR THE GLAZE:

1 medium ripe **peach**, peeled, pitted, and chopped (½ cup)

1½ cups **confectioners' sugar**, sifted, plus more as needed

1. **Make the cake:** Preheat the oven to 350°F. Lightly grease a 10-inch tube pan with vegetable oil spray. Place the pan on a baking sheet.

2. In the bowl of a stand mixer fitted with the paddle attachment, beat the butter and granulated sugar on low speed for 2 minutes, or until light and fluffy. Scrape down the sides of the bowl with a flexible spatula. Add the eggs and extra yolk one at a time, mixing well after each addition. Scrape the bowl again.

3. In a large bowl or on a sheet of parchment paper, whisk or stir together the sifted flour, baking powder, ginger, and salt. Stir the vanilla and almond extracts into the sour cream. On low speed, add the flour mixture to the mixer bowl in three additions, beginning and ending with the flour and alternating with the sour cream mixture,

beating after each addition until well combined. The batter will be thick.

4. Remove the bowl from the stand mixer and use a rubber spatula to fold in the chopped peaches until evenly distributed.

5. Transfer the batter to the prepared pan, smoothing the surface with a spoon. Bake for 60 to 70 minutes, rotating the baking sheet from front to back halfway through, until the cake is nicely browned and cracked on top, and a tester inserted into the thickest part of the cake comes out clean. Let cool in the pan on a rack for 20 minutes.

6. Run a knife around the edges of the pan to carefully loosen it, then dislodge the cake from the pan. Place the cake on a wire rack set over a rimmed baking sheet.

7. **Make the glaze:** In a food processor or blender, combine the peaches and the confectioners' sugar. Purée until the mixture is smooth, opaque, and fairly thick, adding either more confectioners' sugar or a teaspoon of water at a time, as needed, to keep the glaze thick and pourable.

8. Pour the glaze over the cake while it is still slightly warm, letting it drip down the sides. Allow the glaze to set completely before serving.

CORN ICE CREAM

Not long after we bought the farm, so to speak, we ventured over the nearby Blue Ridge Mountains into the Shenandoah Valley and the town of Staunton, Virginia. Enjoying its heyday right about then was the Staunton Grocery restaurant, led by chef Ian Boden, and we parked ourselves at a counter looking into the kitchen as Ian chatted and toiled. That gorgeous meal ended with the perfect dessert: his corn ice cream, with the fresh taste of summer. Ian's now a good pal of ours, and we try to visit his newer restaurant, The Shack, every few months (*Esquire* referred to it as "the incredible restaurant in the middle of nowhere that nobody knows about").

Dwight and I make this dessert—and a corn-themed dinner—nearly every summer when fresh local corn is sweet and plentiful. Picture a sultry Saturday evening outside at the farm, with guests seated around a table surrounded by overflowing hydrangea bushes, while fireflies flit over toward the chicken coop. We start with cocktails using Virginia corn moonshine and move on to corn chowder (page 101), cornbread (page 67), and shrimp and corn stew (page 102), and finish with this ice cream. Get a head start, though: this ice cream's custard base needs to be refrigerated for at least 4 hours or made the day before and chilled overnight.

MAKES ABOUT 1 QUART

---

4 ears of **corn**, shucked

2 cups **heavy cream**

1 cup **whole milk**

1 cup **sugar**

1 **vanilla bean**, cut in half lengthwise

6 large **egg yolks**

1 tablespoon **sorghum syrup** or **honey**

¼ teaspoon **fine sea salt**

1. Slice the kernels from the cobs into a mixing bowl. With the back of a knife, scrape the remaining corn and any "milk" off the cob into the bowl. Halve the cobs crosswise and reserve them.

Transfer the corn (and its milk) to a blender or food processor and purée until smooth.

2. In a large saucepan, combine the cream, milk, and the puréed corn mixture. Add the corncobs, ½ cup of the sugar, and the split vanilla bean. Simmer over medium heat just until the dairy starts to scald, about 7 minutes. Do not let it boil over.

3. Remove from the heat, cover, and let steep for 30 minutes. Transfer the cobs and the vanilla bean to a plate and return the saucepan to the stovetop over medium heat. Simmer the mixture to allow the dairy to scald once more, about 6 minutes. Do not let it boil over.

4. Meanwhile, in a separate bowl, whisk together the egg yolks, the remaining ½ cup sugar, the sorghum syrup, and salt. Whisk 1 cup of the scalded dairy mixture into the yolk mixture to temper it. Whisk all of the yolk mixture back into the scalded mixture, then return the saucepan to the stovetop over medium-low heat. Whisk constantly for 6 to 8 minutes, until the custard is fragrant and thick enough to coat the back of a wooden spoon or spatula.

5. Set a fine-mesh strainer over a large bowl. Press the corn custard through with a spatula or wooden spoon to remove and capture all the liquid. Let the solids sit in the strainer for a minute, then press them once more to ensure all the liquid is extracted. Discard the remaining solids.

6. Place the reserved cobs and the vanilla bean in a nut-milk bag or wrap in cheesecloth (to keep the custard smooth) and return it to the corn custard to further infuse. Cover and refrigerate for at least 4 hours and up to overnight.

7. Discard the cobs and vanilla bean, scraping any clinging custard back into the bowl. Transfer the custard to an ice cream machine and process according to the manufacturer's directions.

8. Scoop the corn ice cream into a container and cover the surface directly with plastic wrap. Seal and freeze until firm, at least 4 hours and up to overnight.

CONDIMENTS

203
BLUEBERRY JAM
with Ginger & Lime

204
**FOGGY RIDGE APPLE
BUTTER & WINTER
SQUASH BUTTER**

206
**GRAND CHAMPION
PEACH JAM**

208
TOMATO JELLY

209
BLACK PEPPER RICOTTA

209
PICKLED RED ONIONS

210
PICKLED RAMPS

211
MUSHROOM STOCK

BLUEBERRY JAM

with Ginger & Lime

I long ago dedicated this recipe to my pal Ann Clark, who drove each August from Virginia to Maine, where she cared for her parents. I had a fantasy that I'd ride up with her one summer, spend some time in Old Orchard Beach, and return home with a backseat full of wild Maine blueberries. Sadly, that never happened, but Ann did bring home some wild blueberries for me on a few of her trips, and I made this jam. If you can find small wild blueberries, so much the better for this recipe, because they pack a concentrated flavor punch. Fresh, plump blueberries are an easy substitution (and I've used frozen wild blueberries in place of a cup or two of the larger fresh berries).

MAKES 3 TO 4 PINTS

NOTE: Powdered fruit pectin and canning jars can be found at hardware stores and seasonally at grocery stores.

4½ cups (28 ounces) **fresh blueberries**, stemmed and rinsed

3 tablespoons **bottled lime juice**

5 cups **sugar**

2 teaspoons finely chopped **crystallized ginger**

¼ teaspoon **pure vanilla extract**

6 tablespoons **powdered fruit pectin**

Freshly grated zest of 1 lime (1 to 2 teaspoons)

1. Sterilize the jars, rings, and lids according to the manufacturer's directions. Set a raised wire rack on a dish towel or layer of newspaper.

2. In a large bowl, crush all but 1 cup of the blueberries with a potato masher or pastry cutter (or even the rounded bottom of a coffee cup, as I do). Transfer the berries and their juices to a large saucepan and add the lime juice. Bring to a boil over medium-high heat, reduce the heat to medium-low and cook for 15 to 25 minutes, depending on how chunky or smooth you like your blueberry jam to be. (The longer it cooks, the more the blueberries will break down and the smoother the jam will eventually become.)

3. Meanwhile, in the same bowl that you used to crush the blueberries, stir together the sugar, crystallized ginger, and vanilla.

4. Add the pectin to the berries in the saucepan, stirring just until incorporated. Once the mixture is bubbling again, cook for a few minutes more until slightly thickened.

5. Add the sugar mixture to the berries, scraping the bowl with a flexible spatula and stirring until the sugar has dissolved. The mixture should be glossy. Once the mixture has returned to a vigorous boil, cook for 1 to 3 minutes more (again depending on your preferred consistency). Remove from the heat and stir in the lime zest. Skim off any foam.

6. Carefully pour the jam into the sterilized jars, leaving ½ inch of headspace at the top of the jars. Wipe the rims of the jars clean and seal them tightly. Transfer the jars to a canning pot and add water to cover by 1 to 2 inches. Boil the jars for 10 minutes. Carefully remove the jars from the water and place them on the wire rack. Let stand for several hours until cooled.

7. Unopened jars of processed jam can be stored at room temperature for up to 1 year; opened jars will stay fresh in the fridge, tightly covered, for up to 1 month.

FOGGY RIDGE APPLE BUTTER
and
WINTER SQUASH BUTTER

I first met Diane Flynt at a James Beard House Virginia-themed dinner years ago when Dwight and I were seated at a table with her in New York City. She and her husband, Chuck, are founders of Foggy Ridge Cider in the Blue Ridge Mountains of Virginia and now are two of our best pals and confidants. Diane continues to be my go-to source on the best apple varieties for whatever I'm cooking up in the kitchen. I'm an apple butter guy, and Diane set me straight on what apples to use (see Notes) and how to cook and flavor it (and to sweeten and spice it up only if necessary). She sent me to Ronni Lundy's award-winning 2016 book, *Victuals*, for the slow-cooker method she uses. It's the way fire halls throughout Appalachia now cook their apple butter for fundraisers; if you'd prefer to do it on a stovetop or in the oven, you'll need to send the cooked fruit through a food mill.

I spent several months playing with the right apple combination until Diane distracted me with her new passion: winter squash butter. She says it's so amazing that she has not made apple butter in years. I offer my takes on both of her butters here: Diane prefers to keep the flavors pure, with little or no spice, but I include some for those needing an extra something. Diane serves the squash butter on steel-cut oatmeal for breakfast and on vanilla ice cream for dessert. It also works well in savory dishes, such as atop pork roast and black-eyed peas, especially if you add a little salt and fresh thyme like Diane does.

APPLE BUTTER

MAKES 4 PINTS

6½ pounds unpeeled **apples** (15 to 18), cored and cut into 1-inch chunks (see Note)

½ cup **granulated sugar**, or to taste

¼ cup (packed) **light brown sugar**, or to taste

½ teaspoon **ground cinnamon**, or to taste

¼ teaspoon **ground mace**, or to taste

¼ teaspoon **ground cardamom**, or to taste

Pinch of **kosher salt**

1. Place the apples in a slow cooker, set it on high, and cook, uncovered, for 1 hour. Stir, reduce the temperature setting to low, cover with the lid, and let the apples cook for 9 to 11 hours, until very mushy and broken down.

2. Stir the apple mixture with a wooden spoon or fork to further break up the pieces. Increase the temperature setting to high, cover, and cook for 1 hour more. Taste and stir in just enough of both sugars, a minimal amount of the spices (start with ½ teaspoon of cinnamon and ¼ teaspoon of mace and cardamom), and the salt. Use an immersion blender to purée the apple mixture directly in the slow cooker, or transfer the mixture to a food processor and purée until smooth (you may need to do this in batches). Cool to room temperature if you do not plan to process the apple butter by water-bath canning.

3. Sterilize the jars (and rings and lids, for water-bath canning) according to the manufacturer's directions. Set a raised wire rack on a dish towel or layer of newspaper.

4. Fill the cooled sterilized canning jars, leaving ½ inch of headspace. Gently rap them on the counter to release any air pockets. Wipe the rims clean. Seal the jars with lids and rings finger-tight and refrigerate for up to 2 months, or process with the water-bath canning method according to manufacturer's directions and store, unopened, for up to 1 year.

WINTER SQUASH BUTTER

MAKES 3 PINTS

6½ to 7½ pounds **winter squash**, cut into halves or quarters and seeded (see Note)

1 **tart apple**, such as Granny Smith, peeled, cored, and cut into small chunks

1 tablespoon **apple cider vinegar**

1 tablespoon **apple brandy**

Pinch of **kosher salt**

¼ cup **sugar**, or to taste

1. Preheat the oven to 375°F. Grease a large rimmed baking sheet with vegetable oil spray.

2. Remove any remaining fibrous bits from the squash. Arrange the chunks flesh-sides up on the baking sheet in a single layer. Roast for about 45 minutes, or until lightly browned and softened.

3. Scoop out 5 to 6 cups of the roasted squash flesh and transfer it to a large Dutch oven or other heavy pot (reserve the remainder for another use). Stir in the apple and vinegar, cover, and cook over medium to medium-low heat for about 20 minutes, stirring occasionally, adding a little water to avoid scorching if necessary, until the mixture is mushy and steamy. Remove from the heat.

4. Use an immersion blender to purée the mixture directly in the pot, or transfer the mixture to a food processor and purée until smooth (you may need to do this in batches). Stir in the apple brandy and salt, puréeing again until well blended. Taste and add the sugar a little bit at a time, only as needed (the natural sweetness of the still-warm squash will sweeten the mixture a decent amount).

5. Transfer the squash mixture to clean canning jars, leaving ½ inch of headspace. (Winter squash butter should not be processed by pressure or water-bath canning.) Gently rap them on the counter to release any air pockets, or use a knife or small spoon to stir through each jar. Wipe the rims clean. Cool slightly, seal the jars with clean lids and rings, and refrigerate for up to 2 weeks. The squash butter can also be frozen for up to 6 months.

NOTES: For the apple butter, Diane suggests using a somewhat dry apple that falls apart when cooked and has a good balance of sweet and tart. Most summer varieties turn mushy when cooked, which is why many people make apple butter with summer apples. Diane uses more than one variety for her apple butter—a good plan that helps when using grocery store apples with little flavor. She also reminds me that cooking intensifies both good and bad flavors, so don't use an apple with bitter or off-flavors. She suggests searching farmers' markets for varieties of Wolf River, Yellow Transparent, Lodi, Summer Rambo, Red Detroit, Buncombe, Golden Delicious, Fuji, and Granny Smith apples.

For the winter squash butter, look for Robin's Koginut (preferred), Red Kuri, and/or Waltham butternut squash rather than acorn squash or anything stringy like spaghetti squash.

GRAND CHAMPION PEACH JAM

This little batch of sunshine started it all, and since several recipes in this book can't live without my peach jam, I'm including the recipe again here, as in our first book.

The first time I made this, peaches were coming into season just as my friend Mary Jones had given me a tub of crystallized ginger, so I combined the two with some spices and cooked up a batch of jam. I submitted the results in the Arlington County Fair (my first entry ever) and won four awards, including first prize, best of show, theme award, and the title of Grand Champion. It led to my story on the front page of *The Washington Post* Food section, and, in a convoluted way, to launching a bakery by following my culinary passion. We use later-season freestone peaches at the bakery, due to our volume and the ease of releasing the pit from each peach. The rich sweetness of the peaches finds a comforting complement in ginger, nutmeg, cinnamon, cloves, and allspice. Nothing tastes better on our Rise & Shine Biscuits (page 55) or our Heavenly Waffles (page 37), and we also use the jam in our Peach Hand Pies (page 49). Sometimes I'll add chopped fresh rosemary and minced shallots to the jam to create a more savory glaze for chicken and fish.

MAKES SIX 1-PINT JARS

1. Sterilize the jars, rings, and lids according to the manufacturer's directions. Set a raised wire rack on a dish towel or layer of newspaper.

2. In a large saucepan, bring the peaches and lemon juice to a boil over medium heat. Add the pectin and return the mixture to a boil. Gradually add the sugar, stirring continuously until it has completely dissolved. While the jam is cooking, use a pastry brush dipped in water to wash down any sugar crystals that may form on the inside of the pot. Stir in the crystallized ginger, fresh ginger, nutmeg, cinnamon, cloves, allspice, and lemon zest and cook at a vigorous boil for about 1 minute, stirring continuously, until well combined. Remove the saucepan from the heat and skim off and discard any foam.

3. Carefully pour the jam into the sterilized jars, leaving ½ inch of headspace at the top of the jars. Wipe the rims of the jars clean and seal them tightly. Transfer the jars to a canning pot and add water to cover by 1 to 2 inches. Boil the jars for 10 minutes. Carefully remove the jars from the water and place them on the wire rack. Let stand for several hours until cooled.

4. Unopened jars of processed jam will keep at room temperature for about 1 year; opened jars will stay fresh in the fridge, tightly covered, for up to 1 month.

About 11 large ripe **peaches**, peeled, pitted, chopped, and slightly mashed (8 cups)

¼ cup **bottled lemon juice**

7 tablespoons **powdered fruit pectin**

7 cups **sugar**

1 tablespoon finely chopped **crystallized ginger**

½ teaspoon **freshly grated ginger**

½ teaspoon **freshly grated or ground nutmeg**

½ teaspoon **ground cinnamon**

Pinch of **ground cloves**

Pinch of **ground allspice**

Freshly grated zest of ½ lemon

TOMATO JELLY

Irene Kerns introduced herself to me when she showed up at the bakery with a jar of her prized tomato jelly. She is the sister of Marion Maggiolo, a fellow business owner in Warrenton who buys our rum cakes each weekend to serve to customers at her Horse Country equestrian store just down the hill. I thanked Irene for the jelly and set it aside for a special occasion. I pulled it out a couple weeks later when I needed a little something to brighten up small ham biscuits for a tailgating event at Great Meadow, home of the Virginia Gold Cup steeplechase races. I saw Irene that afternoon, and I couldn't shut up about how good that jelly was. She handed over her last jar, so I knew I had to track down her recipe if I wanted to have more and not make a pest of myself. Irene makes this year-round—she uses dried basil in the winter—but I've also included the option of fresh basil to go with those summer tomatoes.

MAKES SIX 8-OUNCE JARS

2½ cups **tomato juice** (from 1½ to 2 pounds fresh tomatoes, mashed and well-strained) or canned tomato juice

¾ cup **bottled lemon juice**

5 cups **sugar**

5 to 7 drops **hot pepper sauce**, such as Tabasco to taste

½ teaspoon **dried basil**, or 1 generous teaspoon minced fresh

1 (3-ounce) pouch **liquid pectin**

1. Sterilize the jars, rings, and lids according to the manufacturer's directions. Set a raised wire rack on a dish towel or layer of newspaper.

2. Combine the tomato juice, lemon juice, sugar, hot pepper sauce, and basil in a large nonreactive pot. Over medium heat, bring the mixture to a rolling boil, stirring to dissolve the sugar; the temperature should be 220°F and the mixture should be foaming. Add the pectin and boil at 220°F, without stirring, for no more than 10 minutes, or until thickened enough to coat the back of a spoon and drop off in a thickened "sheet." Skim off any foam.

3. Carefully pour the jelly into the sterilized jars, leaving ¼ inch of headspace at the top of the jars, and skim off any bubbles on the surface of the jelly. Wipe the rims of the jars clean and seal them tightly. Transfer the jars to a canning pot and add water to cover by 1 to 2 inches. Boil the jars for 10 minutes. Carefully remove the jars from the water and place them on the wire rack. Let stand for at least 12 hours.

4. Unopened jars of processed jelly will keep at room temperature for about 1 year; opened jars will stay fresh in the fridge, tightly covered, for up to 1 month.

BLACK PEPPER RICOTTA

My friend William Dissen, chef and owner of Haymaker restaurant in Charlotte, North Carolina, shared this simplified ricotta recipe as part of the Wild Mushroom Tartines with Black Pepper Ricotta (page 89). Making ricotta at home couldn't be easier, and it's so delightfully fluffy that you'll find it hard to go back to using store-bought. Just remember to use full-fat buttermilk here, because it won't work with low-fat or nonfat. This ricotta also works beautifully in our Mushroom-Ricotta Lasagne with Port Sauce (page 140). The cheese is pretty tasty served as a dessert, too, topped with honey and cinnamon.

MAKES ABOUT 3 CUPS

8 cups **full-fat buttermilk**

2 tablespoons **kosher salt**

2 teaspoons **coarsely ground black pepper**

1. Line a large chinois strainer or fine-mesh sieve with a few layers of cheesecloth and place it over a deep bowl.

2. In a medium or large Dutch oven or other heavy-bottomed pot set over medium heat, slowly bring the buttermilk and salt almost to a boil (180°F), stirring just once or twice early on to dissolve the salt. Remove from the heat and let the mixture sit for about 20 minutes, during which curds should form.

3. Pour the contents of the pot into the lined strainer or sieve and let the curds drain for 30 minutes to 1 hour. Sprinkle them with the pepper and fold it in gently.

4. Discard the liquid (whey) in the bowl or reserve for another use. Transfer the ricotta to an airtight container without packing it too tightly. Refrigerate for at least 2 hours and up to 2 days.

PICKLED RED ONIONS

These pickled rings give added zing to so many meals—the Wild Mushroom Tartines with Black Pepper Ricotta (page 89), Sweet Potato & Poblano Enchiladas with Oaxacan Mole Sauce (page 145), Beetloaf Sandwiches (page 79), and even Chunky Meatloaf with Plenty of Bacon (page 143). But that list is by no means exhaustive—try pickled onions atop scrambled eggs, in a burrito, and on a burger. If you don't have access to a ready-made pickling spice blend, you can make one with 1½ teaspoons each of mustard seeds, coriander seeds, whole allspice, whole black peppercorns, and caraway seeds, and a crumbled dried bay leaf.

MAKES 6 CUPS

4½ cups **apple cider vinegar**

¾ cup **sugar**

3 tablespoons **kosher salt**

3 tablespoons **pickling spice**

6 cups thinly sliced **red onions** (about 3 large)

1. In a small saucepan, combine the vinegar, sugar, salt, and pickling spice and bring to a low boil over medium heat, stirring until the sugar and salt have dissolved. Cook for 5 minutes to allow the flavors to infuse.

2. Place the red onions in a large glass jar or heatproof plastic container. Pour the pickling mixture through a fine-mesh strainer over the onions, then discard the spices. Make sure the onions are completely submerged. Cool, cover tightly, and chill for at least 3 hours before using. The pickled onions will keep, tightly covered, in the refrigerator for up to 1 month.

PICKLED RAMPS

Even with three restaurants spread across North Carolina and a family of four at home in Asheville, chef William Dissen finds time to head back into the Appalachia woods where he played as a boy. Foraging for ramps, which are akin to wild leeks, was a big part of his growing up, and he returns to his secret haunts in early spring for the thin bulbs with a garlicky-onion flavor. Annually the team at his Haymaker restaurant puts up more than a hundred pounds of wild ramps so they—and their customers—can enjoy the mountain delicacy year-round. Ramps can be found in April and early May at many farmers' markets in the Mid-Atlantic and Southern states.

MAKES 1 QUART

1 pound **ramps**, green leaves trimmed to 1 inch beyond the stem (reserved for another use, if desired), cleaned

1½ teaspoons **whole black peppercorns**

½ teaspoon **mustard seeds**

¼ teaspoon **caraway seeds**

¼ teaspoon **fennel seeds**

¼ teaspoon **cumin seeds**

1½ cups **white wine vinegar**

1 cup **sugar**

1 tablespoon **kosher salt**

1 **bay leaf** (fresh or dried)

1. Sterilize a quart glass jar by submerging it in boiling water for 10 minutes.

2. Pack the ramps into the sterilized jar and set aside.

3. In a deep saucepan over medium heat, combine the black peppercorns, mustard seeds, caraway seeds, fennel seeds, and cumin seeds. Toast for 1 minute, shaking the pan several times, or until the spices are fragrant and the cumin seeds have slightly darkened in color.

4. Carefully pour in the vinegar and 1 cup water (it may steam up), then add the sugar, salt, and bay leaf. Increase the heat to high and bring to a boil, stirring until the sugar and salt have dissolved. Reduce the heat to medium and simmer for 2 minutes, stirring a few times.

5. Carefully pour the hot pickling liquid (and the spices) over the ramps, making sure they are all submerged (place a weight that fits just inside the mouth of the jar, if needed, until the ramps have wilted enough to remain under the liquid). Wipe the jar rim clean and seal with a new lid and ring until finger-tight. Cool to room temperature, then seal tightly and refrigerate for at least 3 weeks and up to 2 months before using.

MUSHROOM STOCK

This potful of aromatic vegetables, herbs, and dried shiitakes produces a mushroom broth more flavorful than any kind I've come across in grocery stores. If you cook the strained liquid further, concentrating its flavors, it can serve as the sauce base for our Mushroom-Ricotta Lasagne with Port Sauce (page 140) or stand in for the vegetable broth in the Wild Mushroom Tartines with Black Pepper Ricotta (page 89).

**MAKES 7 TO 8 CUPS REGULAR STOCK,
OR 3 CUPS RICH STOCK**

1 large **yellow onion**, thinly sliced

1 **leek**, top green part only, chopped and rinsed well

4 **garlic cloves**, unpeeled, crushed with the flat side of a chef's knife

1 ounce **dried shiitake mushrooms**

1 teaspoon **kosher salt**

½ teaspoon **whole black peppercorns**

8 ounces **white button mushrooms**, stemmed, cleaned, and sliced

2 small **carrots**, trimmed, scrubbed well, and chopped

6 **fresh parsley sprigs**, coarsely chopped

3 **fresh thyme sprigs**

2 **fresh marjoram** or **oregano sprigs**

2 **fresh sage leaves**

2 **bay leaves** (fresh or dried)

9 cups **cold water**

1. Place the onion in a large Dutch oven or other heavy-bottomed pot and pour in just enough tap water to moisten but not cover them completely. Add the leek, garlic, dried shiitakes, and salt. Give the mixture a stir, then cover and cook gently over medium-low heat for 15 minutes.

2. Uncover and add the black peppercorns, button mushrooms, carrots, parsley, thyme, marjoram, sage, and bay leaves. Pour in the cold water and bring to a boil, then reduce the heat to medium and simmer, uncovered, for 1 hour.

3. Pour the stock through a fine-mesh strainer set over a large bowl, pressing as much liquid as you can from the vegetables, then discard the solids.

4. Cool the stock, then transfer it to an airtight container and refrigerate for up to 2 days, if not using immediately, or proceed with the following step to make the rich stock.

5. To make a rich stock: Wipe out the pot and return all of the strained stock to the pot. Bring to a boil over high heat and cook until it has reduced to 3 cups, 15 to 20 minutes. Cool, then transfer to an airtight container and refrigerate for up to 2 days, if not using immediately.

OUR COMMUNITY OF ARTISANS

AR'S HOT SOUTHERN HONEY

Ames Russell of nearby Richmond, Virginia, dropped by the bakery to interest us in his spiced-up honey. Once I saw the bourbon-barrel-aged version, I said yes! We use his hot honey in a good number of bakery items, including our Virginia Peanut Pie (page 170) and our Lexington Bourbon Cake (page 183). My favorite application? Drizzling it on pizza.

hotsouthernhoney.com

BELMONT PEANUTS

The daughter of farmers, Patsy Marks married another farmer, and their family has been growing, roasting, and packing peanuts on their land in Capron, Virginia, for nearly thirty years. We use their bigger, bolder, crunchier Virginia peanuts in our Virginia Peanut Pie (page 170) and carry their peanuts and cashews under the Red Truck Bakery label.

belmontpeanuts.com

BENTON'S SMOKY MOUNTAIN COUNTRY HAMS

For nearly fifty years, the Bentons have been curing meat in the foothills of the Smoky Mountains in Madisonville, Tennessee, and the best chefs in the country haven't stopped lining up for it. Their bacon is the most important ingredient in our BLTs with Avocado Pesto and Mayonnaise (page 74) and shines in our Chunky Meatloaf with Plenty of Bacon (page 143).

bentonscountryhams2.com

BILLY REID

Fashion designer Billy Reid brought his international headquarters to his wife's enchanting hometown of Florence, Alabama, and legions of musicians and artisans followed him there. During the pandemic, Billy unveiled his new lines virtually, and we sweetened the experience for fashion editors and writers by sending baked goods inspired by his family's heirloom recipes. We were honored to be a part of his annual Shindig and served slices of cakes to the masses from the back of our old red truck while our pals the Watson Twins performed on stage. Billy's team surprised me with an outfit for my Grand Marshal stint at our town's Christmas parade, and I'm wearing his clothing most every day, as well as in this book's photos.

billyreid.com

CATOCTIN CREEK DISTILLING COMPANY

Don't you just know we'd cozy up to our local whisky distillery, not far up the road in Purcellville, Virginia. We thought our pals Becky and Scott Harris's rye was the best thing ever, until we started adding their apple brandy to our Caramel Cake with Pecans (page 191) and creating our applejack cake just in time for *The New York Times* to write about our mutual collaboration.

catoctincreekdistilling.com

FAUQUIER EDUCATION FARM

I shoved the bakery's support solidly behind this local organization that teaches students how to farm, with the crops they raise being donated to area food banks and those in need. Our supportive customers quickly rally to help the farm financially every time I put out an urgent request.

fauquiereducationfarm.org

FORT LONESOME

I'm smitten with Kathie Sever, Amrit Khalsa, and Bekah Dubose, the creative goddesses of custom chain-stitched coats, Western shirts, and whatever else any nationally known country singer wants to wear on stage—or what a baker wants to wear on a cookbook tour (see page 219).

ftlonesome.com

MEG NOTTINGHAM WALSH

Meg and I used to work together at the National Trust for Historic Preservation, and I enjoyed seeing her paintings show up at the R. H. Ballard Gallery near us in Little Washington. She loved the idea of creating a painting of my farmhouse (see page 182), and the project became a Christmas gift for Dwight.

megwalsh.com

OUR NORTH CAROLINA POTTERY PALS

The chunky, rough-hewn yet elevated pottery of Bakersville, North Carolina, artisan Shawn Ireland (now in Athens, Georgia) is put to good use every day at both of our bakeries and improves the look of everything I serve at home. You'll see Shawn's clever ceramics throughout this book, including embracing the Roast Chicken with Guava & Pineapple (page 139).

shawnirelandpottery.com

At the 105-year-old Jugtown Pottery, in Seagrove, North Carolina, the Owens family—Vernon, Pam, Travis, and Bayle—have created batter bowls and pie dishes for our use in the bakery, and their renowned decorative vases, figurines, and candlesticks have a special spot on our farmhouse mantel.
jugtownware.com

Sitting just inside the door of our Marshall bakery, potter Daniel Johnston's huge lidded pot greets customers—and they all ask about it. An even larger pot, one of one hundred that lined the dirt road past Johnston's kiln, has a place of honor in our farmhouse, accompanied by smaller serving dishes and pots.
danieljohnstonpottery.com

For twenty years, we've been lining up in Pittsboro, North Carolina, for Mark Hewitt's kiln openings and the mad dash for his scholarly pieces, including our bean pot (see page 149).
hewittpottery.com

SMITHEY IRONWARE

Modern iconic ironware, cast and hand-forged by the team Isaac Morton has assembled in Charleston, South Carolina, are workhorse pieces in my kitchen and at the bakery. I'd be helpless without their cast-iron skillets and their hefty Dutch ovens—and if I could go back in time, I'd make sure my grandmother had these in her North Carolina kitchen.
smithey.com

WOODIE LONG GALLERY

I sure miss our pal Woodie Long. He and his wife, Dot, became friends of ours long before he illustrated a cover of *The Washington Post Magazine* for me in my former life as an art director. I love being reminded daily of him through his whimsical, flowing, brightly covered pieces at both of our stores and in both of our houses.
woodielong.net

WORLD CENTRAL KITCHEN

Matthew Adler and Mollie Moore have been helming chef José Andrés's World Central Kitchen in Washington, D.C., and I volunteered during a government shutdown and again through the Covid-19 pandemic, to help them serve between 7,000 and 10,000 meals each day to frontline workers, furloughed government staffers, and those desperate for a meal. We're big supporters.
wck.org

OUR ARTISANS, PRODUCERS, AND FRIENDS

Kevin Adams and
Gay Street Gallery
gaystreetgallery.com

Big Spoon Roasters
bigspoonroasters.com

B.T.C. Old-Fashioned
Grocery
btcgrocery.com

The Dabney restaurant
thedabney.com

Dwight McNeill,
AIA (architect of our
two stores)
dwightmcneill.com

Garden & Gun magazine
gardenandgun.com

Greens restaurant
greensrestaurant.com

William Dissen and
Haymaker restaurant
haymakerclt.com

Frank and Pardis Stitt
and Highlands Bar & Grill
highlandsbarandgrill.com

Ian Boden and The
Shack restaurant
theshackva.com

The Jacques Pepin
Foundation
jp.foundation

James Beard
Foundation
jamesbeard.org

J.Q. Dickinson
Salt-Works
jqdsalt.com

Kindred restaurant
kindreddavidson.com

King Arthur
Baking Company
kingarthurbaking.com

The Lee Bros.
mattleeandtedlee.com

Angie Mosier, our
book's photographer
**placematproductions.
com**

George Washington's
Mount Vernon
mountvernon.org

Scott Peacock,
biscuit virtuoso and
indigo revivalist
chefscottpeacock.com

Relish Decor
relishdecor.com

Joe Sink's attractive and
functional tableware
joesinkpottery.com

Southern
Foodways Alliance
southernfoodways.org

Thornton River Art
and Heidi Morf
thorntonriverart.com

Williams Sonoma
williams-sonoma.com

World Spice
Merchants
worldspice.com

And my team at
redtruckbakery.com
and **instagram.com/
redtruckbakery**

THE LYRICAL PROSE OF MY FRIEND RONNI LUNDY IS THE PERFECT WAY TO KICK OFF THIS BOOK.
A Kentucky native, Ronni is an expert on Southern and Appalachian foods and their roots, and her home in North Carolina is just over the mountain from where my grandparents lived, a region that plays a big part in my life and this story. Her early book *Shuck Beans, Stack Cakes, and Honest Fried Chicken* is exactly what it sounds like: the heart and soul and Mother Church of Southern cooking. Her 2016 masterpiece, *Victuals*, landed with such force that the James Beard Foundation threw at her not one but two top awards before the dust even settled. Bourbon cake clouds Ronni's memory about how we met, but I first caught sight of her at the Southern Food Writers Conference, which collided with Knoxville's International Biscuit Festival, where I was a judge and don't remember anything about the biscuits but couldn't forget Ronni. I've shipped her so many baked goods that she finally bellowed, "Enough! No more cakes!" and told me if I sent anything more, she'd have to get new shocks for her Chevy Astro van.

A couple of years ago, on an 850-mile drive from her home near Asheville to western Massachusetts, Ronni stopped by the Red Truck Bakery for a late bite and to pick up a cake to enjoy up north with her friends. I didn't know at the time that Ronni's ultimate destination that day was the home of her literary agent, Lisa Ekus, the best in the business. At Ronni's urging I latched onto Lisa, and she became *my* agent—steering, coddling, listening, pushing, encouraging, and championing me every step of the way—and each day I love her even more and find out a few more things that we have in common. My wish had been for Lisa to get this cookbook's proposal into the hands of Clarkson Potter editor Francis Lam, whom I had met at a Southern Foodways Alliance symposium (and to whom I listen each weekend on public radio's *A Splendid Table*). What we didn't know was that Francis was about to become editor in chief of Clarkson Potter, and Francis happily introduced me to Lydia O'Brien, in whose hands *The Red Truck Bakery Farmhouse Cookbook* then landed. Before I was a baker, I was a magazine art director, and I've worked with some of the best editors in the country. That was surpassed with this book, and it was kismet: Lydia is a local, having grown up in Washington, D.C., and has visited the bakery several times with family and friends in tow. Lydia quickly embraced the comfort-with-friends-and-family theme of the bakery and this book, and she has been a true partner of mine throughout the process, with edits that strengthened my words and excellent creative ideas that influenced the design and art direction. This book started with my busted shoulder, and it wrapped up while I was dealing with a serious concussion after a crosswalk accident. Lydia patiently walked me through the final edits while I was having difficulty focusing on the details. Thanks to all of you—Ronni, Lisa, Francis, and Lydia—for taking good care of my book (and me).

Angie Mosier, the food stylist on my first cookbook, is a prized photographer in her own right (just ask chefs Eric Ripert, Sean Brock, Marcus Samuelsson, Vivian Howard, and Rodney Scott). She is the only person I wanted to capture the charm of my farmhouse and bakery (and the food that came out of both), and her gorgeous photography for this book justified that decision. She embraced my desire to include items important to me in the photos shot at my farmhouse: our Southern pottery and folk art, and family heirlooms that included my maternal grandmother's handmade hundred-year-old quilt, my paternal grandmother's beloved kitchen artifacts, and a metal fireplace screen my great-grandmother handcrafted. Perhaps the image that best captures Angie's artistic genius is the stunning slice of lemon chess tart on a bluebird plate (page 167). That picture got others besides me aflutter: Angie was on my farmhouse porch making that photograph when a commotion quickly erupted above her head. "I looked up," she told me later, "and, you won't believe this, I found two excited bluebirds flying around the porch ceiling duking it out while watching me work."

A cornucopia of thanks to recipe tester Bonnie Benwick, with whom I worked at *The Washington Post*, where she was the deputy food editor. Dumping nearly one hundred recipes at one time in her email in-box didn't faze her. Her neighbors were the happy beneficiaries of her testing, and I was happy to have just one person overseeing the entire project, ensuring consistency throughout. While I was sidelined with a concussion, Bonnie—along with Venus Barratt, our former bakery staffer blessed with a superb sense of style—drove out to the farmhouse to make some of the dishes in this book; it was an extraordinary assistance. I appreciate the help of Jura Koncius and her sister Sigita Clark, who doggedly searched out sources for farmhouse-appropriate linens and fabrics to make our food look its best. Special thanks to friends in the business whose work appears in some form here: Rick Bayless, Ian Boden, Carrie Brown, William Dissen, Diane Flynt, Dixie Grimes, Joe and Katy Kindred, Jeremiah Langhorne, Ouita Michel, Justise Robbins, Bill Smith, Annie Somerville, Frank and Pardis Stitt, and Alice Waters.

Clarkson Potter book designer Ian Dingman, who realized quickly that he and I were both type aficionados, captured the feel of my bakery even better than I did in the first book and I'm really pleased that he surpassed his superb work on this book. Thanks, too, to Marysarah Quinn, Stephanie Huntwork, Terry Deal, Monica Stanton, and Jana Branson on the Clarkson Potter team, who reminded me of the most enjoyable parts of my publishing days.

· · ·

IT TOOK THE MENTORING OF baking pros to coax me out of the world of newspapers and magazines and into a professional kitchen. Thanks, first, to Connie O'Meara, who let me talk my way into early-morning training shifts at her bakery on Cape Cod while I was on vacation from *The Washington Post* (she advised me not to give up my day job). Thankfully, Mark Ramsdell (a former assistant pastry chef at the White House) saw my passion and took me under his wing through two years of his classes at the much-missed L'Academie de Cuisine outside of Washington, D.C. Instructor Eric Kastel at the Culinary Institute of America in Hyde Park, New York, encouraged me through strict discipline, special projects, and three a.m. baking shifts for their store and café. King Arthur Baking Company chef and instructor Jeffrey Hamelman introduced me to the magic of his company's philosophy and their products in Norwich, Vermont, and taught me how to run a bakery kitchen. The iconic old red truck I bought for the farm from designer Tommy Hilfiger inadvertently gave the business its name and charm (thanks, Tommy—look what it started).

Launching a bakery in a rural farmhouse was met with skepticism until the locals got a taste of what was coming out of the oven. My next-door neighbors Scott and Lynne Johnson were the first to assist when I was signing my cottage industry food permit application and, along with our mutual neighbors Alan and Joan Davidson, were happy to offer advice on the cooking results. Sandy Gilliam of The Village Green, the nearby country store where I first started selling fresh baked goods, graciously invited me in and handled the weekend sales of items delivered in my red truck. That's where John and Beverly Sullivan of Little Washington found my baked goods, introducing them to their friend, *New York Times* food writer Marian Burros. The story she wrote about me on the front page of the *Times'* Food section sent tens of thousands of readers to my website in one day, introducing my baking to a hungry nation. That leads to immense thanks to Patrick O'Connell and his Inn at Little Washington, who blazed the path forty-five years ago for future artisan food businesses in rural America and taught us the importance of supporting local farmers. It is all so intertwined and I love you all for your help.

I am very thankful to some heavy hitters who have helped me and my bakery. John T. Edge and the awesome team at the Southern Foodways Alliance did more than any other group to introduce me to like-minded Southern food writers, chefs, historians, and guardians. John Currence of Big Bad Breakfast (and the genius behind some of the South's best restaurants) continues to offer wise counsel, encouragement, and praise, and enthusiastically spews the Red Truck gospel. Influenced by her family's heartrending tragedy and subsequent grace, Shelly Colvin, with her husband, Jeff, and their son Judge, guided me through my own medical challenges as this book was wrapping up. Shelly had earlier introduced me to fashion designer Billy Reid and made sure we had a prime spot to show off our cakes—and our big red truck—at the Billy Reid Shindig in Florence, Alabama. Billy enjoyed our products and asked me to re-create a caramel cake (see page 191) in honor of both his great-grandmother and his grandmother. With thanks to Billy, his CEO Mark Daley, and marketing operations manager Mimi Cirenza, we shipped that cake to their A-list of magazine editors and customers, along with a second Billy Reid collaboration a year later based on Billy's wife Jeanne's grandmother's toffee bar recipe. Immense thanks to *Garden & Gun* editor in chief Dave DiBenedetto and his team for introducing us to their readers—among them Dave's mom, Marge, who ships our cakes to her Christmas list each year after a considered vetting of items with me in back-and-forth emails. Dave loved the Billy Reid caramel cake story enough to put it on the cover of their food issue and assigned me a piece to write about it inside. And to Mary Chapin Carpenter, a good sounding board on every subject: I'm sorry for waking you up with stupid little text messages—it's just that I've missed you so much during the lockdown, and we love when you brighten our doorway. Mary Chapin is infused with spontaneous generosity and didn't hesitate a second when I asked if we could shoot some landscape photos at her farm nearby, which offers the best views of the Blue Ridge (and would allow me to spend some time with her gregarious pup, Angus). "Yes! Of course! But you've got to be here tomorrow at 5:30 a.m. for the early morning light, the dew, and the wondrous colors." We were on time and it was glorious, as is she.

Hearty thanks to the Lee Brothers—my friends Matt and Ted—who taught me much at their Cookbook Boot Camp in Charleston and are quick with advice whenever it's needed. In Virginia, Governor Ralph Northam and his wife, Pam, became friends of ours with several invitations to the Executive Mansion, and with Pam's help I concocted a delicious gluten-free and vegan coffee cake that she could enjoy (see page 50). Our US Senator Tim Kaine stops by the bakery when he's in the area, and we make sure he gets a cake on his birthday. He was a big help when a local mother asked if I would send a Shenandoah apple cake to her son, stationed aboard the Coast Guard cutter *Escanaba*, which had just arrived in Portsmouth, Virginia, after months at sea near Greenland. Instead, with Senator Kaine's assistance, we delivered a boatload of cakes to the entire crew. I'm ever thankful to Barack Obama for his White House salutes to our bakery and my story, and to his closest aides, Emily Blakemore and Cody Keenan, who ensure that the former president doesn't miss celebrating Pi Day with a stack of our pies in his office, and who remind me that the Obama family enjoys having our desserts on their dinner table each Thanksgiving. The crafty women at Fort Lonesome in Austin, Texas, documented Obama's good words about our pies in a museum-quality chain-stitched sport coat that I wore on my first book tour (someday I'll tell you what happened to it). Gratitude must be inserted here to Louise Bernard, Anne Gottschalk Scott, Rob Kent, Sophie Loyd, Claire Farhi, and my friend David Ferriero, the now-retired Archivist of the United States. Thanks to Kathie Sever, Amrit Khalsa, and Bekah Dubose at Fort Lonesome, who replaced that coat with a custom shirt—also a museum piece—that is a part of my new book tour and is pictured opposite.

Speaking of the two book tours: thank you to America's best independent bookstore staffs for hosting me. I love them and they love cake, so it's a perfect match. Please support your neighborhood bookstores. And to my chums Vivian Howard, Wendy Rieger, Joe Yonan, and Allan Gurganus: You were swell book-event moderators the first go-around—can we do it again?

Most importantly, every day I appreciate the good work of each member of my bakery team (led by our exceptional general manager, Jen Broderick), now numbering around fifty. A dozen times a day I silently thank my business partner, Peter Schwartz, for his savvy advice, for helping to keep us profitable, and for jumping in to cover for me during my medical absences. Thanks to my investors—friends who have been some of my biggest cheerleaders. And we're doing all this for our loyal customers in our rural county and across America, who have kept us in business even during the darkest times. The entire Red Truck team thanks you.

This book is about family and comfort. I owe much to my relatives, who emphasized both, including my grandmother Willmana Noyes; my parents, Robert and Genevieve Noyes; my siblings, Mark, Cheryl, Diane, and Doug; Uncle Stan and Aunt Darla Noyes; cousins Kathie Pagan and Carol Clark; sisters-in-law Pam Noyes and Karen Wicker; and our Aunt Molly Bland. They are all over this book.

And Dwight: Who knew that the quirky little farmhouse we bought in Orlean would become the catalyst for two beloved bakery locations (designed by you!) and for the two cookbooks they launched? Thanks for the love, encouragement, bakery Christmas decorating, and book-tour cake-slinging. You've made it a fun journey, and I couldn't have done it without you.

—*Brian Noyes*

Adler, Matthew, 213

Aioli, Grilled Chicken Sandwiches with Sage Leaves, Pancetta and, 80, *81*

Animal Cookies, Iced, 122

Apples

Apple Crisp, *176*, *177*

Butternut Squash Soup with Apples, Pears and Pecan Butter, *98*, *99*

Farmers' Market Galette, *38*, *39*

Foggy Ridge Apple Butter, 204, 205

Salted Caramel Apple Pie, 168

Apricots

Apricot Scones with Cranberries and White Chocolate, 35

Blueberry and Apricot Bars, 113

AR's Hot Southern Honey, 212

Atlantic Beach Pie, Bill Smith's, 172, *173*

Avocado, BLTs with Pesto Mayonnaise and, 74, *75*

Bacon

Baked Beans with Molasses, Honey and Bacon, 148, *149*

BLTs with Avocado and Pesto Mayonnaise, 74, *75*

Chunky Meatloaf with Plenty of Bacon, 143

Corn Chowder with Bacon, 101

Creamy Potato Soup with Bacon and Rosemary, 100

Mid-July Tomato Pie with, 130, *131*

Quiche Lorraine with Bacon and Basil, 42, *43*

Baked Beans with Molasses, Honey and Bacon, 148, *149*

Banana Pudding with Homemade Vanilla Wafers, 175

Bars. *See* Cookies and bars

Basil. *See also* Pesto

Heirloom Tomato Bisque with Fresh Basil, 95

Mid-July Tomato Pie with, 130, *131*

Nita's Corn Salad with Tomatoes and Basil, *152*, 153

Pesto, 83

Quiche Lorraine with Bacon and Basil, 42, *43*

Beans

Baked Beans with Molasses, Honey and Bacon, 148, *149*

Conde Road Chili with Oaxacan Mole Sauce, 97

Sweet Potato and Poblano Enchiladas with Oaxacan Mole Sauce, *144*, 145

Beef

Chunky Meatloaf with Plenty of Bacon, 143

Conde Road Chili with Oaxacan Mole Sauce, 97

Beetloaf Sandwiches, 79

Belmont Peanuts, 212

Benton's Smoky Mountain Country Hams, 212

Berries. *See also specific types*

Farmers' Market Galette, *38*, 39

FLOVA's Coffee Cake with, 50, *51*

Birthday Cake, Noyes, *194*, 195–96

Biscuits

Rise and Shine Biscuits with Ham, *54*, 55–56

tips for, 26, 29

Blackberries. *See also* Berries

blackberry buckle, 45

Farmers' Market Galette, *38*, 39

Black Pepper Ricotta, 209

Wild Mushroom Tartines with, 88, 89

BLTs with Avocado and Pesto Mayonnaise, 74, *75*

Blueberries. *See also* Berries

Blueberry and Apricot Bars, 113

Blueberry Jam with Ginger and Lime, *202*, 203

Blue Ribbon Blueberry Pie with Ginger, 162, *163*

Farmers' Market Galette, *38*, 39

Pork Tenderloin with Rosemary and Blueberries, 129

Boden, Ian, 198

Bourbon Cake, Lexington, *182*, 183

Breads, 53–71. *See also* Lunch; Muffins; Rolls; Sandwiches; Scones

Cornbread with Sorghum Butter, 66, 67

Focaccia with Sun-Dried Tomatoes and Goat Cheese, 60, 61–62

Gussied-Up Hushpuppies with Country Ham and Pepper Jelly, 68, 69

Irish Soda Bread with Caraway and Currants, 70, 71

Kindred Milk Bread, 58, 59

Potato and Pesto Flatbread, 83–84

Proper Hot Cross Buns, 63–64, 65

Rise and Shine Biscuits with Ham, *54*, 55–56

tips for, 29

Zucchini Bread with Walnuts and Cream Cheese, 57

Breakfast, 31–51. *See also* Breads

Apricot Scones with Cranberries and White Chocolate, 35

Farmers' Market Galette, *38*, 39

Farmhouse Muffins with Sausage and Jalapeño, 46, *47*

FLOVA's Coffee Cake, 50, *51*

Heavenly Waffles, *36*, 37

Mom's Sour Cream Coffee Cake, 40

Orange Pecan Rolls, 32–34, *33*

Peach Hand Pies, 48, 49

Quiche Lorraine with Bacon and Basil, 42, *43*

Strawberry Buckle, *44*, 45

Sunday Morning Peach Muffins with Candied Pecans, 41

Brown, Carrie, 82

Brownies, Red Truck, *114*, 115

Brunswick Stew, Aunt Molly's, 92, *93*

Buckle, Strawberry, *44*, 45

Butternut squash

Butternut Squash Soup with Apples, Pears and Pecan Butter, *98*, *99*

Foggy Ridge Winter Squash Butter, 205

Savory Hand Pies with Butternut Squash and Country Ham, 86, *87*

Cakes

Caramel Cake with Pecans, *190*, 191–92

Carrot Cake with Chantilly Cream, 181

Flourless Chocolate Truffle Cake, 184, *185*

FLOVA's Coffee Cake, 50, *51*

Lexington Bourbon Cake, *182*, 183

Martha Washington's Great Cake, *186*, 187–88

Mom's Sour Cream Coffee Cake, 40

Noyes Birthday Cake, *194*, 195–96

Orange Cake, 193

Peach Pound Cake, 197

tools and tips for, 27, 28, 29

Triple-Chocolate Cake, 189

Caramel, 29

Caramel Cake with Pecans, *190*, 191–92

Salted Caramel Apple Pie, 168

Carrots

Carrot Cake with Chantilly Cream, 181

Carrot, Parsnip and Leek Potpies, *126*, 127–28

Roasted Heirloom Carrots with Rosemary and Harissa, 154, *155*

Casserole, Squash, with Corn and Crunchy Breadcrumbs, 158, *159*

Castaway Cookies with Lime and Coconut, 118

Catoctin Creek Distilling Company, 212

Chantilly Cream, Carrot Cake with, 181

Cheese

Black Pepper Ricotta, 209

Wild Mushroom Tartines with, 88, 89

Farmhouse Muffins with Sausage and Jalapeño and, 46, *47*

Focaccia with Sun-Dried Tomatoes and Goat Cheese, 60, 61–62

Grilled Halloumi, Watermelon Salad with, *156*, 157

Mid-July Tomato Pie with, 130, *131*

Mushroom-Ricotta Lasagne with Port Sauce, 140–42, *141*

Pimento Cheese, Fried Green Tomato Sandwiches with, 76, 77–78

Potato and Pesto Flatbread with, 83–84

Quiche Lorraine with Bacon and Basil, 42, *43*

Savory Hand Pies with Butternut Squash and Country Ham and, 86, *87*

Savory Pie and Quiche Crust with, 128

Squash Casserole with Corn and Crunchy Breadcrumbs, 158, *159*

Sweet Potato and Poblano Enchiladas with Oaxacan Mole Sauce, *144*, 145

Zucchini Bread with Walnuts and Cream Cheese, 57

Cherries
    Farmers' Market Galette, *38*, 39
    Icebox Fruitcake, 123
    Sour Cherry Pie with a Hint of
        Almond, *164*, 165
Chess Pie, Chocolate, with
        Graham Cracker Crust,
        174
Chess Tart, Lemon, 166–67, *167*
Chicken
    Aunt Molly's Brunswick Stew,
        92, *93*
    Baked Chicken with Oaxacan
        Mole Sauce, 136–37
    Grilled Chicken Sandwiches
        with Sage Leaves and
        Pancetta, 80, *81*
    Old-School Chicken Soup, 94
    Peanut Ginger Chicken with
        Cucumber Salsa, 134,
        135
    Roast Chicken with Guava and
        Pineapple, *138*, 139
    Tarragon Chicken Salad on Irish
        Soda Bread, 85
Chili, Conde Road, with Oaxacan
        Mole Sauce, 97
Chocolate. *See also* White
        chocolate
    Billy Reid's Toffee Bars,
        110–12, *111*
    Chocolate Chess Pie with
        Graham Cracker Crust,
        174
    Flourless Chocolate Truffle
        Cake, 184, *185*
    Noyes Birthday Cake with, *194*,
        195–96
    Red Truck Brownies, *114*, 115
    Triple-Chocolate Cake, 189
Chowder, Corn, with Bacon, 101
Classic Piecrust, 169
Cobbler, Peach, Dot's, with
        Crystallized Ginger, 180
Coconut
    Castaway Cookies with Lime
        and Coconut, 118
    Icebox Fruitcake, 123
Coffee cakes
    FLOVA's Coffee Cake, 50, *51*
    Mom's Sour Cream Coffee
        Cake, 40
Coleslaw, Eileen's, 151
Condiments, 201–11
    Black Pepper Ricotta, 209
    Blueberry Jam with Ginger and
        Lime, *202*, 203
    Foggy Ridge Apple Butter and
        Winter Squash Butter,
        204–5
    Grand Champion Peach Jam,
        206, *207*
    Mushroom Stock, 211
    Pickled Ramps, 210
    Pickled Red Onions, 209
    Tomato Jelly, *208*, 208

Cookies and bars, 107–23
    Billy Reid's Toffee Bars,
        110–12, *111*
    Blueberry and Apricot Bars,
        113
    Castaway Cookies with Lime
        and Coconut, 118
    Chewy Granola Bars, *108*, 109
    Homemade Graham Crackers,
        120, 121
    Homemade Vanilla Wafers, 175
    Icebox Fruitcake, 123
    Iced Animal Cookies, 122
    Moravian Ginger Cookies, 119
    Orange Poppy Seed Cookies,
        116, *117*
    Red Truck Brownies, *114*, 115
Corn
    Corn Chowder with Bacon, 101
    Corn Crab Cakes with Jalapeño
        Mayonnaise, *132*, 133
    Corn Ice Cream, 198, *199*
    Nita's Corn Salad with
        Tomatoes and Basil, *152*,
        153
    Squash Casserole with
        Corn and Crunchy
        Breadcrumbs, 158, *159*
Cornbread
    Cornbread with Sorghum
        Butter, *66*, 67
    Corn Crab Cakes with Jalapeño
        Mayonnaise, *132*, 133
    Gussied-Up Hushpuppies with
        Country Ham and Pepper
        Jelly, 68, *69*
Country ham. *See* Ham
Crab
    Corn Crab Cakes with Jalapeño
        Mayonnaise, *132*, 133
Cranberries
    Apricot Scones with Cranberries
        and White Chocolate, 35
    Chewy Granola Bars, *108*, 109
    focaccia with raisins and
        cranberries, 62
    Zucchini Bread with Walnuts
        and Cream Cheese and,
        57
Crisp, Apple, *176*, 177
Cucumbers
    Cucumber Salsa, Peanut Ginger
        Chicken with, 134, *135*
    Watermelon Salad with Grilled
        Halloumi, *156*, 157

Desserts, 161–99. *See also*
        Cookies and bars
    Apple Crisp, *176*, 177
    Banana Pudding with
        Homemade Vanilla
        Wafers, 175
    Bill Smith's Atlantic Beach Pie,
        172, *173*
    Blue Ribbon Blueberry Pie with
        Ginger, 162, *163*

Caramel Cake with Pecans,
        190, 191–92
    Carrot Cake with Chantilly
        Cream, 181
    Chocolate Chess Pie with
        Graham Cracker Crust,
        174
    Corn Ice Cream, 198, *199*
    Dot's Peach Cobbler with
        Crystallized Ginger, 180
    Farmers' Market Galette, *38*,
        39
    Flourless Chocolate Truffle
        Cake, 184, *185*
    Lemon Chess Tart, 166, *167*
    Lexington Bourbon Cake, *182*,
        183
    Martha Washington's Great
        Cake, *186*, 187–88
    Noyes Birthday Cake, *194*,
        195–96
    Old-Fashioned Strawberry
        Shortcakes, 178, *179*
    Orange Cake, 193
    Peach Hand Pies, *48*, 49
    Peach Pound Cake, 197
    Salted Caramel Apple Pie, 168
    Sour Cherry Pie with a Hint of
        Almond, *164*, 165
    Strawberry Buckle, *44*, 45
    Triple-Chocolate Cake, 189
    Virginia Peanut Pie, 170, *171*
Dinner, 125–45. *See also* Soups
        and stews
    Baked Chicken with Oaxacan
        Mole Sauce, 136–37
    Carrot, Parsnip and Leek
        Potpies, *126*, 127–28
    Chunky Meatloaf with Plenty of
        Bacon, 143
    Corn Crab Cakes with Jalapeño
        Mayonnaise, *132*, 133
    Mid-July Tomato Pie, 130,
        131
    Mushroom-Ricotta Lasagne
        with Port Sauce, 140–42,
        141
    Peanut Ginger Chicken with
        Cucumber Salsa, 134,
        135
    Pork Tenderloin with Rosemary
        and Blueberries, 129
    Roast Chicken with Guava and
        Pineapple, *138*, 139
    Sweet Potato and Poblano
        Enchiladas with Oaxacan
        Mole Sauce, *144*, 145
Dissen, William, 89, 209, 210
Dubose, Bekah, 212

Egg Salad Sandwiches, Jimtown,
        82
Enchiladas, Sweet Potato and
        Poblano, with Oaxacan
        Mole Sauce, *144*, 145
Equipment and tools, 27, 29

Farmers' Market Galette, *38*, 39
Farmhouse Muffins with Sausage
        and Jalapeño and, 46, *47*
Fauquier Education Farm, 212
Flourless Chocolate Truffle Cake,
        184, *185*
FLOVA's Coffee Cake, 50, *51*
Focaccia
    BLTs with Avocado and Pesto
        Mayonnaise, 74, *75*
    with cranberries and raisins, 62
    Focaccia with Sun-Dried
        Tomatoes and Goat
        Cheese, *60*, 61–62
    Potato and Pesto Flatbread,
        83–84
Foggy Ridge Apple Butter and
        Winter Squash Butter,
        204–5
Fort Lonesome, 212
Fruitcake
    Icebox Fruitcake, 123
    Martha Washington's Great
        Cake, *186*, 187–88

Galette, Farmers' Market, *38*, 39
Gazpacho, Summer, *104*, 105
Ginger
    Blueberry Jam with Ginger and
        Lime, *202*, 203
    Blue Ribbon Blueberry Pie with
        Ginger, 162, *163*
    Dot's Peach Cobbler with
        Crystallized Ginger, 180
    Grand Champion Peach Jam
        with, 206, *207*
    Lexington Bourbon Cake, *182*,
        183
    Moravian Ginger Cookies, 119
    Peanut Ginger Chicken with
        Cucumber Salsa, 134, *135*
Goat cheese
    Beetloaf Sandwiches with, 79
    Focaccia with Sun-Dried
        Tomatoes and Goat
        Cheese, *60*, 61–62
    Sweet Potato and Poblano
        Enchiladas with Oaxacan
        Mole Sauce, *144*, 145
Graham crackers
    Chocolate Chess Pie with
        Graham Cracker Crust, 174
    Homemade Graham Crackers,
        120, 121
    Icebox Fruitcake, 123
Grand Champion Peach Jam, 206,
        207
Granola Bars, Chewy, *108*, 109
Green Pea Salad, Aunt Darla's,
        150
Greens restaurant, 140
Greens, Savory Hand Pies with
        Butternut Squash and
        Country Ham and, 86, *87*
Guava and Pineapple, Roast
        Chicken with, *138*, 139

Halloumi, Grilled, Watermelon Salad with, *156*, 157
Ham
 Aunt Molly's Brunswick Stew, 92, *93*
 Gussied-Up Hushpuppies with Country Ham and Pepper Jelly, 68, *69*
 Rise and Shine Biscuits with Ham, *54*, 55–56
 Savory Hand Pies with Butternut Squash and Country Ham, 86, *87*
Hand pies
 Peach Hand Pies, *48*, 49
 Savory Hand Pies with Butternut Squash and Country Ham, 86, *87*
Harris, Becky and Scott, 212
Heavenly Waffles, *36*, 37
Hewitt Pottery, 213
Hot Cross Buns, Proper, 63–64, *65*
Hushpuppies, Gussied-Up, with Country Ham and Pepper Jelly, 68, *69*

Icebox Fruitcake, 123
Ice Cream, Corn, 198, *199*
Iced Animal Cookies, 122
Ingredients, 26
Ireland, Shawn, 212
Irish Soda Bread with Caraway and Currants, *70*, 71
 Tarragon Chicken Salad on, 85

Jalapeños
 Farmhouse Muffins with Sausage and Jalapeño, 46, *47*
 Jalapeño Mayonnaise, Corn Crab Cakes with, *132*, 133
Jams
 Blueberry Jam with Ginger and Lime, *202*, 203
 Grand Champion Peach Jam, 206, *207*
Jelly, Tomato, 208, *208*
Jimtown Egg Salad Sandwiches, 82
Johnston, Daniel, 213
Jugtown Pottery, 213

Kerns, Irene, 208
Khalsa, Amrit, 212
Kindred Milk Bread, 58, *59*

Lasagne, Mushroom-Ricotta, with Port Sauce, 140–42, *141*
Leeks
 Carrot, Parsnip and Leek Potpies, *126*, 127–28
 Mushroom-Ricotta Lasagne with Port Sauce, 140–42, *141*

Lemon(s), 26
 Bill Smith's Atlantic Beach Pie, 172, *173*
 Lemon Chess Tart, 166, *167*
Lexington Bourbon Cake, *182*, 183
Lime
 Bill Smith's Atlantic Beach Pie, 172, *173*
 Blueberry Jam with Ginger and Lime, *202*, 203
 Castaway Cookies with Lime and Coconut, 118
Long, Woodie, 213
Lunch, 73–89. *See also* Soups and stews
 Beetloaf Sandwiches, 79
 BLTs with Avocado and Pesto Mayonnaise, 74, *75*
 Fried Green Tomato Sandwiches with Pimento Cheese, *76*, 77–78
 Grilled Chicken Sandwiches with Sage Leaves and Pancetta, 80, *81*
 Jimtown Egg Salad Sandwiches, 82
 Potato and Pesto Flatbread, 83–84
 Savory Hand Pies with Butternut Squash and Country Ham, 86, *87*
 Tarragon Chicken Salad on Irish Soda Bread, 85
 Wild Mushroom Tartines with Black Pepper Ricotta, *88*, 89

Marks, Patsy, 212
Martha Washington's Great Cake, *186*, 187–88
McNeill, Dorothy, 123, 180
Meat
 Chunky Meatloaf with Plenty of Bacon, 143
 Conde Road Chili with Oaxacan Mole Sauce, 97
 Pork Tenderloin with Rosemary and Blueberries, 129
Mid-July Tomato Pie, 130, *131*
Milk Bread, Kindred, 58, *59*
Mole Sauce, Oaxacan, 137
 Baked Chicken with, 136
 Conde Road Chili with, 97
 Sweet Potato and Poblano Enchiladas with, *144*, 145
Moore, Mollie, 213
Moravian Ginger Cookies, 119
Muffins
 Farmhouse Muffins with Sausage and Jalapeño, 46, *47*
 Sunday Morning Peach Muffins with Candied Pecans, 41
 tips for, 28–29

Mushrooms
 Mushroom-Ricotta Lasagne with Port Sauce, 140–42, *141*
 Mushroom Stock, 211
 Wild Mushroom Tartines with Black Pepper Ricotta, *88*, 89

Northam, Pam, 50
Noyes Birthday Cake, *194*, 195–96

Oaxacan Mole Sauce, 137
 Baked Chicken with, 136
 Conde Road Chili with, 97
 Sweet Potato and Poblano Enchiladas with, *144*, 145
Okra and Tomatoes, Shrimp Stew with, 102, *103*
Onions, Red, Pickled, 209
Orange(s)
 Orange Cake, 193
 Orange Pecan Rolls, 32–34, *33*
 Orange Poppy Seed Cookies, 116, *117*
Owens family pottery, 213

Pantry ingredients, 26
Parsnips
 Carrot, Parsnip and Leek Potpies, *126*, 127–28
 Parsnip Purée, 151
Pâte Sucrée, 166
Peaches
 Dot's Peach Cobbler with Crystallized Ginger, 180
 Farmers' Market Galette, *38*, 39
 FLOVA's Coffee Cake with, 50, *51*
 Grand Champion Peach Jam, 206, *207*
 peach buckle, 45
 Peach Pound Cake, 197
 Sunday Morning Peach Muffins with Candied Pecans, 41
Peanuts
 Peanut Ginger Chicken with Cucumber Salsa, 134, *135*
 Virginia Peanut Pie, 170, *171*
Pears, Butternut Squash Soup with Apples, Pecan Butter and, *98*, 99
Peas
 Aunt Darla's Green Pea Salad, 150
Pecans
 Candied, Sunday Morning Peach Muffins with, 41
 Caramel Cake with Pecans, *190*, 191–92
 Icebox Fruitcake, 123
 Orange Pecan Rolls, 32–34, *33*
 Pecan Butter, Butternut Squash Soup with Apples, Pears, and, *98*, 99

Pesto, 83
 Pesto Mayonnaise, BLTs with Avocado and, 74, *75*
 Potato and Pesto Flatbread, 83–84
Pickles
 Pickled Ramps, 210
 Pickled Red Onions, 209
Pies and tarts
 Bill Smith's Atlantic Beach Pie, 172, *173*
 Blue Ribbon Blueberry Pie with Ginger, 162, *163*
 Carrot, Parsnip and Leek Potpies, *126*, 127–28
 Chocolate Chess Pie with Graham Cracker Crust, 174
 Classic Piecrust, 169
 Farmers' Market Galette, *38*, 39
 Lemon Chess Tart, 166, *167*
 Mid-July Tomato Pie, 130, *131*
 Pâte Sucrée, 166
 Peach Hand Pies, *48*, 49
 Quiche Lorraine with Bacon and Basil, 42, *43*
 Salted Caramel Apple Pie, 168
 Savory Hand Pies with Butternut Squash and Country Ham, 86, *87*
 Savory Pie and Quiche Crust, 128
 Sour Cherry Pie with a Hint of Almond, *164*, 165
 tips for, 29
 Virginia Peanut Pie, 170, *171*
Pimento Cheese, Fried Green Tomato Sandwiches with, *76*, 77–78
Pineapple, Roast Chicken with Guava and, *138*, 139
Plums
 Farmers' Market Galette, *38*, 39
Poppy seeds
 Orange Poppy Seed Cookies, 116, *117*
Pork
 Pork Stew with Sweet Potatoes, 96
 Pork Tenderloin with Rosemary and Blueberries, 129
Port Sauce, Mushroom-Ricotta Lasagne with, 140–42, *141*
Potatoes
 Corn Chowder with Bacon, 101
 Creamy Potato Soup with Bacon and Rosemary, 100
 Potato and Pesto Flatbread, 83–84
 Potpies, Carrot, Parsnip and Leek, *126*, 127–28
Pottery artisans, 212–13
Pound Cake, Peach, 197
Powers, Kevin, 79
Preserves. *See* Condiments

Pudding, Banana, with Homemade Vanilla Wafers, 175

Quiche
Quiche Lorraine with Bacon and Basil, 42, *43*
Savory Pie and Quiche Crust, 128

Raisins, focaccia with cranberries and, 62
Ramps, Pickled, 210
Red Onions, Pickled, 209
Reid, Billy, 110, 212
Ricotta, Black Pepper, 209
Wild Mushroom Tartines with, 88, 89
Rise and Shine Biscuits with Ham, *54,* 55–56
Rolls
Kindred Milk Bread rolls, 58
Orange Pecan Rolls, 32–34, *33*
Proper Hot Cross Buns, 63–64, *65*
Rosemary
Creamy Potato Soup with Bacon and Rosemary, 100
Focaccia with, 61–62
Pork Tenderloin with Rosemary and Blueberries, 129
Roasted Heirloom Carrots with Rosemary and Harissa, 154, *155*
Savory Pie and Quiche Crust with, 128
Russell, Ames, 212

Sage Leaves and Pancetta, Grilled Chicken Sandwiches with, 80, *81*
Salads. *See* Sides
Salads
Aunt Darla's Green Pea Salad, 150
Nita's Corn Salad with Tomatoes and Basil, *152,* 153
Watermelon Salad with Grilled Halloumi, *156,* 157
Salsa, Cucumber, Peanut Ginger Chicken with, 134, *135*
Salted Caramel Apple Pie, 168
Saltine cracker crust, Bill Smith's Atlantic Beach Pie with, 172, *173*
Sandwiches
Beetloaf Sandwiches, 79
BLTs with Avocado and Pesto Mayonnaise, 74, *75*
Fried Green Tomato Sandwiches with Pimento Cheese, 76, 77–78

Grilled Chicken Sandwiches with Sage Leaves and Pancetta, 80, *81*
Jimtown Egg Salad Sandwiches, 82
Tarragon Chicken Salad on Irish Soda Bread, 85
Wild Mushroom Tartines with Black Pepper Ricotta, 88, 89
Sauces
Oaxacan Mole Sauce, 137
Pesto, 83
Sausage and Jalapeño, Farmhouse Muffins with, 46, *47*
Savory Pie and Quiche Crust, 128
Scones, Apricot, with Cranberries and White Chocolate, 35
Sever, Kathie, 212
Shortcakes, Old-Fashioned Strawberry, 178, *179*
Shrimp Stew with Okra and Tomatoes, 102, *103*
Sides, 147–59
Aunt Darla's Green Pea Salad, 150
Baked Beans with Molasses, Honey and Bacon, 148, *149*
Eileen's Coleslaw, 151
Nita's Corn Salad with Tomatoes and Basil, *152,* 153
Parsnip Purée, 151
Roasted Heirloom Carrots with Rosemary and Harissa, 154, *155*
Squash Casserole with Corn and Crunchy Breadcrumbs, 158, *159*
Watermelon Salad with Grilled Halloumi, *156,* 157
Smith, Bill, 172
Smithey Ironware, 213
Soda Bread, Irish, with Caraway and Currants, *70,* 71
Tarragon Chicken Salad on, 85
Somerville, Annie, 140
Sorghum syrup, 26
Sorghum Butter, Cornbread with, *66,* 67
Soups and stews, 91–105
Aunt Molly's Brunswick Stew, 92, *93*
Butternut Squash Soup with Apples, Pears and Pecan Butter, 98, 99
Conde Road Chili with Oaxacan Mole Sauce, 97
Corn Chowder with Bacon, 101

Creamy Potato Soup with Bacon and Rosemary, 100
Heirloom Tomato Bisque with Fresh Basil, 95
Old-School Chicken Soup, 94
Pork Stew with Sweet Potatoes, 96
Shrimp Stew with Okra and Tomatoes, 102, *103*
Summer Gazpacho, *104,* 105
Sour Cream Coffee Cake, Mom's, 40
Squash. *See* Summer squash; Winter squash
Stews. *See* Soups and stews
Stitt, Frank, 166
Stock, Mushroom, 211
Strawberries
Old-Fashioned Strawberry Shortcakes, 178, *179*
Strawberry Buckle, *44,* 45
Summer Gazpacho, *104,* 105
Summer squash
Squash Casserole with Corn and Crunchy Breadcrumbs, 158, *159*
Sweet Potato and Poblano Enchiladas with Oaxacan Mole Sauce, *144,* 145
Zucchini Bread with Walnuts and Cream Cheese, 57
Sweet potatoes
Beetloaf Sandwiches, 79
Carrot, Parsnip and Leek Potpies with, *126,* 127–28
Pork Stew with Sweet Potatoes, 96
Sweet Potato and Poblano Enchiladas with Oaxacan Mole Sauce, *144,* 145

Tarragon Chicken Salad on Irish Soda Bread, 85
Tartines, Wild Mushroom, with Black Pepper Ricotta, 88, 89
Tarts. *See also* Quiche
Farmers' Market Galette, *38,* 39
Lemon Chess Tart, 166, *167*
Pâte Sucrée crust for, 169
Tips and tricks, 28–29
Toffee Bars, Billy Reid's, 110–12, *111*
Tomato(es)
BLTs with Avocado and Pesto Mayonnaise, 74, *75*
Focaccia with Sun-Dried Tomatoes and Goat Cheese, 60, 61–62

Fried Green Tomato Sandwiches with Pimento Cheese, *76,* 77–78
Heirloom Tomato Bisque with Fresh Basil, 95
Mid-July Tomato Pie, 130, *131*
Nita's Corn Salad with Tomatoes and Basil, *152,* 153
Shrimp Stew with Okra and Tomatoes, 102, *103*
Summer Gazpacho, *104,* 105
Tomato Jelly, 208, *208*
Watermelon Salad with Grilled Halloumi, *156,* 157
Tools and equipment, 27, 29
Triple-Chocolate Cake, 189

Vanilla Wafers, Homemade, Banana Pudding with, 175
Virginia Peanut Pie, 170, *171*

Waffles, Heavenly, *36,* 37
Walnuts
Billy Reid's Toffee Bars, 110–12, *111*
Savory Hand Pies with Butternut Squash and Country Ham and, 86, 87
Zucchini Bread with Walnuts and Cream Cheese, 57
Walsh, Meg Nottingham, 212
Washington, Martha, 187
Watermelon Salad with Grilled Halloumi, *156,* 157
White chocolate
Apricot Scones with Cranberries and White Chocolate, 35
Castaway Cookies with Lime and Coconut, 118
Wild Mushroom Tartines with Black Pepper Ricotta, 88, 89
Winter squash
Butternut Squash Soup with Apples, Pears and Pecan Butter, 98, 99
Foggy Ridge Winter Squash Butter, 205
Savory Hand Pies with Butternut Squash and Country Ham, 86, 87
Woodie Long Gallery, 213
World Central Kitchen, 213

Zucchini
Squash Casserole with Corn and Crunchy Breadcrumbs, 158, *159*
Zucchini Bread with Walnuts and Cream Cheese, 57

Published in the United States by Clarkson Potter/
Publishers, an imprint of Random House, a division
of Penguin Random House LLC, New York.
ClarksonPotter.com

CLARKSON POTTER is a trademark and POTTER
with colophon is a registered trademark of Penguin
Random House LLC.

Library of Congress Cataloging-in-Publication Data
is available upon request.

ISBN 978-0-593-23481-5
Ebook ISBN 978-0-593-23482-2

Printed in China

10 9 8 7 6 5 4 3 2 1

First Edition

Photographer: Angie Mosier
Food Stylists: Angie Mosier, Venus Barratt,
Tamie Cook, and Savannah Sasser

Editor: Lydia O'Brien
Designer: Ian Dingman
Production Editor: Terry Deal
Production Manager: Jessica Heim
Composition: Merri Ann Morrell
Copy Editor: Kathy Brock
Indexer: Thérèse Shere
Marketer: Monica Stanton
Publicists: Jana Branson and Lauren Chung